CW01263141

Chasing Ghosts

Chasing Ghosts

an account of an attempt at
flying the Atlantic by
microlight aircraft

Brian Milton

NEP Travel

First published in Great Britain 2002
© Brian Milton 2002
No part of this publication may be reproduced by any means or in any form without the written permission of the author
Set in Bembo by Bookcraft, Stroud, Gloucestershire
Printed by Antony Rowe, Chippenham, Wiltshire
Published by NEP Travel, 2 Cyprus Street, London E2 0NN
ISBN 1-8724102-3-5

It is not the critic who counts; not the man who points out where the strong man stumbled, or where the doer of deeds could have done better. The credit belongs to the man who is actually in the arena; whose face is marred by dust and sweat and blood, who strives valiantly; who errs and comes short again and again; who knows the great enthusiasms, the great devotions and spends himself in a worthy cause; who at the best knows in the end the triumphs of high achievement; and who at the worse, if he fails, at least fails while daring greatly; so that his place shall never be with those cold and timid souls who know neither defeat nor victory.

Franklyn Delano Roosevelt

Contents

Acknowledgements	viii
Introduction: My own personal howler	ix
A modest proposal	1
Origins of the Atlantic attempt	6
Alcock and Brown, Lindbergh and the Atlantic flights	19
A brief history of the New Aviation	39
Biographical values	50
Sponsorship	78
Technical preparations	87
American preparations	94
New York to Newfoundland	127
More down-time days	153
The fateful decision	185
The secret diaries	195
Going for it	209
Aftermath	219
Colour plates between pages	*118–127*

Acknowledgements

I was going to blow all my savings on this adventure, but in the event, I had backing from a number of people.

I would like to thank Paul Loach, Tony Canning and Rollo Clifford, of Lion Capital Partners, for being sportsmen, in the original nineteenth century sense, about backing this flight. I remain in their debt. I could not have found a steadier or more loyal friend than Jim Cunliffe, of Mainair Sports, who provided the Blade 912, which, if it hasn't quite achieved the fame it should have done on this adventure, is surely destined to on the next. Steve Allinson, MD of Lynx Avionics, provided all the intercom and interface equipment. without which I would not have been able to handle four video cameras and record hours of flying. I would not have been able to actually contemplate the flight with any equinamity without having the use of a small altitude warning device made by Larsen and Brusgaard in Denmark; it would have costs thousands of pounds trying to develop an alternative. I want to thank the BMAA's chief executive, Chris Finnigan, for unstinting help, and the BMAA doctor, Carl Hallam, for his sage and committed advice. I set out to try and raise the profile of a charity which I think is the future, the Artificial Heart Fund, run by Nikki King, daughter of a Dambuster pilot, and though I did not raise it as much as I wanted to, I tried. And there were dozens of friends, some of long-standing like Stephen Lewis and John Hunt and Dave Simpson, some who are "just" beautiful like Moira Thomson, Helen Dudley and Valerie Thompson, and some I made en route like Guyon Nelson of MacDan Aviation in New York, and three families in Stephenville, Newfoundland, the Dennis's, Shepperd's and Skinner's, all names with a long and honourable English history. I also want to thank the Connor family, of Grand Falls, Windsor, who found me in extremis, and without whom I would never have got to the start line.

This book is dedicated to you all.

Introduction

My own personal howler

"So why did you go?" Paul asked.

"The weather was good in the Atlantic," I said.

"It wasn't very good where you were, though, was it?"

"The Atlantic proper was only 40 miles away, and once over that, I would have had the best weather I had seen for six weeks."

"But you didn't get there, did you?"

We were in Chez Gerrard, an upmarket wine bar and lunching restaurant, down from Bishopsgate on the east side of the City of London. I was getting the first of a series of bollockings, this one, importantly, from Paul Loach. I knew more were coming, and I knew I had to take them.

We were interrupted from an unexpected quarter, a former colleague on the *London Financial News*, Mike Foster, out at lunch even though it was a Friday, when most of that newspaper was written. Mike was, ironically, the indirect means of my first meeting with Paul Loach, because four years earlier he had set up the introduction that led to my friendship with Paul. It was different this time.

"You're to stop now, ok," roared Mike, paying no attention to the other diners. *"It's got to stop, stop right now, and I mean it. Your friends are worried. I was talking to Malcolm Callaghan and we're both agreed it's too risky. Go back into journalism. Go back into journalism, ok? But you've got to stop what you're doing. They'll take you back on the newspaper."*

It was like getting a Howler in a Harry Potter novel. There was no way I could escape it. Mike Foster was one of the two journalists I respected most in the world. He was a man full of an edgy integrity, in which he constantly consulted an inner guru to determine right from wrong. He had all the best qualities of a journalist, including disrespect for authority, a healthy disbelief in anything he heard, the determination to get to the truth, and the ability to recognise a good story. But at heart he was very kind, and his Howler was genuinely in concern for my welfare.

Mike continued for about a minute, giving me the public bollocking that Paul was giving me in more privacy. Eventually, with another *"Stop it, stop it now, I mean it"* he walked off, his face shiny with sweat, to find whomever he was lunching with.

"You certainly have some good friends," said Paul, smiling.

He meant it. It wasn't sarcasm.

I still felt I was right to do what I had done, but I had not the energy or the courage to argue then, with Paul or Mike. I tried writing about it a few days later, ahead of another bollocking with Paul and his two partners, Tony Canning and Rollo Clifford, each of whom was down £20,000 apiece for backing me in this venture. On paper, it was money from their company, Lion Capital Partners, but in fact, because no one else on the board believed in the adventure, it was their personal money. Paul Loach had persuaded them about my worth. It was my venture, so the outcome was mine.

But how had I got into it?

Could I have not failed?

1

A Modest Proposal

The first reaction to a proposal to fly the Atlantic by microlight is, "surely that is impossible!" That was said to me by David Bremner, Editor of *Microlight Flying*, a few weeks before I left for New York to attempt it. I sent him a paper outlining why I thought it was not impossible. Later, in the middle of the fight to make the Atlantic flight work when it was falling around my ears, I was asked to prepare a paper outlining the safety measures I would take, and I used the arguments I had sent to David as a basis for my case. It was not then thought helpful, and I was advised to drop the whole argument, but looking at it now, it still has the force I felt it had then, and should have been considered:

Night flight over the Atlantic in a flex-wing

Night-flying a flex-wing is quite different from making that sort of flight in a standard 3-axis aircraft. A flex-wing is inherently stable, like a sailing boat. Hands-off in pitch it will rest in equilibrium. It does not spin, and tends to mush rather than stall. Where a 3-axis machine in a stall can go violently into a spin which disorientates the pilot, and is prolonged unless corrected, that does not happen with a flex-wing.

Compare my Lion Atlantic Flyer with Lindbergh's "Spirit of St Louis". He deliberately built his Ryan monoplane with a small tail. Told that this characteristic would make the aircraft unstable and liable to go into a quick spin, Lindbergh said that was what he wanted, because it would wake him up if he dropped off.

I have taken exactly the opposite view to Lindbergh, and wish to play to my aircraft's strengths. If a hand throttle is set on a flex-wing to maintain height, it does not matter if there are minutes or even half hours of inattention over the Atlantic, because there is nothing to hit. The only danger in a quick nap would be to lose height, and I have taken precautions against that. Whereas on a motorbike or car, a second's inattention can be fatal, this is not true on a flex-wing. On the world flight there were minutes when I struggled to change camera film, especially during turbulence in the mountains. I let the control bar go and the aircraft flew where it will, and I was confident that so long as I was not near a mountain, nothing bad could happen to me.

Duration

Though my web site quotes 33 hours for the Atlantic flight, in the right conditions it is likely to be 24 hours. The 33 hours was quoted to establish a symbiotic link between my flight and Lindbergh's, who took that time (plus half an hour) between New York and Paris in 1927. Alcock and Brown took 16h30m to make the 1,915 mile flight from Shannon to Clifden in Ireland in 1919. My flight to Shannon is slightly longer, 1,943 miles, but that is because Shannon is up a long estuary; my last few miles will be overland.

The Mainair Blade 912 cruises at 62 mph, about 25 mph slower than A&B's Vickers Vimy. They had a fresh to strong west wind, and I wish to await such conditions for my own flight. I was informed by our Met Office in Bracknell that these conditions are common in the summer months, especially in July. Ideal conditions would be a deep stable High pressure area in mid-Atlantic, with a Low over Greenland, and few or even no fronts from Newfoundland to Eire. With an 18 mph moderate following west wind (and at my latitude it's more likely to be fresh to strong, even better), I will complete the flight within 24 hours or less. This is a duration of wakefulness easily within the grasp of any partying teenager, and certainly within *my* grasp when one considers the alternatives.

Sleep

I visited Dr Barbara Stone for advice; she's an expert on sleep and sleep deprivation at DERA, a Defence establishment near Bracknell. She described a 3-hour danger period when entering a sleep-cycle at between 1.30am and, say, 4.30 in the morning, after which the body enters a second cycle of wakefulness. She demonstrated with graphs how taking two caffeine tablets an hour, starting at midnight and covering this period, was effective in warding off sleep and keeping the subject alert until the sleep cycle ended. She suggested I take a type of caffeine tablet, of which I have an adequate supply. Dr Stone also suggested taking a sleeping pill on the night before the big flight, to ensure a prolonged period of rest before it.

Even accepting that I will be at 80–85% of efficiency the following morning as the long Atlantic flight is ending, I only really need to make 180 degree turn and put the aircraft safely on the ground. All the other brain functions that Lindbergh had to preserve, which he needed for navigation, do not need to be at that level for me. My navigation is simple, because I have three GPS's (Global Positioning Systems, satellite navigators), each powered by the generator but each with six hours available of independent battery-powered operation.

Back-up

I have two Protrack parachute alarms with me, one fitted into my helmet visor, the other a reserve. Their normal purpose is to warn free-fall parachutists, who often become intoxicated by the experience of rushing through the sky, that they must open their parachutes. There are three levels of warning; polite, strong, and very rude. They have been specially adapted by their Danish manufacturers, Larsen and Brusgaard, for my needs. I don't require any other function than the warnings. I have them set for very rude at 3,000 feet, with the strong and polite warnings at 3,500 feet and 4,000 feet. I prime them before the flight (I can re-prime them in flight) and they become active when I am above 4,000 feet.

If I settle down to fly at 5,000 feet and I drop off, these alarms are my back-up. If I do not descend, then I will not hit anything, and no harm is done. If I fly in circles for half an hour and wake up 30 miles off course, why does it matter? On the 1,000 mile flight from New York to Stephenville, I had a consumption of 11.3 litres/hour, with a load of 180 litres, about what I would have as darkness descends in the Atlantic. With a total load, including reserves, of 426 litres, I can conservatively fly for 35 hours. Every hour I fly the load lightens and I can expect to reduce the revs and therefore the fuel consumption. Losing an hour mid-Atlantic is not a serious problem.

To get back on course again, I do not have to climb through freezing cloud to get a sun or a star shot, like Alcock and Brown or Lindbergh, with all the risk they took doing so. I merely press the GPS goto buttons and my course is laid out for me.

Lighting

The most important instrument on the Atlantic flight is the Skyforce Skymap II GPS. It has six internal batteries, but is also powered by the aircraft's battery, charged by the Blade's generator. The Skyforce has internal illumination. All my engine instruments on the *Flydat* are illuminated. On the dashboard I have a small map-light to illuminate the other instruments, much like a Cessna. These are a turn-and-bank indicator, ASI (Air Speed Indicator), VSI (Vertical Speed Indicator), transponder (identifies me to radar), fuel flow meter and fuel gauge. In addition, and attached to the metal ring of the life-jacket I will wear at all times, are three fully-charged torches. In the simple cockpit I inhabit in a flex-wing, I have adequate internal lighting.

Food

I have been advised by the BMAA medical expert, Carl Hallam, a GP and former marine doctor with considerable experience of Arctic soldiering. He recommended against the practice I developed on the world flight, where I ate no breakfast and made each daily flight on will-power and chewing gum. I expect to eat and drink sparingly throughout the flight, to keep my body fuel levels up, and avoid the confusion and weakness induced by low sugar levels.

The Moon

The next full moon night is July 5th. I would like to choose a day to make the Atlantic flight between ten days before the full moon, and ten days after it. I would take off from St Johns early in the morning, not long after dawn. Because I am flying east, by the time my body clock starts to say it is tired, about 20 hours into the flight, it will already geographically be morning again. I will be less likely to want to sleep as the sun comes up, and I am filled with excitement at seeing the last 300 miles on the GPS map. I have done 300-mile flights in a flex-wing often enough to know how much they take out of you, so I can pace myself through the last difficult period.

Brian Milton
Stephenville, Newfoundland
Thursday, June 14, 2001

2

Origins of the Atlantic Attempt

I was down in a small old house I have in France in August 1999, struggling to put together a novel and keeping half an eye out for two microlight pilots, Mike Blythe and Olivier Aubert, endeavouring to fly around the Pacific Rim. I had been the first man to fly a microlight around the world, completing the journey the previous year. Now I was following the attempt at a similar journey, in terms of distance covered, by two very experienced pilots. Mike was a South African, and Olivier a Swiss. They each flew their own flex-wing, but operated as a pair, as much for company as for safety. Four years earlier, they had flown from Cape Town up the east coast of Africa and across the Mediterranean to the North Cape in Norway, the furthest north that Europe goes. They found funding for their flight in bits and pieces, and enjoyed the leisurely experience of the journey, never under time pressure as I had been because of the way I outlined my projects to sponsors, against the clock. If Mike and Olivier liked somewhere, they stayed to enjoy it better.

Their flight around the Pacific took them up the west coast of South America, and they were due to go on up the North American coast via Canada and Alaska to Siberia, then down roughly the route I took on the world flight, through Japan and China and Malaysia and Indonesia to end in Australia. They had all the usual adventures expected on such a flight, but as they reached the United States, the political problems of getting through Russia and Japan daunted them. The authorities in both these countries, for separate reasons, put the intrepid pair off. Mike and Olivier had seen what had happened to me in Russia and could not find their own way through. At the same time the Japanese, who do not want foreign microlights flying through their country, opened negotiations (and closed them again, probably giggling as they had with me) by suggesting a landing fee at each airfield of $25,000. Mike and Olivier decided, mid-flight, they would change their ambition and fly around the Atlantic Rim instead.

It was a matter of a few days, calling on the precedent of my flight across the North Atlantic route, to get their permissions changed to allow them to cross Canada via Quebec, Labrador and Innuitland. They took a slightly different course to me to reach Greenland, flew over that, and then "hopped" to Iceland, adding a long flight missing out the Faeroes Islands to get to Scotland.

Their new route would take them through France and across Spain, and essentially around the west coast of Africa to Cape Town. There was an epic quality that I would not have enjoyed myself in some of the flights they made in Africa, especially in those two dreadful centres of corruption, Nigeria and Cameroun. But while they were still in Europe I managed to get an invitation through to them from Villefranche du Perigord, and they stopped the night at my house to swap stories and dream. I had a flight in both their machines, just to see how they handled.

Olivier and I soon fell out. He believed I had too easy a flying life, raising sponsorship before making the flights I had done. In his opinion I should be more earthy about my flights and do it in a different spirit, seeking freedom, as he does it. And having heard from Keith Reynolds in England why Keith had left me in Siberia, Olivier wanted to challenge me about that too. He was sitting out on my terrace, chilling out with some exotic weed after we had aired blunt views about our different approaches to adventures, and Mike and I were chatting in the kitchen in a desultory fashion.

What was he going to do after he finished in Cape Town?

He thought he would settle down for a bit and recover, financially as much as physically, and wanted to spend time with his family. We looked over possible flights, Everest, Pole to Pole, and eventually, the Atlantic proper, the way it was first done, rather than the way he and Olivier and I had done it, around the edges.

"What is the distance from St Johns in Newfoundland to Ireland," I asked, idly, " the way Alcock and Brown did it?"

Mike had a computer with a programme that enabled him to make this calculation easily. He mumbled away for a few moments.

"It looks like 1,915 miles," he said.

"Is that nautical miles, or statute miles?"

"Statute."

"Do you know, that's do-able!" I exclaimed, and then wondered if I had blurted out too much. Among pilots whom I thought would also have a go, when it was generally realised that we were capable of making such a flight in microlights, Mike was a prime candidate. But it did not catch Mike's attention in quite the same way it caught mine. I was afire with the idea. In still air, which I would not have but you have to calculate that way, it would take more than 30 hours to make such a flight. How much fuel would I need? On my longest Atlantic hop, from Kulusuk in eastern Greenland to Reykjavik in Iceland, 450 statute miles, I had used 11 litres an hour with 8 hours, 15 minutes flying. I needed a safety margin, a big one, so if 30 hours used 330 litres, I probably needed 400 litres. I knew that a Frenchman, Guy Delage had carried 350 litres on his microlight flight across the South Atlantic back in 1992. Would current British microlight wings be capable of carrying the same load?

After I saw Mike and Olivier off the following day, heading for Spain, I drafted a one-page proposal which I had ready at any time to present to a potential sponsor. This is the gist of what I proposed

> *The distance between St John's, Newfoundland, and Shannon on the west coast of Ireland, is just 1,915 statute miles (3,064 kms). It was first flown in 1919 by John Alcock and Arthur Whitten Brown in a Vimy bomber. They took 16h30m to reach Ireland, flying at 100mph with a tailwind.*
>
> *It is possible to cover this huge distance non-stop in a flex-wing microlight, flying at 65mph, and assuming a tailwind of a mere 15 mph (for which I will wait) and do the flight in 24 hours. But in the worst-case scenario, I would have a still-air speed of 60 mph, and no tailwind, taking 33 hours to reach Ireland. This is the same time as Lindbergh took, non-stop, to reach Paris from New York in 1927.*
>
> *The microlight in which I want to repeat their flight is a Pegasus Quantum Sport 912, the same type of microlight I flew around the world in 1998. It has a Rotax 912 engine, developing 80hp, and using 11 litres/hour; 4-stroke, 4-cylinder, dual ignition, it is one of the most reliable engines in the world. I will carry 400 litres of fuel, a tenth of A&B's, but fly slower than them. Navigation would be by GPS – global positioning system – so I don't need to fly in the ice-forming regions above cloud, as they did.*

> *The flight will be made in June/July and take advantage of the better weather forecasts we have today. It is not really about being technically competent; my engine is so much better than A&B's. It is about character and stoicism. For sponsors, this is a huge event, with a chance to promote themselves world-wide, repeating one of the most famous flights ever made, non-stop from America to Europe.*

Over the next sixteen months, I wafted this idea in front of anyone I could find who might be interested in sponsoring it. Whenever I saw an advertisement for a product that aimed to come across to the public as adventurous, I found out who the marketing agency was, and wrote proposing they sponsor my flight. I culled biographies of rich and powerful businessmen from the financial pages of newspapers, especially if I saw they had a private aircraft, or really wanted to be a fighter pilot, and sent them letters with the idea.

Nothing came of it.

The year 2000 could reasonably be described as the worst of my life. Nothing seemed to work. I tried for jobs in television, and even if suited, at 57 I was too old. I got as far as a screen test as a financial reporter, ad libbing two minutes off the FTSE screen, and being deemed excellent. But it did not lead on to work. I lived by occasional talks drummed up by the London Speaker Bureau, and selling part of my store of shares.

It was towards the end of that year that I felt enough was enough. The following year, 2001, was not going to be the same. I had two adventures on the stocks, one the flight across the Atlantic the second to chase the ghost of an early American aviator, William Devoe Coney, across America. Coney was the first man to fly coast to coast across the USA in a flying time of less twenty-four hours, though because of poor weather back in 1921, his elapsed time coast-to-coast was 57 hours, 27 minutes. I wanted to race that time in a microlight. I had got close once to raising the sponsorship for the Coney Run, which would have covered all my expenses and left me enough for the Atlantic, and even got as far as drafting a contract and sending it out. But the stock markets in which my potential backer was invested either went through the floor, or did not go through the floor quickly enough. Anyway, he called it off. Perhaps in the future, he said, but not now.

In the late Autumn I talked things over with my children, James and Jade. James, 25, was a First Lieutenant in the Army at the time, an Arabic specialist, while Jade, 22, was in her third year at Trinity College, Dublin, studying English and History. I told them I was dying of frustration and that I proposed selling my liquid assets and funding my own adventure. There might, I said, be a possibility that I could sell a TV documentary about one or other of the adventures, but in any case, I wanted to do them both, the Coney Run and the Atlantic. It was their inheritance I proposed spending, but James and Jade both agreed. They are accustomed to seeing me on adventures, and this was just another one. Jade might have worried about who was going to pay her university fees if anything happened to me, but I made adequate provisions against an accident in my last will and testament, which I always leave behind on such adventures.

I had an adequate aircraft, the GT Global Flyer, with about 550 hours on it. Of these, 405 hours were spent going somewhere on the world flight. There was at least another 650 hours of life before I would have to pay out for a major overhaul of the engine, so both adventures were easily within its current service life. The GT Flyer was built by Pegasus Aviation near Marlborough in Wiltshire. It had carried 117 litres of fuel on the world flight, 50 litres in a belly tank, 25 litres each in tanks slung either side of me, and 17 litres on the floor of the cockpit. I needed to carry much more fuel than that, but would the wing take it?

I phoned Dr Billy Brooks that autumn, the aircraft designer, whose name I had successfully put up for an award coupled to the Segrave Trophy. Billy mumbled while he made his calculations, and then said he thought the wing would take the weight. I asked if they could build me a fuel tank to fit on to my existing wing. He grew vague.

My relationship with Pegasus was an arms-length one. The company had been founded at least 15 years earlier by amalgamating a firm called Solar Wings which made hang glider wings, with other companies that built microlight trike units. I had owned 25% of Solar Wings, and had always used their wings while hang gliding or microlighting. When I flew around the world I had paid the market price for everything, including the aircraft, and during the flight the official Pegasus line was, "nothing to do with me, guv". Pegasus boss Bill Sherlock was worried, as was most of the British microlighting community, that I would crash and burn in my modified aircraft. Pegasus disclaimed any responsibility for what I had done to make the GT Flyer capable of flying around the world, and for my flying it.

This attitude changed instantly once I had got back safely. From "not me, guv", the company then spent more than a year, heavily advertising in the aviation media that they had built the first microlight to fly around the world. A photograph (my copyright but who cared? or even asked?) of me flying across the New York skyline was the centrepiece of the advertising. Unknown to me at the time, the company produced a limited edition of ten Quantum 912 microlights, all looking like the GT Flyer. I found it disconcerting to fly into a meeting at Popham, for example, to see four other aircraft almost exact clones of my own. It would have been nice to have known. I think it is reasonable to say that my flight around the world benefitted Pegasus.

I thought Billy Brooks would be excited about designing a one-off tank for a flight across the Atlantic. In fact, nothing happened for weeks. I phoned again and checked that it was possible to build one, and again Billy said it was. Next, I had a phone call, I think it was from Pegasus marketing man John Fack, with whom I had flown hang gliders for 25 years, demanding a formal letter exonerating Pegasus from anything I was going to do with the big tank. I sent off such a letter, nothing happened again for more months. I lost heart. If Pegasus were not interested, I still had one of their aircraft, but where could I find a fuel tank big enough for the job?

There are three significant microlight manufacturers in Britain; the other two are Medway Microlights near Rochester in Kent, for whom Keith Reynolds had been test pilot, and Mainair Sports up in Rochdale, Lancashire. Colin Bodill had flown a Mainair Blade 912 around the world. Mainair was owned by Eileen Hudson, widow of a man I had done a lot of hang gliding with, John Hudson, but the company was run by Jim Cunliffe. I had met Jim once, a big straight-speaking Northerner with a shy manner, when I saw Colin off on his world flight. Jim had been closely involved in Colin's flight, but we hardly knew each other well. One day I phoned Jim and told him about my dilemma, saying I had no sponsors, was planning the Atlantic flight on my own using an aircraft built by his main rival, but would Mainair build me a huge fuel tank? Without hesitation, Jim said yes.

The more I talked to Jim, the better I liked him. I went through what I required in detail, and he was so friendly and helpful that I asked, in the end, whether he would rather I did the flights on his aircraft. He said he would. I told him I could not afford to buy a brand new Blade, costing more than £20,000, but I would find the money for all the modifications, including the big tank. In return, I would give him whatever publicity I could get on the Coney Run before the Atlantic.

"Will your wing be able to take such a load, though?" I asked.

Again, we went through the calculation stage, this time with Mainair's chief designer, Roger Pattrick. After calculations, Roger said it would, but that the safety margins would come down. If I pulled more than 3.5G the wing would collapse. I could pull 3.5G with a 90 degree wingover, well outside the envelope of the wing, if I was so foolish enough to attempt it.

"What about the design of a tank? Guy Delage had one which was virtually part of his aircraft. Could you fit a 400 litre tank into a Blade?" I asked.

Again Roger said he could, but that he needed time to design one. I ended the conversation happy to have allies, and was particularly taken with Jim Cunliffe, an opinion, unlike others, I have had no cause at all to revise after all that happened.

I needed an organiser, and already had a volunteer. Two years earlier at the British Microlight Aircraft Association AGM, I had met Liam Abramson, a smart-looking South African living in north London. I was selling *Global Flyer*, my book about the world flight, and Liam came up to buy one. From the first he was very impressive, intelligent, decisive, and, I thought, full of character. He urged me to consider him as an organiser if ever I went on another adventure, and I filed away his name. His normal job was lecturing on the business side of music, but he assured me he would be able to fit whatever I needed into his working life.

When I decided on a shoestring budget that both adventures would go ahead, it was a terrific relief. Whatever happened, I could start to plan, and I felt I had come back to life. I phoned Liam and outlined what I was doing. Even though two years had gone by since his initial approach, he was keen to be involved. He had made a couple of microlight flights, in 3-axis rather than flex-wing, but I thought then that actually having experience of flying was secondary to being a good organiser. We met and came to an agreement. He would do the organising for the flights, and look after the media for both of them. I would not pay him a huge sum of money, just £300 a week for a set number of weeks, but the understanding was, if I raised any sponsorship money then his pay would rise to £600/week, much more reasonable income, plus his expenses.

Normally, I do adventures for what the Irish call the *craic*, because they are there. This time I wanted to involve a charity. I had met Nikki King at aviation functions, introduced to her by Tony Iveson, a former 617 "Dambuster" Squadron pilot and a friend. Nikki had the special attraction for me of being the daughter of Dave Shannon, one of Guy Gibson's pilots on the famous

Dambuster Raid in World War Two. She had recently taken over fund-raising for the Artificial Heart Fund, based at the John Radcliffe Hospital in Oxford. The AHF was said to be one of the two foremost pioneers into artificial hearts (the other being a hospital in Texas). These were used either as a way of resting an existing heart which may suffer temporary damage, or as replacements for worn-out hearts. The supply of human organs from accident victims was, of necessity, limited, and there was always a much bigger demand than there was a supply.

At that time in Britain, artificial hearts had been used four times. The hearts themselves, made in the USA and costing £50,000 each, were about the size of a human thumb, but the battery pack to drive it, worn outside the body, was somewhat bigger. The first use of such a heart in this country was on a 19 year old girl called Julie, who was thought certain to die when her heart was infected by a virus. But pioneer surgeon John Westerby inserted an artificial heart in Julie for just over a week, stopping her own heart and giving it time to recover. He later restarted her by-now rested organ and removed the artificial one. Julie recovered fully and went back to leading a normal life.

AHF's latest patient, Peter Houghton, who had survived 11 months when I met him, with the functions of his real heart taken over by an artificial one, planned to walk from John O'Groats to Lands End to raise money for the charity, and to show how fit he was. I was to give him his first microlight flight.

Nikki was happy to allow me to associate her charity with my flight, essentially to raise its public profile rather than as a direct fund-raiser. I had no experience of raising money for charity through adventures, and we could not think of a way to do more than get publicity.

I started planning the flights in detail in early 2001, first the Coney Run and then the Atlantic. I spent as much time researching the Coney adventure as I did the Atlantic flight, and it threads through the Atlantic story. Much of February, for example, I spent in America, eight days in Washington tracking down the official reports on Coney's 1921 flight, and ten days in his home town of Brunswick, Georgia, finding his grave and the original house he lived in, still standing. I would not have been able to take all the financial costs had it not been for the network of campanologists that I was introduced to by a girlfriend at the time, Elva Ainsworth, one of the country's top bell-ringers.

In early March, Liam invited me to a reception at a legal firm in the City of London. He told me his brother John was an up-and-coming lawyer at

LeBoeuf, Lamb, Greene and MacRae, a large international law firm. One reason I was invited was because of my world flight, as a "notable" pilot, and there I met a couple of American women pilots who were due to set out on an air race to Australia.

At that reception I was introduced to a man who seemed central to the aviation establishment. He was called David Gleave, his card described him as Chief ATC Investigator for a company called Aviation Hazard. He was a client of Liam's brother, which gave him great credibility, both in my eyes and in Liam's. Gleave was very taken with the proposed Atlantic flight and volunteered his help, specifically with Canadian permissions. He seemed to know a great deal about the subject, who to speak to, the procedures to be completed, and we welcomed his offer. He also volunteered two other jobs, to find us a large Russian aircraft called an Antonov 124 to get me and the microlight to America, and to get me permission to fly off an Antonov wing in my trike, (when it is on the ground, of course), to demonstrate its flying characteristics.

From time to time over the next three months I checked with Gleave that all was well, both by e-mail and by telephone. I was assured it was, that there were no problems he was not capable of coping with, and he would let me know if there were. I met him again at the annual fly-in at Popham, full of charm and enthusiasm. It turned out that getting a lift to America by Antonov 124 just never quite happened, and nor did the wing take-off. But at least the Canadian permissions were going without a hitch.

There were two odd aspects about the flight that I feel worth recording. The first is that I now often saw Helen Dudley, the amateur actress who was then a PA in a City company, and who had been a muse on the world flight. We used to meet at her flat near Bow, or my house in Bethnal Green, for dinner. Helen had once had her stars read by my friend Stephen Lewis, a brilliant City economist whom I had known for 15 years, and trusted more than any man in the world. Fluent in both forms of Roman Latin and in Ancient Greek, Stephen had regularly led the institutional polls as best economist in the City in the 1980's, and we had got to know each other when I was TV-am's Financial Correspondent. Stephen had learned all the various forms of astrology in the certain belief that one cannot understand Greek or Roman (or Chinese) history without such knowledge. He thought Helen was very gifted in these airy arts – reading palms, astrology, tarot cards – in which I myself do not believe. But when a beautiful woman offers to read your Tarot cards, what do you say? One evening early in January, I picked nine tarot cards and Helen read my future. I do not claim to understand what it was all about, but they were these:

1. *King of Staves – light colour, fair skin, slimly built. Likes me but is not getting involved with me. Cheers me up. Good at marketing.*
2. *Justice – Fairness, balance, taking the outcome as good. Fairness in a wider sense. Terrific if joint venture is to be entered. If marriage, would work. Agreement through discussion, even if I am honest and others are not, I am right.*
3. *Three Cups (R = Reversed) – A fun card (wedding? a child? housewarming?). Even a reverse is fun, frivolity or sex. Expected marriage. If an affair, marriage will not follow.*
4. *Strength – Someone ill recovers soon. Tired, down-hearted, then things will improve. I will overcome obstacles, even against pressure. Achievements and success ahead. It's a good card for interviews. Quiet courage of the unexpected kind. Good wins over evil.*
5. *King of Swords (R) – Aggressive man stirs up trouble. Lawyer in opposition? Medical, professional man whom I will be against. May be evil because he cannot help it. Expect aggression, tantrums, even violence from this man.*
6. *Death – Never means death (except sometimes with old and sick). Means change. Current situation will change. Death of old self, new way of life. Initially unpleasant, even financial losses, a change in health, but always a chance to make good. Changes from unnecessary past rubbish to a new start.*
7. *Knight of Swords (R) – Tough, brave, intelligent, young man will help me soon. Assertive dark young man. Reverse is an aggressive destructive dark young man, or just active ambitious man, will come into my life. Arguments. Medical, surgical treatment soon.*
8. *Page of Staves – Intelligent, restless youngster shows up when I'm on a journey. Young visitors a long way off. Surprising news on the way about work and old friends, minor property matters go ahead now.*
9. *Six Coins (R) – Money shared out soon. May be the result of an inheritance. Too many people are draining me of energy. Also, could be in a good position to help out others.*

Then Helen asked me to think of the most important question in my life this coming year, and pick a card. I thought the question was: Will I be alive at the end of it? I pulled a card called Magician.

This is said to depict new opportunities, new relationship, more likely business than romance. There will soon be a chance to use existing skills, education, perhaps something in politics? Bold step, chancy element, but the card says, go ahead, have a go. Put ideas into practice, get rewarded. It presupposes self-reliance.

From time to time as this story unfolds, go back to this tarot reading.

The second oddity came from another woman, Judy Leden, a friend for twenty years ever since she came into hang-gliding, when she felt that I had steered her into becoming a great pilot. As she was at one time and simultaneously, the British, European and World Woman's hang gliding champion, and also held, in three separate flights, the British, European and World distance record, she was undoubtedly great. In microlighting, in 1994, she and a second separate pilot, Ben Ashman, flew two microlight aircraft – each 100 kgs overweight – from London to Amman in Jordan. In the process, they raised £100,000 for a cancer fund commemorating a young Jordanian girl, Yasmin Saudi (Judy's daughter was named Yasmin) whose death prompted the journey. Judy's book, *Flying with Condors*, was beautifully written and there was talk of it being filmed.

Now married to another good pilot, Chris Dawes, and with two children, I had seen much less than usual of Judy in recent years. But she sent me a note before I left on the Atlantic flight, commenting on the feeling that sometimes comes over her when friends get into danger. Her husband had recently broken his leg hang gliding (in horrendous conditions) and Judy, who was 20 miles away, *knew while it was happening that it was going on*. She was already on the way to find him long before anyone else knew about the accident.

She told me that when she had last seen the great young American hang glider pilot, Chris Bulger, back in 1985, she clung to him crying, as if she knew it was the last time she would see him; he was killed soon afterwards, ahead of their next rendezvous. Judy said she had these insights as a matter of form, even though she did not like them. Her 6-year old daughter, Yasmin, may have the same "gift"; Yasmin was at home when her mother took off recently into difficult conditions, and the nanny heard Yasmin say, at the exact time of take-off, "Be careful, Mummy".

At no time during my world flight, or earlier during my Australia flight, did Judy have these feelings about me. She "knew" I was going to be all right. She told me that so far she had not had these feelings about my Atlantic Flight. It was a question of, so far, so good. I was not sure I wanted to know if Judy ever *did* get these feelings.

There was little risk attached to Coney, but much more to the Atlantic flight. Was I capable of doing it? I had been "on the road" for 121 days on the flight around the world, but never been more than 10 hours in the air on any one day. This is a lot of hours, especially as there is no automatic pilot and all the flying is "live", but it was still less than a third of what I was planning in repeating Alcock and Brown's flight. My normal daily diet on the world flight had been simple; eat and drink as little as possible in the morning so as not to want to go to the toilet in the air, chew gum all day, and in the evening eat and drink as much as I could.

Dr Carl Hallam, the BMAA's doctor and a Blade 912 Flyer, was a former Royal Marine with experience of work in the Arctic. He suggested a number of precautions I must take:

"I am not an expert in the academic sense, although having worked for three winters in the Arctic, I am very conscious of the practical problems. I suppose that it is fair to say that if all goes well with electric clothing, that you will probably not get cold at all throughout your flight. However, at the expense of being tedious I would like to outline the mechanisms by which we generate heat and keep warm as this knowledge will make the experts advice more understandable.

We need fuel, but have no reliable fuel gauge, so P.P.P.P.P.P. is our only reliable safeguard (Proper Planning Prevents Piss-Poor Performance).

To generate heat, all our food is ultimately broken down in our bodies into glucose, our actual fuel. When we move our muscles, we metabolise the glucose, carried in our bloodstream from our gut. This produces carbon dioxide and water with the release of energy, which actually makes the muscle contract and heat, which keeps us at 37C. We blow off the carbon dioxide in our expired air. The blood, acting like a central heating system carries the heat from the muscles to the rest of the body. The bigger the muscles, the more heat they generate; digging the garden or running on a hot day makes us very hot. Standing motionless on a very cold day will make us even more cold. Therefore moving the large muscles like legs and arms will be your only source of heat if other systems fail. I am anxious that you will not be able to do this, strapped into your Blade.

This whole process can only continue provided there is a sufficient supply of fuel. We are not talking about huge quantities here. Our daily ration pack in the Arctic provided 5,500 Calories in two meals which enabled us to ski with large packs both uphill and downhill, as well as keeping warm. These activities at minus 20C or less in fact made us very hot.

Various parts of the body can function below 37C, hands and feet for instance, but the brain has a very narrow temperature tolerance, and must be kept at or near 37C to function normally. Below this, one becomes progressively confused and ultimately unconscious.

The problem is the lack of a fuel gauge to give us an "at a glance" estimation of our nutritional state.

Bearing in mind the 'reward' aspect of eating, all you need do is literally fill a bag of all your favourite treats and munch your way across the Atlantic. This way you will undoubtedly consume sufficient calories and your spirits will be far higher than if you were sucking some awful sweet and sticky fluid through a tube. You MUST of course actually eat your goodies and not be so British that you arrive in Shannon with them still all wrapped up in the bag.

You will need at least two litres of fluid, either plain water or two litres of the rehydration mixture correctly made up that I gave you.

As for Heat Loss, at every breath we take in about 1 litre of air at say, 0 – 5C at night. We breathe the same air out at 37C. We have to heat every litre of air to 37C in order to exchange gasses in our lungs. That means, unfortunately, that however well insulated you are in trendy Goretex nicks, socks, Long Johns etc. we cannot prevent the heat loss of respiration. You can see the links that exist between heat gain and heat loss and the crucial role that fuel plays in keeping us warm ..."

It is as well Carl Hallam did not consider the diet of Alcock and Brown on the original 1919 flight, with Alcock in particular partial to swigging whisky to keep himself warm in the air. I decided I needed to know more about the two principal ghosts I was going to race against, and the third, Charles Lindbergh, under whose flight-path I was going to travel.

3

Alcock and Brown, Lindbergh and the Atlantic flights

The ghosts of great aviators haunt me. I understand that the past is a foreign country and they do things differently there, but however fleetingly, I also want to capture something left of the faint quality of those heroic aviators. I had already done so on previous flights.

Once, on my way to Australia by microlight in early January, 1988, leaving Sittwe in Burma, I climbed into the air above the airfield, built next to a beach. Looking east through jungle growth and colonial buildings that we – the British – had built before the Japanese occupation, I saw mountains in the blue distance. I knew that beyond those mountains was Rangoon. Turning right to look back at the airfield it was a shock to see, with the hair standing up on my arms and the back of my neck, that also carved out of the jungle next to the runway I had just left, was a ghostly runway, a shadow in different coloured grass. I realised it had been the runway in use in 1919 when Ross and Keith Smith came through to meet up with those gallant but losing French aviators, Poulet and Benoist. It had been used by Bert Hinkler in 1928 and by Amy Johnson in 1930. It was the goal of Sir Charles Kingsford-Smith on his 1935 record attempt from England to Australia before he disappeared with flames appearing from his engine in the Bay of Bengal.

I was looking down on the same scene they had looked at. My situation was similar to theirs, and in particular, to Hinkler's and Johnson's, in that they were lone flyers as I was. I could feel the holiness of the moment reaching across decades so they were no longer sepia-tinted figures staring at me from old books, impossibly romantic.

They were, briefly, as I am. In turn, I was as they are.

I knew a great deal about Ross Smith on that Australia flight, but rather less about the eight American aviators who were the first to fly around the world in 1924, and whose ghosts I raced by microlight in 1998 and beat. Was it because the latter were American Army pilots, and on an official mission, backed by all the resources of the US Government, and therefore less human and personal to me? I spent months, though, chasing down accounts of the 1919 flight by John Alcock, and Arthur Whitten Brown, the first non-stop across the Atlantic. It was also easy to find accounts of the New York-Paris flight made by the American, Charles Lindbergh, in 1927. These three ghosts fascinated me, and the even fainter ghosts of the men they had beaten, and whose experience I wanted to rediscover in my own flights.

The first Atlantic flight

After World War One there was a ferment to fly big distances. The first major target was the Atlantic, less than ten years from the day that Louis Bleriot had put a marker against the Royal Navy by flying the 22 miles of the English Channel. Five teams set out to Newfoundland, at the time still an independent Dominion and not part of Canada. None of the teams were of "enemy origin", which meant they were eligible to win a prize of £10,000 put up by Alfred, Lord Northcliffe, who owned the *Daily Mail*. This was for a flight "from any point in the United States, Canada or Newfoundland to any point in Great Britain or Ireland, in 72 consecutive hours (or vice versa)". The distance between St John's, Newfoundland, and the nearest part of the west coast of Ireland, is 1,915 statute miles (3,064 kms). One could re-fuel, if one wished, in mid-Atlantic.

The most famous pilot at that time preparing in Newfoundland was Harry Hawker, whose name was later adopted by the Sopwith Company, which went on to make aircraft like the Hurricane and Typhoon. Hawker was planning to fly a Sopwith single-engined machine called *Atlantic* specially designed for the flight, in which the pilot sat beside and a little behind the navigator. He planned to drop the *Atlantic's* undercarriage after take-off to give himself an extra 7 mph, and to skid to a landing at the far end. The aircraft was capable of 100mph, and carried 330 gallons of fuel (1,561 litres); if it ditched, the upper part was designed to act as a lifeboat. His navigator was Kenneth MackenzieGrieve, a Royal Navy commander with no flying experience at all before the big flight.

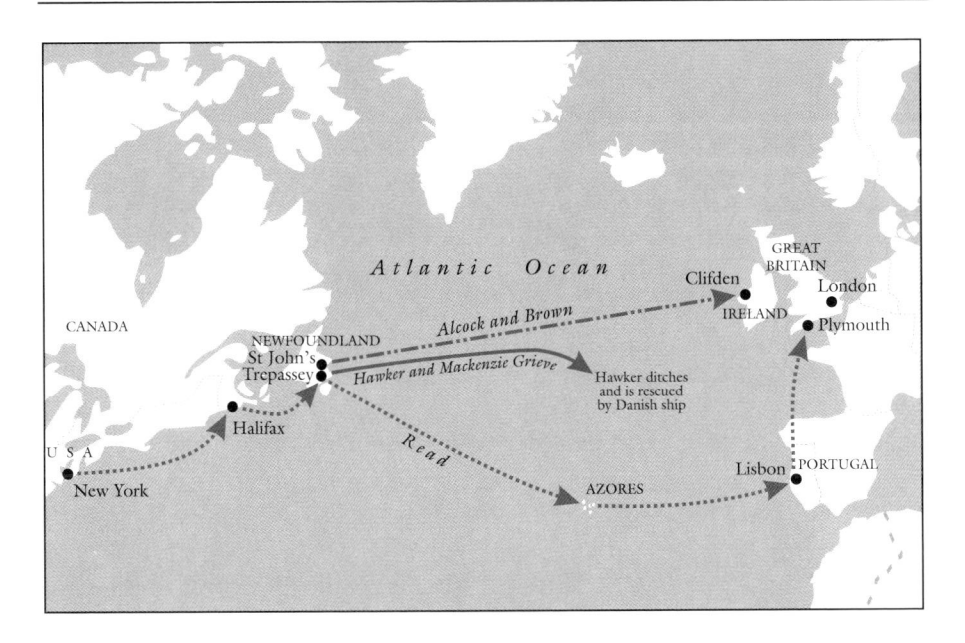

1919 Transatlantic flights

A second entry came from the Martinsyde Company, with a small single-engined two-seater aircraft called *Raymor*, faster than the Sopwith at 110 mph, and carrying 393 gallons of fuel (1,860 litres), capable of flying 2,750 miles non-stop. The pilot was Freddie Raynham, and his navigator was a one-legged ex-Royal Navy Captain called Fairfax Morgan, who claimed to be a descendent of Henry Morgan, the pirate. Morgan had lost his leg when he was shot down in the war, and his artificial leg was made of cork (it would float.)

A third British entry came from Handley Page, with its new V/1500 biplane bomber originally designed to bomb Berlin. It had four engines, a crew of two, and a commander, a 55 year old Admiral, Mark Kerr, the same age I had been on my world flight. The Kerr team set up in Harbour Grace, apart from everyone else, about 60 miles from St Johns.

The last British team to enter was from Vickers, a twin-engined Vimy bomber crewed by two ex-prisoners of war, Captain John Alcock and his navigator, Lieutenant Arthur Whitten Brown. Alcock had been shot down fighting the Turks, but had already established his pre-War reputation as a brilliant pilot, enough to impress Vickers. Brown, his navigator, born in Manchester of American parents, volunteered for the Royal Flying Corps in 1914, and was shot down fighting the Germans. One leg was so badly injured

Brown could never walk properly again. He had hobbled in to Vickers looking for a job, and was asked if he could navigate an aircraft across the Atlantic. As he inspected the aircraft with Alcock, the latter tapped his walking stick and said, "you won't be needing that. We're flying, not imitating Moses".

Separate from this largely-British effort to cross the Atlantic non-stop, the Americans had their own ideas. The US Army Air Corps had expanded explosively when America entered the War in 1917, and in 1919 it was contracting just as fast. An aggressively energetic general called Billy Mitchell was urging his pilots to break every aviation record possible, racing across America, around the coast of the United States, up to Alaska and back, and soon, around the world. Mitchell wanted good positive stories in his campaign to create a US Air Force separate from both the Army and Navy. In 1919, the air arms of the US Navy as well as the US Army were fighting for their political lives. The US Navy determined to send its own team to be first across the Atlantic, not non-stop but in stages from New York via Nova Scotia, Newfoundland, the Azores and then Spain and England.

All the teams except Kerr's, lodged in the Cochrane Hotel in St John's, Newfoundland's capital. It was then the best hotel in the city, a four-story wooden building with a palm court and a billiard room, run by the four Dooley sisters. Hawker and Raynham were ready to make their flights even before Alcock and Brown had set off from England, but the weather in the area – notorious then as it is now – was against them. They had day after day of rain, winds blowing the wrong way, and when they had sun, out in the Atlantic it was not possible to guarantee a following wind. Worse, each team had to build a separate aerodrome, because there were no flying facilities on the island of Newfoundland. Until the competition started, no one there had seen an aeroplane.

On April 11, 1919, at Glendenning's Farm, six miles from St Johns, Hawker took the Sopwith out for a test flight, which was successful. They were watched by Raynham and Morgan, who had arrived that day by ship at St Johns from Liverpool with their aircraft still crated. Newfoundland prohibited the sale of alcohol at the time – a wartime measure – and Martinsyde smuggled crates of whisky and gin in to drown their sorrows if Hawker won, or to celebrate if they beat him. Five days after their arrival, after working night and day at their own "airfield" by Quidi Vidi Lake, Raynham and Morgan were ready to challenge

Hawker. The weather remained awful, and the full moon night of April 16, earmarked as a likely take-off day, went by unflown.

Both teams watched nervously as an American survey party turned up that week to look over the harbours to the south of Newfoundland to begin their own sea-plane flight across the Atlantic.

A whole month was to go by in fruitless waiting before the weather was deemed safe enough to fly.

On May 8th, Alcock and Brown were nearing Halifax Harbour when three American Curtiss flying boats, NC-1, NC-3 and NC-4, look off from Long Island, New York, and set out on the thousand mile journey to Newfoundland. NC-4 had engine failure in the Gulf of Maine, landed on the sea, and taxied safely to port and repairs. The other two were moored in Halifax as Alcock and Brown passed through. The two British aviators took a train from Halifax to North Sydney on Cape Breton Island, a ferry across to Port aux Basques, and then a tedious 39-hour railway journey to St Johns, passing via Stephenville Junction where I was to be held up for so long 82 years later. They were greeted with great enthusiasm at the Cochrane by Hawker and Raynham – old friends – on May 13th. In pre-war days, Alcock, Hawker and Raynham had been rated among the 10 best pilots in Britain. At that hotel meeting Alcock and Brown were depressed to hear about the weather, and the complete lack of an airfield, though the newcomers were offered fields being used by their competitors … after their competitors had set out on their Atlantic attempt. They may have been friends, but winning was winning.

Two days later they were electrified to hear the American seaplanes were preparing to leave, on a direct route south east between Newfoundland and the Azores patrolled by 27 US Navy destroyers, available to rescue the airmen if they ditched at sea. The two seaplanes, NC-1 and NC-3, had made it to their start point, but as they were ready to leave for the Azores without the third aircraft, they heard NC-4 circle overhead. They waited until it landed, and resolved to leave the following day, together. British spectators called them the "Nancies", after NC.

On May 16th the American seaplanes left, flying in formation, but soon separating at night. NC-4, the late arriver, proved the fastest, and arrived at Horta in the Azores at 11 o'clock the following day after a flight of 15 1/2 hours. The others were not so lucky. NC-1 ran into fog near the islands, opted to land on the sea, sprang a leak, and the crew baled furiously for 6 hours until rescued by a passing steamer, just as the aircraft was on the verge of sinking.

NC-3 also came down on the sea in the bank of fog, but misjudged the landing, split the hull, and tore off the float from its left wing. The crew were 200 miles from land, their drinking water had been ruined, their radio equipment was broken. For two days, exhausted and seasick, they baled out water, and taxied their aircraft through gales of up to 60 mph to the island of San Miguel. The crew took it in turns to lash themselves to the tip of the starboard wing to keep the NC-3 on an even keel and the port wing out of the water. When an American destroyer discovered them, the crew refused rescue and taxied on into Ponta Delgada to a hero's welcome.

It was another ten days before the successful NC-4 was able to leave the Azores for a 900 mile journey to Lisbon in Portugal.

On May 18th, Alcock and Brown, after a fruitless search for an airfield of their own, their Vimy still at sea in crates, returned to the Cochrane to find Hawker and Raynham working feverishly. They had received that day a "good" weather forecast. The sun shone for the first time in many days, and reports from ships at sea indicated good weather in mid-Atlantic. There was a gentleman's agreement that each would warn the other that they were about to start, and Hawker and Mackenzie-Grieve gave such a warning to Raynham and Morgan. Hawker added a dinner invitation in London.

At 3.48 that afternoon, Hawker flew his heavily-laden Sopwith off the uneven ground into a moderate to fresh wind after a run of 300 yards. He headed first for St Johns, flying over Raynham's ground at Quidi Vidi (seeing the white faces of their rivals looking up) before crossing the coast where they released their undercarriage and climbed into the distance. Raynham was not unduly worried; his was the faster machine, and he wanted to complete his last careful preparations. An hour later he and Morgan climbed into their flying suits, both being teased by local girls about the piece of tube each was trailing from one trousered leg as toilet arrangements. At 4.48pm they started their take-off run, and after 200 yards rose struggling into the air. But a strong cross-wind hit them and knocked them back on to the ground again, where the grossly over-loaded aircraft broke the undercarriage and it buckled into the ground. The crowd rushed up, expecting to find the airmen either dead or severely injured; they climbed out, apparently unhurt. But Morgan's face had crashed into the cockpit dashboard, the glass had splintered and entered his skull and he was rushed off to hospital. Raynham "had little to say but what he did say was forceful".

Heavily laden take-offs in Newfoundland were obviously difficult. The airfield at Quidi Vidi was at right angles to that at Glendenning's Farm, so the head wind that had helped Hawker take off was a cross-wind for Raynham

That evening, Raynham offered Alcock and Brown the use of his field at Quidi Vidi, which they gratefully accepted. It was not long enough for a fully-laden Vimy, but they were happy to have an air-strip so close to St Johns. Raynham made his generous offer despite plans to have another go at flying the Atlantic.

(He did so on July 17, 1919, this time with a different navigator – Morgan was sent back to England for treatment – but again Raynham crashed on take-off. Discouraged by his bad luck, he dismantled his aircraft and shipped it and himself back home).

No one slept that night of May 18th at the Cochrane, waiting for news of Hawker and Mackenzie-Grieve. What had happened to them?

For the first four hours of the flight, all went well. They climbed to 10,000 feet over the ever-present fog-banks off Newfoundland, averaging a steady 105 mph. The wireless proved useless, and Mackenzie-Grieve soon stopped fiddling with it. They ran into pillars of cumulus clouds up to 15,000 feet, and without the power to climb above them, Hawker dived into the clouds, enduring lashing rain and temperatures dropping to freezing point. North winds blew them off course. As the sun was setting Hawker noticed the radiator temperatures were too high. He could not account for this. The shutters on the radiator were fully open (he thought, though when the wreckage was discovered, the shutters were found fully closed) but he did not have many hours' experience in this type of aircraft.

Hawker cut the throttle and glided from 12,000 feet to 9,000 feet. To his relief, when he opened up again, engine temperatures remained normal. He climbed back to 12,000 feet, but steam soon came from the radiator. He began diving until the temperature was normal, then climbing again. He and Mackenzie-Glieve flew through the night like this, rarely ungluing their eyes from the temperature gauge. They were unable to see the Atlantic below them, but once Mackenzie-Grieve got a good star shot and found they were 150 miles south of their intended track. As it happens, this put them close to the shipping lanes.

After the sun came up, they had no alternative but to enter a huge towering storm. The turbulence threatened to pull the aircraft apart. Hawker tried to dive beneath the storm, then suddenly, the engine stopped. Instruments showed everything to be normal, but they could not restart. They were diving towards the surface of the sea, pumping petrol into the engine, when at the last moment it burst into life again. They realised, as they started to climb, there was little water left in the cooling system, and they were doomed to ditch. As the storm gathered pace, they turned right to fly south into the main shipping lanes, looking for a ship.

They spent two hours at about 200 feet, the aircraft being thrown around the sky, and between violent spasms of sickness Hawker was still able to fly. They gave themselves little chance of survival on their own. Then out of the murk, Hawker spotted a small steamer called *Mary*. They flew alongside, and Mackenzie-Grieve fired a red flare to attract attention. Hawker circled until they saw a man come out of the wheelhouse and stare up at them. They ditched in the ship's path, climbed into their "boat", and the aircraft was left, half out of the water, buoyed up by the petrol tanks.

It took ninety minutes in those awful conditions for the steamer finally to get a boat into the water and pick the two airmen out of the rising sea.

They had flown for fifteen hours and were just 500 miles from Ireland when they ditched. The steamer had no radio, so for more than a week an anxious world, including their companions in the Cochrane Hotel, came to believe they had been lost at sea. The Government was attacked by journalists contrasting the elaborate efforts of the Americans to look after their pilots, against the hands-off policies of Westminster. King George V sent a telegram of condolence to Mrs Hawker and her baby daughter. Finally, on May 26th, *Mary* rounded the Butt of Lewis and signalled to Lloyd's tower there:

"Saved hands sop-aer-opl-ane"
"Is it Haw-ker?"
"Yes"

A special destroyer was laid on to get them to Scapa Flow quickly. All the way to London by train, they were greeted as heroes. A hundred thousand people packed around King's Cross Station to see them to the Royal Aero Club. Lord Northcliffe gave them a cheque for £5,000, and the King gave them each Air Force Crosses. Even their aircraft was rescued, found floating ten days after the ditching, salvaged and brought home to be exhibited in Selfridges. Their air mail letters were recovered, and delivered.

Two days after Hawker and Mackenzie-Grieve reached Scotland, the NC-4 completed the first crossing of the Atlantic by aeroplane, by landing in Lisbon. She reached Plymouth Harbour on June 1st, 17 days after setting off from Newfoundland, alighting close by the steps where the Pilgrim Fathers had set off in 1620.

Back in Newfoundland, that left a damaged Martinsyde, a secretive Handley Page, and the Vickers Vimy of Alcock and Brown, which finally arrived at St Johns on May 26th. Fences had to be knocked down as the crates with aircraft parts were tugged through the city's streets by cart horses handled by a Mr Lester. It took a whole day to travel just one mile. Alcock alternated between settling claims for damage, and begging Lester not to wreck his aircraft. By lunchtime the following day, all the bits were safely stowed away, and they began to plan assembly.

Raynham's hangar was too small to do this job indoors, so it was all done in the open. For three days it rained almost without ceasing, and the Vickers team worked up to fourteen hours of daylight in a biting wind. There were no cranes, and sheerlegs had to be rigged from telegraph poles. A soldering iron immediately cooled when pulled from the fire, and hours were spent constructing a shelter to enable the soldering to be done safely, only for the wind to blow it away.

The race was on against Mark Kerr's Handley Page, of which team they knew little. They were always stopping to listen, wondering if they would hear the HP's engines passing overhead.

During the first week in June the Vimy started to look like a real aircraft. Crowds of local people visited it every day, most of them never having seen an aeroplane before. They sucked their teeth at the news that the Vimy intended to keep its undercarriage.

"What use will your wheels be to ye when ye land in the sea?" they demanded.

Alcock pointed out that they intended to fly the Atlantic, not fall into it. Others wanted to know if they filled the aircraft with gas to make it light so it could fly. The weather, always uncertain in the region, remained relatively fine.

Alcock worried constantly about the take-off run. He was offered the use of a field by a local chancer, proposing to hire it to him for £5,000, at a time when one pound Sterling could *buy* ten acres of Newfoundland. But one day Lester drove him out to a field where Alcock could pace out 500 yards, and then offered it to him for nothing. Lester even provided labour for three days to remove trees and boulders and fill in soggy ground, to enable a runway to be constructed. It became known, famously, as "Lester's Field". It was ready by June 8th.

"T'will do, t'will do," said Alcock, "but I hope we only have to use it once."

That afternoon, as they were doping the fabric of the Vimy, they heard engine noises and looked up to see the Handley Page pass overhead at 5,000 feet. They heard in the evening at the Cochrane Hotel that it had flown for six hours, and everyone presumed it was ready for the Atlantic flight. The betting odds, once 3–1 on the Vimy, shortened on the HP. Alcock resolved to test-fly the Vimy the following day, two weeks after the aircraft had been landed in St Johns harbour.

Next morning he and Brown filled the Vimy with just enough petrol and oil for a short flight, and were able to get off from Quidi Vidi without any problems. They flew over St Johns, and, lightly loaded, "she was as nippy as a scout." The two men did think of flying to Harbour Grace to wind-up the HP team, but had not enough fuel for the gesture. They completed the flight with one landing on Lester's Field. Alcock sent Vickers a very English cable that night:

"Machine absolutely tophole."

As always, nothing went perfectly. Their fuel, stored in barrels with a rubber lining, was found to be useless. The rubber had dissolved to produce a sticky deposit. Fred Raynham, still unready to fly, gallantly offered them fuel from his own reserves. Their wireless broke down on the test-flight. The weather deteriorated and a 24-hour watch was instituted, with men standing next to the tied-down aircraft waiting to hear the sound of tearing fabric and splintering wood. Alcock played patience and was irritable (that happens to me, too). Brown went fishing.

On June 12th the wind dropped and they heard the Handley Page cruise by overhead, and were fearful it was actually on the Atlantic attempt. But it turned back to return to Harbour Grace. Alcock and Brown took the Vimy up for another test flight and said it was perfect; even the wireless worked. When they landed the gale blew up again and flying became impossible. That evening a Vickers director, Maxwell Muller turned up. He was anxious at the delays; the company board in England could not understand why their aircraft was not already in the air. Alcock explained, and Muller saw conditions for himself. Alcock promised to leave in the morning.

Friday was Alcock's "lucky" day, and 13 Brown's "lucky" number, so on Friday, June 13th, the two men leapt out of bed to a near-gale with rain driven noisily against the windows of the hotel. Brown was dubious, but Alcock said he was sure they would leave that day. They drove Muller out of bed, he also thought they were mad to be so optimistic with such rotten weather, and the three men went to Lester's field to find the Vimy bucking and lurching against the tie-down ropes. Alcock remained optimistic, cheering everyone up. The compass was swung, food stored on board, and Alcock began boiling every pint of water that went into the radiator. What happened to Hawker, he resolved, would not happen to them. The weather forecaster, Lieutenant Clements, turned up and said the gale would continue until the middle of the following day.

Alcock did not believe him, and ordered the Vimy to take on board its huge fuel load of 865 gallons (3,932 litres) of petrol, and 40 gallons of oil. It was pumped in by hand from barrels. No one had ever put this much fuel on board an aircraft before, and no one knew what would happened.

Suddenly, there was a snapping noise. A shock absorber mounted on the axle had broken, under the load. No one looked at Alcock. He laughed and said, "maybe it wasn't 13 that was lucky, maybe it was 14 instead" and everyone else laughed too. They off-loaded the fuel and water and repaired the damage. Neither of the airmen slept well that night.

Their team worked from dusk to windy dawn repairing the axle, re-loading the fuel and water, and putting a final coat of dope on to the fabric surfaces.

On June 14th Alcock woke to a gentle breeze, kicked Brown out of bed, and was halfway to the car when Brown shouted that he was still in his pyjamas. They dressed, drove to the field, and then the wind started and stopped in vicious gusts. Alcock, all impatience, wanted to leave immediately. Brown and Muller urged caution. Lieutenant Clements arrived to say that all the winds in the Atlantic were westerly, with fine weather for the next 24 hours. He cautioned Alcock to wait for better weather later in the day. Alcock started each engine, listened to them running perfectly, switched off, and agreed to wait.

A boy arrived on a bicycle with sandwiches and coffee from the Cochrane Hotel. The boy started a rumour that someone had seen the Handley Page in the air. Local people in St John's wanted *their* team of Alcock and Brown to beat ("that Outport") Harbour Grace's team of Admiral Mark Kerr's, so there was a lot of disturbance at this rumour. Unseen by the pilots, one of the mechanics, Harry Cough, pulled out a cast-off horse-shoe and screwed it firmly under the pilot's seat.

By one o'clock the weather had improved, and the wind dropped to a steady 30mph. A petrol pipe, broken against one of the tie-down ropes, had been replaced. Alcock and Brown walked to the aircraft. The restraining ropes were removed, and the Vimy juddered.

Alcock said, "if we don't leave now we never will."

Brown agreed.

Lieutenant Clements said the high winds would drop over the Atlantic, and they would have a moderate westerly to Ireland. A bag containing 197 air mail letters was put on board. Doctor Campbell, who had helped Alcock get around Prohibition and the dearth of alcohol by giving the pilot medical prescriptions, ran up and give Alcock a bottle of whisky. Alcock thanked him and took a huge gulp! Forty volunteers took up places against the wing and tail. The engines were started, warmed up, checked OK, a hand raised, the wheel chocks removed, engines roared, volunteers dropped to the ground, and they all watched the lurching take-off.

Gradually the Vimy gained speed. Horses in nearby fields bolted. Fred Raynham, watching, three weeks after his own crash, must have had mixed feelings. Alcock kept the aircraft low until just a hundred yards was left, then slowly raised the nose and cleared the boundary dyke "by inches". It was 1.45pm. local time, 1615GMT.

They flew inland, and were lost from sight and a crash was feared. But they flew into wind, in bumpy air, as Alcock struggled to gain height at less than 200 feet/ minute. When they reached 1,000 feet, Alcock turned the Vimy, and they flew at that height over St Johns, and out over the sea, dotted with ice-bergs, heading for Ireland. Within half an hour they were doing 140 knots. They were soon enveloped in fog.

Their radio failed. A propeller-driven dynamo powered it, and the propeller sheared off. They shrugged and carried on climbing, Brown demanding height so he could get a "fix" on the sun. They lived in their own small world. Suddenly, there was a heavy clattering, and they looked to see the exhaust pipe on the starboard engine splitting away! It turned white-hot, and then melted, and the exhaust gases blew out in an absolutely raw state with no silencer at all. Flames belched backwards, but Brown could see no ill effects on the fabric of the wing. The noise, though, was deafening, and they could communicate only by notes.

After two hours they ate sandwiches. Alcock had a slug of whisky, while Brown finished a beer and gaily slung the bottle over the side. They were still in cloud, now at 5,000 feet, hand-pumping fuel into the tanks that directly fed the engines. Alcock took the aircraft up slowly, looking to break into clear air, with Brown worrying about navigation. Then for ten minutes they flew into a hole in the clouds, Brown took a sun-shot and found they were just a few miles south of track. At 9.30 it started to get dark. Their electric flying suits slowly failed, leaving them cold. Brown stood up every half hour for the rest of the night, playing a torch on each engine to see if they were OK.

At 12.05 Brown wrote, "I must see the stars".

Alcock could hear what he imagined was a change in the rhythm of both engines, running on three-quarter power. Nevertheless, he opened the throttles, they climbed and eventually burst out into a starry night with a near-full moon. They discovered they had covered 850 nautical miles at 106 knots, which was brilliant. Brown thought they should celebrate. He took out chocolate and more sandwiches, laced the coffee with a generous measure of whisky, and passed it to Alcock. Alcock started to sing, though Brown could not hear the words. They descended to 4,000 feet, still with the moon visible. The Atlantic below was hidden by a blanket of clouds.

At 3.30, just before dawn, they ran straight into the centre of a storm. Rain turned to hail, and the Vimy was slung around the sky. Lightning flashed around the wings, and the air speed indicator jammed at 90 knots. The Vimy stalled and fell in a spiralling dive towards the sea. Both men were disorientated, still in cloud but with flashes of lightning. Falling almost vertically, the altimeter unwound, 4,000 feet … 3,000 … 2,000 … 1,000 feet, Brown grabbed the log book and watched, in a detached way, while Alcock struggled with the controls … 500 … 300 … 100 feet … the needle was almost at zero when they fell out of the cloud and saw the sea immediately below them. Alcock, now knowing which way up he was, hauled back on the control column, levelled the wings, and opened the throttles. They seemed close enough that the spray of the white horses touched their undercarriage, but they were flying again. Brown looked at the compass a few minutes later and saw they were heading west back towards Newfoundland. He nudged Alcock, who burst out laughing, turned, and they were back on course.

They climbed back to 6,500 feet, but were now in a slight headwind – so much for weather forecasts, Alcock said later, with some bitterness – and soon they were again in a storm. Rain turned to hail, the aircraft was covered in snow, but Alcock kept climbing, hoping to break out above, perhaps to get another sun fix.

At 8,800 feet Brown saw that the air intakes on the engines were covered in snow, and they could soon be in serious danger. Brown, despite his gammy leg, released his safety belt, pulled off his mittens, and climbed out on to the wing. Alcock tried to pull him back but Brown savagely pushed him away, gripping the wooden strut that held the port engine. He dug out his jack-knife, and in the 90 mph winds and hail, chipped the ice off the air intakes. The engine began to pull cleanly again. Brown struggled behind Alcock's back to the starboard side, and despite the flames whistling past his face just a few inches from him, cleared the air intakes there too. Then, exhausted, he found his way back to the cockpit.

This he did five times in all during the storm.

At 7.20 am they climbed through 11,000 feet and got above the storm. The aircraft was covered in ice and difficult to control. Brown "fixed" the sun and wrote a note saying Ireland was within reach and it would be better down below, where it was warmer "and where we might pick up a steamer". Alcock descended back into cloud. The starboard engine started mis-firing loudly; the carburettor was iced-up. The shutters of the radiator had become a solid block of ice, and water temperatures were rising quickly. Visibility dropped to zero, and Alcock decided to throttle back to tickover. The explosions stopped, but started again whenever he opened the throttle. He resolved to glide down as low as possible in the hope that warmer air would clear the icing.

They were struck by turbulence, but also an eerie silence, or it felt that way after the roaring and clattering of the past 15 hours. They could talk to each other, but had nothing to say. They went down through 10,000 feet, 7,000, 5,000 and could see the effects of the warmer air. Ice on the wing surfaces was melting, and there was less stiffness in the controls. Below 1,000 feet they were unhappy to be trusting their instruments, but could still see nothing. At 500 feet they burst out of cloud to see the ocean and Alcock opened both throttles. The engines responded without a falter. Brown raided the locker again for a scrappy breakfast.

At 8.15 they came across two small islands, which Brown identified as being north of their projected course. They crossed the Irish coast at 8.25 and found the town of Clifden. People ran out, the airmen thought, to greet them, waving when they lined up on a smooth green field. But they were warning that it was a bog, and the Vimy ended, nose-up, in it. Both airmen survived the crash unscathed, and radio messages were soon going out from the nearby Marconi station to say they had arrived.

They, too, like Hawker and Mackenzie-Grieve, were greeted as heroes, even in an Ireland not far from independence from Britain as they took a train through to Dublin, but after arriving in England their welcome was tumultuous. They picked up the *Daily Mail* cheque for £10,000 – actually handed over by Winston Churchill – and the following day they were both knighted, a personal decision by King George V.

Brown married his long-suffering fiancee Kathleen Kennedy in July of that year, having put off the wedding to make the Atlantic flight. Alcock went back to test flying for Vickers. He was killed flying to Paris before the end of that year, crashing in fog over Normandy. Brown never flew again, and, heart-broken at the loss of his only son at Arnhem in 1944, died in Swansea four years later.

Charles Lindbergh

By 1927 the world had Atlantic fever again, this time looking for a winner of a cheque for $25,000 put up by a star-struck Parisian hotel owner, Raymond Orteig back in 1919. The prize, backed by the Aero Club of America, was called the Orteig Trophy, for the first non-stop flight of nearly 4,000 miles between New York and Paris, or vice versa. For years no one tried, because it was beyond the capacity of aircraft in the early 1920's. But in 1927, there were 24 separate attempts at crossing the "pond"; only four of them, one in six, succeeded in getting to the other side.

The tone was set the previous year by a French World War One ace, Rene Fonck, who tried to set off from New York on September 21st, with a crew of three in a Sikorsky tri-motor bi-plane, heavily overloaded with fuel (2,380 US gallons, 9,000 litres). The runway at Roosevelt Field on Long Island was a mile long, and when, more than halfway down it Fonck realised he was not going to get airborne, he tried to abort his flight. He cartwheeled over the ground and the aircraft crashed and burst into flames. Fonck and his American co-pilot escaped, but the French wireless operator and Russian mechanic on board were killed.

Early in 1927, the man with the best chance of winning on paper was a US Navy Lieutenant Commander, Noel Davis, with co-pilot Stanton Wooster, in a tri-motor monoplane ex-bomber called a Keystone Pathfinder funded with $100,000 from the American Legion. Unlike many of the other contestants, Davis had actually flown his aircraft with a full fuel load on board, and if he got away safely, had an excellent chance of making it. But heavily over-loaded as all the Atlantic aircraft were, and leaving from Langley Field, Virginia, on April 26, 1927, they only made an altitude of 20 feet before swerving to avoid trees and crashing into a swamp. Both men were killed instantly.

In France, Charles Nungesser, a former fighter pilot of unbelievable dash and courage, put together a project to fly east-west, Paris to New York. Nungesser had been his country's third highest scoring ace in the Great War, but had faded from fashion afterwards; the Atlantic flight was to re-establish himself again in French society. He took a one-eyed navigator, Captain Francois Coli, flying a single-engined aircraft designed by Pierre Levasseur, and backed financially by a group of wealthy Parisian sportsmen. Nungesser planned to take off from Le Bourget in northern Paris and jettison his under-carriage to achieve a higher speed. But doubts were expressed about whether he had enough fuel to complete the journey, even though he was carrying more than twice as much (883 gallons, 3,340 litres) as Charles Lindbergh did. On May 8th, 1927, with a huge unruly crowd held back by 50 bayonet-wielding soldiers, and a rare easterly wind forecast, Nungesser and Coli took off, covering more than a mile of the airfield's two-mile runway in the effort. They were sighted off Ireland five hours later, but battling a headwind. A false newspaper report the following day caused huge excitement and city-wide celebrations in Paris, complete with detailed accounts of how the pair had landed in New York harbour, and quotes about their experiences. But, they were never seen again.

Among the others who failed that year were Princess Anne Lowenstein-Wertheim, 62 years old, the widow of a German prince, born Lady Anne Saville in England. She wanted to be the first woman to cross the Atlantic in an aeroplane, so she hired two competent pilots, Leslie Hamilton and Fred Minchin, bought herself an aircraft, a Fokker F VIIa, told journalists it was a "great adventure", and the three set off. They were sighted once in mid-Atlantic, and then they, too, were never seen again.

Another woman attempting to be the first of her sex to cross the Atlantic by aeroplane was Ruth Elder, a 23 year old fashion model. She sat next to her pilot, George Halderman, as they set out for Europe via the Azores, but the aircraft's oil pressure fell to zero 400 miles from the islands and they ditched. Miss Elder was able to radio an SOS before they hit the sea, and they were picked up by a Dutch tanker.

The unluckiest pilot was Clarence Chamberlin, flying a Wright-Bellanca monoplane, which even Lindbergh thought was the best aircraft for the job. Chamberlin was hired by a rich young New York businessman called Charles Levine, and the two men test-flew their aircraft far more than any others had done. They established a duration record of more than 51 hours in one flight, easily enough for the New York – Paris journey, but they were plagued by a law suit from a disgruntled navigator who had been dismissed from the project, and it kept them on the ground when the weather finally turned right for a serious attempt from New York.

(They succeeded not long afterwards in making the longest single flight in the world, landing close to Berlin, 300 miles beyond Paris, but by then the Orteig Prize had been won by a man who became one of the most famous of his generation.)

Among all these well-funded attempts, 25 year old Charles Lindbergh, a former barnstormer and mail-plane pilot was a rank outsider. He could not persuade any of the better known aircraft manufacturers either to back him, or to sell him an aircraft with the $15,000 he had raised for the attempt, most of it provided by a group of St Louis businessmen. He had wanted the Wright-Bellanca, but the company was worried about a possible failure with such an unknown pilot. Lindbergh was forced to chose a small West Coast company called Ryan to build him his monoplane, at a cost – including a Wright engine – of $10,580.

Ryan was facing severe cash shortages, so Lindbergh's offer was opportune. They had a Ryan M-2, capable of carrying five passengers, and a designer, Donald Hall, who had worked for the company only 3 weeks. He modified the M-2 to fit Lindbergh's exacting standards, placing a huge fuel tank between the engine and the pilot who had no forward view. The tailplane was deliberately left too small, so the aircraft would be naturally unstable; Lindbergh wanted it to jink around the sky to wake him up. When they had installed the engine, a mechanic dropped a spanner on it, chipping one of the air cooling vanes; Lindbergh insisted they change the whole engine.

"Who will know the difference?" he was asked, angrily.

"I will know the difference."

"Why does it have to be so damned perfect?"

"Two reasons," said Lindbergh. "I am not a good swimmer, and I've always been taught that perfection pays off."

The aircraft was built in sixty days, working against the clock, Ryan Aviation staff working on nothing else, always worried that one of the other competitors was going to get there first. There was a terrible scare when they heard that Nungessor and Coli had made New York, but that passed. On test flights, with just 300 gallons on board, not three quarters of the 425 US gallons the aircraft was capable of carrying, the undercarriage was visibly strained. Lindbergh decided to test no more. The only fully-loaded flight would be the real thing.

They named the aircraft, *Spirit of St Louis*.

Lindbergh set off on May 10th to fly east, stopping only once at St Louis to show his sponsors the aircraft, and suffered carburettor icing over the Rockies which nearly drove him to crash-land. He arrived at Curtiss Field in New York on May 12th surrounded by storms, and straight into a barrage of publicity which, from then on for the rest of his life, never stopped. He was not thought courageous for flying alone, but foolhardy. On May 19th, the day before he departed, the New York *Daily Mirror* carried a photo under the headline "Flyin' Fool Adopts Mystery Air, Indicating Quick Take-off".

Waiting for the right weather conditions, Lindbergh kept an eye on his competitors. These included Commander Richard Byrd in a Fokker Trimotor, fresh from his (now disputed) flight over the North Pole, and Charles Levine and Clarence Chambertin in their Wright-Bellanca, still plagued by a law suit.

The forecast for May 20th was for a high pressure to be mid-Atlantic, indicating mainly westerly winds, and though visibility in New York was poor, Lindbergh decided to go for it. He went to bed early the previous night, posting a friend on the door to guard against reporters, but as he was drifting off the friend burst in and said: "what am I going to do when you're gone?" Lindbergh spent the rest of the night sleepless. At 2.30 in the morning, he drove to his aircraft. Byrd's hangar at Curtiss Field was dark, and Lindbergh's crew towed his Ryan aircraft to the longer Roosevelt Field. At dawn he was on the west end of the runway, only a few feet from where Fonck had crashed the previous year. The wind was from the west, but light. Lindbergh decided on a down-wind take-off, despite his heavy fuel load, because he was afraid the clay runway would be cut-up by his towing tractor. In his little cockpit he had sandwiches, a canteen of water, and a pee-tube.

At 7.54am, with the engine on full throttle and his crew heaving at the trailing edges to get him started, Lindbergh went for take-off. He was chased down the runway by friends in a car, each brandishing a fire extinguisher. He went past the halfway point, still on the ground. The aircraft wanted to fly, but the fuel load was a serious drag. With less than 300 yards left, nothing like enough to abort, the aircraft struggled into the air, and he held it low to gather speed before clearing the telegraph poles at the far end by 20 feet.

The route Lindbergh took out of New York was the same route I consciously took 74 years later, and mirrors in the early stages the fatal flight taken by John F Kennedy Jr and his wife Caroline a couple of years ago, along Long Island to Martha's Vineyard and out into the Gulf of Maine, heading for Nova Scotia. Sleep already began to plague him.

Lindbergh navigated a Great Circle route, changing his heading every hour to stay on the best route to Paris. He was only six miles off course at Halifax. It was dusk, after 11 hours flying, when he crossed St John's Harbour where Alcock and Brown had flown from, and he flew into the Atlantic proper. He had better weather than the British pioneers. He did enter cloud once but saw that ice formed on his wings, so he chose to stay out of cloud – and seemed to have been able to do so – flying north and south of them whenever they appeared in front of him.

After 18 hours flying, 48 hours awake, dawn came, and Lindbergh had terrible problems fighting against sleep. He began to hallucinate, seeing land where there was none, drifting in and out of reality. He stopped keeping a log, and lost track of his course changes. The unstable aircraft jinked around the sky, forcing wakefulness upon him. When he felt himself losing consciousness, he stuck his head out of the window and into the slipstream; this broke the spell.

At 27 hours out of New York, 16 hours out of St Johns, he came across several small boats, and circled them three times, shouting, but no one appeared on any deck, so he flew on. When he did hit land he recognised it was Valencia and Dingle Bay on Ireland's west coast. He crossed Ireland and the western tip of England, and darkness came again as he followed the River Seine up from Le Havre to Paris. To get his bearings he circled the Eiffel Tower, then set off north for Le Bourget, which he guessed was the big blank space beneath him, not lit by street lights. When he landed he was engulfed by tens of thousands of people who had been waiting for him. One of them stole his helmet, and wearing it, the bogus Lindbergh was introduced to the American ambassador while some French pilots rescued the real and weary Lindbergh from the crowd. Souvenir hunters began picking pieces of his aircraft, which was hustled into a hangar. Lindbergh finally met the US ambassador and slept in the Embassy after 63 hours awake.

When he woke he was the biggest hero of the age, bigger even than Jack Dempsey.

These flights were all part of the heroic age of mainstream aviation, when pilots were urged to chance and dare, to win and often lose, and were rewarded with fame and honours. That age has long gone. But in another generation, I wanted to measure my form of flying against the achievements of the original aviators. Though I started the adventure by believing that it would be possible to duplicate Alcock and Brown's flight in a flex-wing microlight, as it developed I thought I might also fly the route Lindbergh flew. I wanted to look down on the same countryside and coast-line that he looked at, to begin in New York and end in Paris. I could not repeat Lindbergh's flight non-stop at 65 mph in a microlight, because I could not stay awake long enough and the fuel load would be really gross. But because of my slow speed, I could cover Alcock and Brown's distance between St John's and Ireland in one flight, but probably complete my journey in the same time, 33 1/2 hours, as Lindbergh took flying from New York to Paris. The added bonus was that in America, where I hoped to sell a television documentary, no one had heard of Alcock and Brown, and most Americans still think that Lindbergh was the first man to fly an aeroplane across the Atlantic.

I saw the whole venture adding significantly to the achievements of the New Aviation, only 30 years old that year.

4

A Brief History of the New Aviation

As background, you should know that aviation history started again on May 23, 1971. That would have been the 123rd birthday of Otto Lilienthal, the great German pioneer who showed everyone that flight was a possibility, but who was killed in 1896 flying near Berlin. He made over 2,000 foot-launched flights, and fits the mainstream of innovators who brought man the gift of flight. These include the Italian genius Leonardo da Vinci who designed the first working hang glider (though he didn't build it and get it to work), the English baronet Sir George Cayley, inventor of the "vaulted arch" (what we now call the cambered wing), and Alphonse Penaud, the French inventor of the rubber-band powered aircraft who lost heart at the age of 30 because no one took any notice of him and committed suicide in 1880. After him came Lilienthal, whose experiments and death inspired the Americans, Wilbur and Orville Wright, to do their own research. They made the first powered flight on December 17, 1903.

After the Wrights, mainstream aviation consciously sought to fly higher, further, faster, in machines that grew in size and power. It tested itself against physical and psychological barriers. Bleriot's crossing of the Channel in 1909, for example, signalled the end of Britain's psychological isolation behind the Royal Navy. The heroic age of mainstream aviation lasted through a number of pioneer flyers, and is marked by great journeys, Alcock and Brown across the Atlantic, the Smith Brothers from England to Australia, Lindbergh non-stop between New York and Paris, Kingsford-Smith across the Pacific, Jean Mermoz across the South Atlantic.

That age ended on July 14, 1938 when Howard Hughes flew around the world in 3 days 19 hours and 8 minutes in a twin-engined Lockheed Electra.

He stepped out afterwards and said, "Anyone could have done it, they just need the right airplane".

After World War Two, pioneering flights were rare, and to do with exploring Space. The best pilots were at the top of a huge pyramid of scientists and workers. At the sharp end, for every sung hero there were thousands of unsung workers at the base. But the more we knew and understood about flight, the more conservative we became.

When the Russians sent up an unmanned satellite called Sputnik in 1957, and Yuri Gagarin became the first man into space in 1961, the Americans went into a frenzy of activity. President John F Kennedy promised to put an American on the moon before 1970; NASA did so with five months to spare. On earth, though, regulation upon regulation was heaped on pilots of big and small aircraft, all in the name of safety. In England and Europe, it became expensive, but everywhere also got smugly complicated. Chuck Yeager, best of the early space pilots celebrated by Tom Wolfe in *"The Right Stuff"*, said recently that when he went through the Sound Barrier in 1946, he just did it. Nowadays, he said, you would need a committee of 600 people to consider all the ramifications of doing it, especially including wannabe victims who needed compensating.

The New Aviation was a reaction against this deadening bureaucracy, and harked back to the original spirit of flight, a man, a wing and the air itself. We began what is, in truth, a second history of aviation. We are still working through it, and going in an entirely different direction to the Mainstream. Though we all want to stay alive, we also have values separate from the values they developed to stay alive themselves.

While the Mainstream was in full power, between Wilbur Wright's culture-shocking visit to France in 1906, and Neil Armstrong's arrival on the moon, there was always a small band of men unhappy about the way aviation was going. They wanted a more *personal*, a more intimate form of flight. In any film documentary of the history of aviation, there is often a section devoted to these wonderful men. There were dozens of failed experimenters, earnest, it is implied, but foolish. You see them on your television screens, almost all pedalling furiously until collapsing into a heap. Though they were laughed at and derided, they persisted. I call them the holy lunatics.

In 1948, an obscure scientific couple in America, Dr Francis Rogallo and his wife Gertrude, patented a wing which they called "a simple, practical, inexpensive and reasonably safe flying machine." Their idea was to construct "a flying machine with no rigid element or element designed to produce rigidity; a completely new concept, never seen before, with no model in science". They set up a wind tunnel in their kitchen and conducted experiments. The Rogallo Wing was entirely flexible. Suspension lines did as much to give it shape as the cut of the sail. It achieved a certain popularity as a kite for children, but no commercial future was seen for it. The Russian venture into Space changed that.

During the early American space frenzy, the authorities threw $50 million into secret experiments with the Rogallo Wing in the hope it could be used to lower space capsules to earth again. In 1962 they decided against this, and released pictures and data to magazines about some of their experiments. These pictures were of special interest to two men, Richard Miller, a student in California, and John Dickenson, an engineer in Australia.

Miller is said to be a typical product of the 1960s Age of Aquarius, full of strong ideas on individual freedom, personal motorless flight, even "transcendental aerodynamics". From 1964 onwards he began constructing "Bamboo Butterflies", rogallo wings made from bamboo and polythene, held together with sellotape. They cost no more than $10 each. Miller hung from a box-like structure under the wing, two parallel bamboo struts buried in his arm-pits, much like Lilienthal. And like the great German original, Miller threw his legs and lower body around to steer the contraption. He flew off sand-dunes in Southern California; one early rule of thumb was, *don't fly higher than you are prepared to fall.*

Meanwhile in Australia in 1963, John Dickenson, an electronics' engineer, was a member of the Grafton Water-ski club in New South Wales. In his spare time Dickenson experimented with gyrocopters. The annual Jacaranda Festival was coming up, and his water-ski colleagues asked him to design a kite they could fly off water-skis. It was a feature of that festival that the flat-kites in use at the time caused great hilarity among spectators, but inevitably resulted in hospital visits for the participants.

When NASA released the Gemini photograph showing a space capsule suspended under a rogallo wing, Dickenson saw it in a magazine and was inspired. Using only the photograph, with no dimensions and no back-up information, he started to make models based on the flex-wing principle. The resulting aircraft had a weight-shift single hang-point and the triangle A-frame that is common to all modern rogallo hang gliders. It was that A-frame that Lilienthal could have done with back in 1896; the whole history of aviation would have been different had he invented it.

Dickenson had a working model of the hang gliders we fly today back in our Stone Age, 1963. But though two rough-neck Australian showmen, Bill Moyes – now known as the Father of Hang Gliding – and Bill Bennett, went into competition with each other flying Dickenson's invention, it did not really catch on for years. Moyes and Bennett may have been seen as merely wild men; Moyes told me once he had broken virtually every bone in his body, and Bill Bennett also looks a battered man.

In Southern California in the beginning of the 1970's, another group of holy lunatics – Moyes and Bennett deserve to be so-described – were linked together by a magazine. It was produced on a Roneo machine, a duplicator, and was at first called *Low, Slow and Out of Control*. Later it became just *Low and Slow* (and much later, of course, *Groundskimmer*, and then *Hang Gliding*). The readers, who included the man-powered flight pioneer Paul McCready, bounced ideas off each other, built fantastic contraptions, bruised themselves trying to get into the air, and always went back to the drawing board.

In 1971, Richard Miller wrote a letter to a colleague, Jack Lambie, a Californian school teacher who was getting his pupils to build full-scale models of bi-plane aircraft designed in 1899 by the French/American mainstream pioneer, Octave Chanute. Lambie gave these a real 1960's name, the "Hang Loose". Miller's letter read, "The 123rd anniversary of Otto Lilienthal's birth will be on May 23, 1971. What can we do to celebrate?" Lambie organised a meeting, which took place on a Southern Californian sand-dune. Fourteen men turned up with foot-launched flying machines, 12 of them Hang Loose's. One of them was a single wing machine, but the fourteenth, built by a man called Taras Kiceniuk, was a rogallo wing.

As Lambie put it later, "Kiceniuk in his Bamboo Butterfly had learned to fly, with the arm rests, beautifully. He looked like Nureyev doing a ballet in that thing."

The longest distance flown that day was 196 feet, and the longest time in the air 11 seconds. But after this meeting, now known as the First Lilienthal Meet, publicised in the local newspapers and in the *Reader's Digest* as *"the flyingest flying there is"*, everyone who participated started getting up to 3,000 letters a week. The writers all wanted to know, not about the Hang Loose, but about the rogallo. There was a quick marriage between the Lilienthal-type machine Kiceniuk had built that day, and the Moyes/ Bennett (i.e. Dickenson) machines. Moyes and Bennett became established manufacturers. Hang gliding exploded. It took a year to reach Britain where our own version of Bill Moyes, a tomato-grower called Ken Messenger, leapt off Mount Snowdon in a Bennett hang glider and was the subject of newspaper articles. It soon spread around the world. The first World Championships were in 1975 in Kossen, Austria. Two years later the rogallo had evolved from little more than a noisy steerable parachute (the sail flapped like a single-cylinder motorbike) into a real wing. Pilots began flying cross-countries. In 1978, the first 100-mile flight was done.

It was this period in the 1970s that gave hang gliding its reputation as a dangerous sport which it still has not lost, and which has spread to its children in the New Aviation, microlights, paragliding and para-motoring.

We flew then – I learned in 1974 – without parachutes. In the early days there was no set method of teaching. I was a BBC Radio journalist, keen to fly, and was taken to the biggest local hill they could find, 450 feet at Devil's Dyke in Brighton. At the end of a day in which I watched people fly and pilots told me what they were doing, they threw me off the hill. My last instruction before getting into the air was to "run like a pig". In the minute before I hit the ground, I was expected to learn how to fly. Thankfully, I did.

The accident rate, mostly because of pilot error but sometimes because of equipment failure, peaked in 1978. We lost ten people in Britain that year, in a community of about 3,500. That compares with the Mainstream accident rate in British aviation in 1912 of 13 deaths, in a community of 750 pilots. It was different back then, of course. There was something noble in learning, and suffering was part of that nobility. After 1978, enough of us had parachutes to make it safer, and the competition to produce safe equipment, as well as performing wings weaned out the cowboys.

Twenty years on, hang gliding is one of the safest forms of light aviation, but it still attracts only a certain type of individual. You cannot fake flying a hang glider, but because it is a great posing machine, people still try. It should be an Olympic sport, it passed the tests back in 1985, but for all sorts of reasons, including the fact that it is little practised in Africa, it isn't.

We stuck engines on rogallo wings, soon known as flex-wings, as soon as we could. The problem was, where did you attach them? For a short while the engines and propeller went on the pilot's back, but if you trip up behind a triangle control-bar and fall, carrying an engine can break your neck (backpack engines work much better 20 years later with paragliders). With hang gliders, we stuck engines on top of the king-post, at the bottom of the king-post with a long shaft going back to the keel, at the back of the keel itself, and dangling off the cross-boom (two of them). A particularly popular model known as the 'Soarmaster' kit had the engine above the pilot with a long shaft to the back of and underneath the keel and the propeller about 18 inches away from the pilot's feet. It was this model, in passing, that those two brave Arabs used to attack Israel in 1987, and which triggered off that particular *Intifada*. Both pilots were shot dead.

Each of these experiments killed people. At the time we said, "it doesn't work there" and went back to the drawing board to find out why, and looked at sticking the engine elsewhere. I personally flew the type with two engines dangling off the cross-boom, and later, I flew a Soarmaster-type unit. Though I lived through these experiments, I was lucky. At 3.15 on a Monday afternoon on November 13th, 1978, in front of BBC TV cameras, I turned a Soarmaster-type unit upside down, the wings folded, and I plummeted 250 feet to the ground. The farmer had ploughed the field the previous day and it had rained overnight, so I was not killed. But it not only made my eyes water, it put me off playing with power for 6 years. It also left me with a legacy of nervousness that affects all the flights I make in a microlight.

The US Army back in the 1950s *had* found a way of safely adding power to rogallos, but had not told the rest of us. It was the French in 1980 who developed the trike, 25 years after the Americans first flew one, effectively a buggy to hang off a wing, with the engine on the buggy rather than the wing. This gave the aircraft a pendular stability – the French still call them "Pendulars" – with the thrust-line between the pilot and the wing. Unlike a conventional 3-axis aircraft, it is naturally stable, especially in pitch. It was no longer foot-launched flight, but it was still weight-shift, a flex-wing, as Lilienthal flew. Trikes were initially used to get a hang glider pilot high so he could turn off his engine and glide, but that soon went out the window. Trikes – and microlights – developed a life and a culture of their own, but inherited hang gliding values. These place much more reliance on individuals than on simple obedience to rules, because we are still writing them.

Almost all this development went on separate from the Mainstream. We had people in hang gliding who represented us in the aviation corridors of power, but we were Johnny's-come-lately to flying, at the bottom of the pecking order. We were condescended to, barely tolerated. In the late 1970s, for example, people who flew conventional sail-planes in the same air that we were aspiring to fly hang gliders actively considered legal means to get us banned from "their" air. This involved telling farmers and journalists how dangerous we were, and using a narrow and peculiar interpretation of aviation law to stop us flying. This campaign, later rather than sooner, was sorted out – some hang glider pilots spent bitter months unfairly banned – but the experience encouraged us to develop separately.

In microlighting in Britain (though not in France), there has been the same experience. In general, because of our slow flight ("a complete bore in the circuit"), and the perception that we are noisier than GA (general aviation) aircraft, we were banned from many established airfields. That meant we developed our own airfields, and a culture outside not only Mainstream regulations, but also Mainstream thought.

Again, stories were spread that we were dangerous, certainly more dangerous than Mainstream Aviation, though even a brief glimpse at our accident statistics will show exactly the opposite. The microlight-flying community is comparable in size to the sail-plane community, and we have roughly the same number of aircraft, but our accident rate is *half* theirs, and yet theirs is considered a more benign form of aviation. It is, oddly, partially the fault of the nature of our type of flying that we have such a reputation. The experience of flight in a trike is so breath-taking, so full of exhilaration, that if it is not dangerous *it jolly well should be*. I have lost count of the number of journalists I have carried in the back of my trike who later described the experience as if they had just survived a fatal accident.

Why does this matter? Only that now microlights constitute one third of all the aircraft registered in Britain, and in five years we will fill half the register. Now that the weight-definition of a microlight has been raised to 450 kgs, we are the future of small aviation.

It was inevitable that as soon as we found our wings worked, we went out to fly 50 miles in one flight, and not long afterwards, went through the rites of passage of microlighting by flying across the English Channel. We began to look at the great goals of Mainstream Aviation. Could we emulate those pioneers?

In 1978, an Englishman called David Cook became the first man to fly the English Channel in a foot-launched powered-hang glider. It was not a flex-wing, but a curious hybrid aircraft. It had a solid wing and a skinny fuselage and a tail, a rudder and elevators, just like a GA machine. This wing was called the VJ-23, designed by the elderly American, Volmer Jensen, another one of the 14 men at the First Lilienthal Meet. David Cook later developed this machine into the CFM Shadow, which was a microlight in weight, but otherwise just a smaller more diminutive version of a GA aircraft. Two of us flew CFM Shadows to Australia, an Englishwoman called Eve Jackson in 1986/7, the first person to do so, completing the journey in more than a year, and me in 1987/8, flying from London to Sydney in 59 days. Though Eve won all sorts of awards for her flight, there was a curious way in which they were not considered microlight flights at all, because they were 3-axis instead of flex-wing.

The first flex-wing to fly the Channel was flown by Gerry Breen in 1979, closely followed by Len Gabriels in the re-built wing that I had crashed to the ground a few months earlier. I followed Len's flight safely as an observer in a helicopter, still nervous about powered "rag-wings".

The first important, and in relative terms, among the greatest of flex-wing journeys was in 1985/6, when an Old Etonian called Richard Meredith-Hardy flew a weight-shift microlight, a Mainair Flash, from London to Cape Town, South Africa. Richard flew with an unreliable two-stroke engine, and spent 8 hours crossing the Mediterranean in a truly epic flight. He did it at a time when anyone else flying a flex-wing was considered Superman if he flew 50 miles. It was a genuine eye-opener.

Richard's flight was an echo of the Mainstream pioneers, Colonel Pierre Van Rynveld and Christopher Brand who flew London to Cape Town in 1920, using three aircraft (Van Rynveld crashed the first two). Eve Jackson's flight was not done with any speed – I seem to have introduced that – but we were following the pioneering brothers, Ross and Keith Smith along the classical London-Sydney route flown in the heroic age by many of the great Mainstream pilots like Bert Hinkler, Alan Cobham, Charles Kingsford-Smith and Amy Johnson.

In 1988, the organiser of my flight to Australia, Neil Hardiman, bought a flex-wing machine and emulated the original Australian pioneer, Kingsford-Smith, in circumnavigating Australia's coast-line. Hardiman did it in 179 days, much slower than Kingsford-Smith, but only paid for his accommodation on 5 of those days.

In 1990, a German pilot called Zoltan Ovari flew from Europe to Australia on a British-built weight-shift Raven wing, the first man to make that flight on a flex-wing, taking about fifty flying hours longer than me. He had a lot of political and permission problems, being impounded in Burma for months. Still broadly on that route, in 1997/8 an Englishman, Colin Bodill, flying a flexwing Mainair Blade 912, took 49 days to fly from London to Sydney, establishing a new speed record, and beating my 59 days.

After a terrific battle with the Danish authorities, also in 1990, a brave and bold Dutchman called Eppo Harbrink Numan – a holy lunatic if ever there is one – succeeded in flying the North Atlantic in a flex-wing. His whole journey took 14 months, because every time Eppo landed, he was harassed half to death by the authorities allegedly concerned for his safety. Really, of course, they were indulging in tick-book regulation, comparing his actual aircraft with what their book said an aircraft should be. When it didn't comply, they banned him from flying on. He ruined his life financially, spending £40,000 from the forced-sale of his restaurant, just to complete the flight, eventually wearing down everyone until they would rather have seen him dead than take another phone call from him. For Eppo, flying was so much easier, and safer of course, than the harassment.

Eppo flew east to west, jumping to the Faeroe Islands, Iceland, Greenland, and Baffin Island, because at those latitudes the prevailing wind is from the east. He succeeded, where Mainstream pilots like Nungessor had failed (I believe they found Nungessor's body in isolated countryside in Maine in the last two years.)

Another microlighting pioneer crossed the South Atlantic in one flight in December, 1992. Frenchman Guy Delage, 41 years old, married, with two children, was the man who later swam the Atlantic. Delage trained for months for his epic microlight flight, emulating the great French pioneer pilot, Jean Mermoz who did the same 'jump' across 2,350 kms of water in one go back in 1933. Delage did it in 26 hours in a weight-shift machine, carrying 350 litres of fuel, and surviving a storm within the infamous *Pot au Noir* which he said drove him so low he hit a flying fish leaping out of the sea. He averaged 56 mph, so he had a headwind much of the way.

We had flown the North Atlantic, the South Atlantic, England-Australia, London to Cape Town. In 1998, inevitably, an attempt was made at flying a microlight around the world. Two of us set off from London in one microlight, the GT Global Flyer. One hundred and twenty days later, I came back alone. My then-companion, Keith Reynolds, forced by the authorities to relinquish his seat to a Russian navigator in Siberia, had seen it in his best interests to go home instead of waiting for me in Alaska. I flew the rest of the way, tracing Phileas Fogg's fictional route, totally alone.

The last great microlight flight of the last century, as I mentioned earlier, was that by Mike Blythe and Olivier Aubert, which set me off on my own Atlantic dreams.

The new century saw an Englishman, Colin Bodill, accompanied by two helicopters and a 14-seater Cessna Caravan acting as gear-carrier, go out to beat my time for a flight around the world in a microlight, again in a flex-wing machine. Colin did in 99 days what I took 120 days to complete. Like one of the helicopters, piloted by Jennifer Murray, Colin is claiming a "first solo" circumnavigation, though Jennifer is certainly the first woman to make such a flight.

We have attempted a few other Mainstream feats, and for various reasons, failed at them. Two attempts have been made to date at flying over Everest, without success. There was a microlight flight made from London to Beijing, but that was stopped inside China for political reasons. Blythe and Aubert were stopped from completing a journey around the Pacific Rim in 1999 because of hassles from the Russians as well as the Japanese.

It is worth saying here where we are going in the New Aviation, if we are allowed to, separate from the Mainstream. Everest, of course, is a noble goal, and one we will succeed at eventually.

In hang gliding, we are learning how to migrate. The biggest single distance flown in a hang glider was set in 2001 by Manfred Ruhmer of Austria, probably the best hang glider pilot in the world, at 462 miles, nearly 700 kilometres. Routes are being pioneered all across Europe which will allow someone, one day, to fly south with the birds on the great migration routes for the winter. They will do this on their own skills, and powered by the heat of the sun and the winds. A competition called the 444, in which 444 kilometres must be flown in 9 days with no help from anyone, is now current among a small group of French, Swiss and Austrian pilots. It is a forerunner of this type of flight. So far the best has been a flight of 1,100 kilometres completed over 3 months through 5 countries by the Swiss, Didier Favre.

In microlighting, one day, we will fly to Australia, also powered by the sun. It has already been done coast-to-coast across the United States. Our aircraft will have engines powered by photo-electric cells. This will lead on to a flight around the world, possibly easier doing it over the Poles than the more classical route I took, looking for the longest sunlight. Those pilots that set off on such flights, and I want to be one of them, will call on the experience of Meredith-Hardy, Delage, Numan, and Bodill rather than on Mainstream Aviation. Philosophically, I can hardly think of anything more anarchic, and arousing of deep suspicion in Mainstream Aviation, than such a flight. All control in aviation is exercised through airfields and the provision of fuel, but such sun-powered flight in microlights will not actually need either. Can you imagine how the authorities will view the regulation of such aircraft?

By contrast with the history of Mainstream Aviation, which was littered with corpses, our safety record on big flights is 100%. We had terrific problems at times, not least on my flight to Australia. But because we are using modern engines, and can navigate by GPS, we have always been able to save the day, and make our flights successfully. Yet the myth persists that we are dangerous. This originated out of our hang gliding past. In fact, we have evolved our own rules, not quite the same rules as Mainstream Aviation, but still rules we abide by for our own safety.

The clash between the two cultures, a feature of all the great microlight flights, dominates my attempt at Alcock and Brown's flight.

5
Biographical Values

In the light of what was to happen, I feel I should abandon the "Boy's Own Story" I normally set out to write about these adventures, in which values are implicit. In the last few years, I used to hear an echo of understanding in talking to other people about adventures, but this has grown fainter recently and often disappeared. In discussion with a journalist about the Atlantic flight during the run-up to the departure for New York, I talked about the flight of Charles Lindbergh, assuming she obviously knew who I was talking about and what he had done. It was with a sense of growing horror that I realised she had never heard of him. That Battle of Britain pilot who went down to a Home Counties school to talk about the tremendous victory over Hitler's Luftwaffe in 1940 must have felt the same way when he discovered that not only did the children not know about the battle; the teacher didn't either. Without that common history, those reference points, how could there be any understanding of what I was setting out to do? In ignorance, what judgements could be made? On a wider level, how could decisions be made about good and bad courses of action if there was no history?

It is always easier to understate values. You do not get up people's noses if you do not dangle your beliefs in front of them. They can object to the actions prompted by those beliefs, without serious challenging the beliefs themselves. I often assume I am talking to people like me, and just describe what happened, with only a brief explanation about why. It is a given, in books I have written about previous adventures, that the whys and wherefores for me must be the same for you. I think of myself as normal, the same sort of person as other people who do what I do. So I felt a natural sense of unease when the wife of one of these people, Nikki Meredith-Hardy, whose husband Richard is one of the world's great pilots, fell down the phone laughing – "you and Richard normal, are you joking!"

Biographical Values 51

I had always felt, ever since I set out on my first genuine adventure, that it would be a real test of my values. But what were those values? Where did they come from? What are the touchstones that drive me to go on when logic and good sense say I shouldn't?

Reluctantly, I need to go back and look at where I got those values. Bear with me.

I was born in Hitchin, in Hertfordshire, in 1942, in the middle of an air raid I am told, though why Hitchin should be bombed I don't know. The confinement was long, 19 hours, and nearly killed my mother. My baptism certificate says, "Robert Brian Milton, being in danger of death … ." I had scarlet fever and a few other illnesses.

My parents, Tom and Eileen, were both Irish Catholics from Dublin, and both, I would say, of working class origin. My mother's family, the Durnans, were Irish back to Brian Boru. She was one of eight sisters, the second-youngest, and her family were strongly nationalist. My Auntie Rose used to tell a horror story about being picked up by her pig-tails by a Black and Tan soldier in 1919 during the "Troubles".

My father's family had been Irish for about three generations. I think my great-great-grandfather came from the English West Country in the middle nineteenth century. His grandson, my grandfather, tried to get off to fight in the Boer War at the age of 16, but he was hauled back by his mother before the ship sailed. I believe he went through four years in the trenches in the 1914–18 War. I met him once when I was five, and remember little about him except that he had been a baker much of his life. He must have passed on a strong set of beliefs to his sons, because my father, Tom, at least, was a Catholic Unionist. Dad thought it was an historic mistake for Ireland to have become independent in 1922, and especially to have been neutral in World War Two. It was not something he shouted out loud. That would have been unhealthy.

My father was educated by the Christian Brothers in Dublin, where everything was beaten into you with a stick. He left school at 16 in 1927 and went to work for the *Irish Independent* newspaper, where he was a printer throughout the week but wrote football reports on Saturdays. He worked through the great depression of the 1930s, but in 1936 threw in his job, left Dublin for England, and after six weeks – doing what, I wonder? probably labouring for wages – he joined the RAF as a lowly aircraftsman. When war was declared in 1939 he volunteered for aircrew, but was turned down for being too tall, and told – "come back in six months". At the time they said they wanted shorter men than his 5 feet 9 inches. While waiting to re-apply, he joined the Signals section, and then he was refused air-crew status because he knew too much, and they could not afford to have him shot down.

He spent the rest of the war, and much of the rest of his life, in Wireless Intelligence, what is called Y-Service. It was not his shift, but it was his unit, that identified the *Bismark* when she was trying to escape the British Fleet in 1941 after sinking *HMS Hood*.

In 1941, aged 30, my father went back to Dublin and married my mother, who was then 26. I have a battered picture of them on their wedding day. Dad looks like he's had a few and Mum has a glint in her eye. I was born the following year, my brother Colin – now a doctor in Melbourne, Australia – in 1944, and my sister Geraldine – also in medicine in Australia – in 1945. I believe my mother had a bad miscarriage on her fourth child and could have no more, otherwise I would have had a lot more brothers and sisters in the Irish Catholic way.

I was brought up a service brat, travelling wherever my father was posted in the RAF, moving every two years. I went to Hong Kong in 1945, to Northern Ireland in 1947, to the island of Sylt in Germany in 1949, Berlin in 1951, and then between England and Germany until I was 19, when I joined the RAF myself. This meant I was educated in four primary, and four secondary schools. There is nothing to say about the primary schools, but the secondary schools were Salesian College, Oxford for two terms, Sir William Borlase School in Marlow for two years, Prince Rupert School (PRS) in Wilhelmshaven in Germany for two years, and Harrow County Grammar School until I went off on a Scholarship to RAF College Cranwell.

My schooling was traditional, in that teachers were called Masters, and they used the cane. In geography, many of the maps we worked with had countries which were coloured red, which meant we owned them. This included Australia, Canada, New Zealand, India – which was already independent but we had owned it for a long time – and much of Africa. History was about heroes, not just about how we beat the Germans, twice, but how through the last thousand years we had fought all sorts of people and we had always won. I learned about heroes, about Crecy and Agincourt and the Hundred Year's War, about Henry the Eighth and the Reformation, about

Marlborough and General Wolfe in Canada beating Montcalm taking the Heights of Abraham, about Nelson at Trafalgar and Wellington at Waterloo. I learned about the Indian Mutiny and the Relief of Lucknow and Mafeking. We were not taught that much about the First World War, because it was not really history then, but everyone knew about the Battle of Britain. Those men who had won it were still young men.

I learned about Scott of the Antarctic and about George Leigh Mallory on Everest. I was 11 years old when Queen Elizabeth II came to the throne, marked by Hilary and Tenzing climbing Everest, and I remember seeing the Coronation on a fuzzy television screen.

My boyhood heroes came from sport and the comic papers, Bradman and Bedser and Dennis Compton – the Brylcream Boy – and Dan Dare, The Great Wilson, Battler Brittan, Rockfist Rogan. I only had one ambition in life and that was to be a fighter pilot. I do not remember having many books in the house, but we must have had some. When I read a book called *Tiger Squadron* at the age of 15, about the death of the Great War pilot Micky Mannock, I burst into tears.

This isn't a detailed autobiography. I am trying to find touchstones, events that I reach back to and remember, often because they hurt. I was bullied at each of the schools I went to. I did not know the right way to get accepted in any class I was sent into, and after a while, inevitably, the bullying would start. For a few years I was not really able to cope with it. It constrained me, put me off lessons – I scored 1% in a Latin exam one year – and I don't think my education, in the sense of giving me a perspective on the wider world, started until after I was 21 years old.

I remember being picked on one day at Borlase for a debagging, and fighting my way out, kicking and punching. I wanted to excel at something when I was 13, still at Borlase School, and took up cross-country running. I won the first two races, it went to my head, I started training so hard my feet hurt, and then I came halfway down the pack and lost heart with that.

I was only 12 when I fell in love for the first time. Her name was Veronica Francis. She was almost exactly a year older than me; her birthday is September 22, mine September 17. We used to meet at ballroom dancing classes. I had no idea what to do about being in love, and did not know how fatal it was to tell anyone else about it. Inevitably someone found out I was stricken with her and told her. Back came the message, "he can go and jump in the lake". This opinion, so lightly delivered, devastated me, and affected the rest of my teenage years by completely destroying any confidence I had with girls. I danced with Veronica weekly, and for a while, I was a good dancer, but when I moved elsewhere it took me years to pluck up the courage to risk that dreadful rejection again. As a result I lost my virginity, ironically to a Canadian waitress, at what (for the 1960s) was the grand old age of 22. I had tried so hard to lose it before that.

I remember the bullying vividly. At PRS I recall being kicked, and not retaliating, by a bigger and stronger boy called Clive Bennett. Another time, I think it was for my parents being Irish, a much bigger boy called John Papworth threw me into the bushes and gave me a good thumping. I do not remember putting up much of a fight, and this is still humiliating to me. It seemed as if I kept dodging the brickbats, doing badly at exams, and just trying to stay alive. It was not as if I was thick, though I was often accused of this, because a few years later I got into Mensa with an alleged IQ – who knows about these things? – of 156. I just was not at all street-wise.

When my father, now a Warrant Officer, moved back to England, I went to Harrow County Grammar (my brother and sister and I had all passed the Eleven-Plus), where Michael Portillo's brother Charles was a year ahead of me, and the younger Portillo started after I left. Soon the bullying started again. At the milk crate one day – we drank gallons of milk then, it was considered healthy – someone started pushing me around. Rather quickly, I just hit him, and when he bounced off the wall, I hit him again, twice, in the face. He stopped bullying me. A few days later, in a classroom waiting for a Master to appear, the same thing happened, more bullying, this time rather thoughtlessly by someone I considered a friend. I hit him all the way to the end of the classroom and when I stopped hitting him he stopped bullying me (and also stopped being a friend).

Soon I joined a gang. We used to hang out around the school stage and dare each other to walk the beams above. We set up a card table 30 feet about the stage and learned poker. When volunteers were asked to join the House boxing team. two of my "friends", one, Colin Hunter, whom I still see occasionally, hoisted me up and said, "Milton can box, sir!".

I had three fights over two years, all won on TKOs, technical knock-outs. My technique was simple and primitive. I asked a friend to hold me by the ankle in my corner of the ring and not let me go until the bell went. Then I struggled and growled while waiting, as if I could not wait to get at my opponent. When the bell went my ankle was released, and I rushed over and thumped my opponent for 3 minutes. There was no finesse at all. I had been in a boxing ring when I was 11 years old, learning all about stance and movement, and some little bugger had come into the ring and thumped me all around it. I gave up boxing then, but now I was in the ring once more, I thought I would do the same to the poor unfortunate chap in there with me. No fight went beyond the second of three rounds. I was profoundly relieved that I did not get someone else like me in there.

The effect of all this was to give me breathing space to be alive. It never really helped with my education, only five O-levels and one A-level. I know it sounds silly to say this; if I had a Mensa IQ, why did I not know I was intelligent? The answer is, I always seemed to be in the wrong.

All the way through my teens into my early twenties, I cannot say I had an original thought. I had all the normal prejudices of a growing English boy, which would now be described as right-wing. My view of history was set; we the British were right and everyone else, including the Americans, were wrong. Foreigners were foreigners, even though they couldn't help it. We were kind and looked after people, but if they wanted a fight we would go out and beat them. I had Catholic views of right and wrong, governed by the Ten Commandments, and until I went off to America at the age of 21, I still went to Mass most Sundays.

I learned to fly on a Flying Scholarship in 1960, at White Waltham to the west of London. My instructor was Joan Hughes, who flew with Amy Johnson in the ATS, delivering aircraft in World War Two. In 1961, despite my poor A-levels, I went to RAF College Cranwell, where I lasted less than a year. Though I tried, I thought, as hard as I could to fit in, there were a number of ways in which I didn't. I could fly all right, it was the rest of the three-year education there I seemed to fail on. Being chopped, essentially for having the wrong attitude, in June, 1962, was devastating. I wandered around England in a daze for 18 months, working first as a labourer, then as a clerk, before emigrating to the United States in November, 1963. It was still easy then for an Englishman, almost as easy as it is now for an Irishman. I chose San Francisco as a base; who knows why? This was before the song was written, "I left my heart in San Francisco." President John F Kennedy was murdered ten days after I arrived.

I wanted a college education in America, and then I thought I would join the US Air Force and be a fighter pilot. I found an apartment, a job as an accountant in the evening, and signed on at the City College of San Francisco. It was 1964. The Vietnam War was cranking up but still over the horizon. The Beatles had arrived in America and blown everyone away. I read Plato's "Republic" and was blown away myself. Philosophy was one of the courses I had signed up for, looking for credits towards a Business degree, but I did not know what philosophy was. When the teacher began examining first one proposition of reality, and then another, I thought he was being silly. I barely restrained myself from saying so. He persisted, I got into barneys with fellow students, and somewhere in the middle of all this, I began an investigation into right and wrong that swept away, not just my religious belief, but any belief at all in God. I found I could, and did, attack every system of thought put up to me, and work out why it wasn't true. When the dust first settled years later, I found I was describing myself as an existentialist. This is a very bleak philosophy in which an individual is responsible for all that he does, and the only quality that transcends reality is courage.

Losing God had its moments of drama.

One moment followed a party at 421 Laguna Street. I was one of a group of young people joined by a man of great age, all of 42 years old. We were passing a marijuana joint around and taking a puff, but when it got to me, I just passed it on. Because John Lennon was also an Englishman, English people were deemed cool – we even used that word then – and I could get away with not participating in smoking a joint. The "old" man really sucked at it. I learned his name was Neal Cassidy. I later discovered, in the hundreds of books I threw myself into when I realised – after Plato – that I had a mind, that he was the model for Dean Moriarty in Jack Kerouac's "On the Road". Three weeks after meeting Cassidy, who died a couple of years later, appropriately alone, by a railroad track, I was on the road myself.

The journalist in me sees that meeting as just chance. The poet, if there is one, sees it as marking a particular stage of my life.

I spent nine weeks travelling, hitching rides, walking, jumping freight trains, sleeping under bridges, burned up crossing the Great Salt Flats, freezing in Minnesota nights. I ended that journey by spending six weeks washing dishes in a place called Bar 4, a DEW Line – Distant Early Warning Line – station 300 miles inside the Arctic Circle. It was during this journey that I lost my virginity in Winnipeg, and just before that, God too.

I had run out of money on my first visit to Winnipeg, and hitched down to Grand Forks, North Dakota and out into the country to Cooperstown to see a banker I had visited previously when I still had some money. Vaguely, I was going to ask him to grub-stake me to go back to pick up that dish-washing job, which paid $100/week and expenses. We spent the weekend with him waiting for me to ask him, but I couldn't work up the nerve. On that Saturday night we went out into Cooperstown and drank far too much beer. It was my turn to drive back, and we came off the road at the only bend in it at 115 miles an hour and crashed across the countryside. The car was a write-off, but we were uninjured. I obviously could not stay there any longer, and set off next day to Grand Forks, absolutely penniless. On the road I found some coins in a heap, amounting to $2.25. This I had with me, still unspent, when I arrived at Grand Forks. About 250 miles to the north was Winnipeg, where I had a job offered, and 250 miles to the south was Minneapolis, where someone owed me $7.

I spent an hour there, agonising.

Mine was the type of religion where, in any doubt, ask God. In all this time, I didn't say a word to Him. He was not part of the decision. I paced up and down and argued with myself, and veered first one way and then another. How was I going to survive in Winnipeg until I was flown north? Begging in the streets was really frowned on back then, and I did not think I could do it. It never even occurred to me, but I am sure if I was really hungry, it would have. But would $7 be enough? There was a friend, Jimmy Wilson, who was also due in Minneapolis at that time. I thought I could stay with him, and be supported, which was the deciding factor in going south. At no time had I involved anyone else in the decision, including God. For a good catholic boy, which I suppose I still saw myself at the time, this was crucial.

In fact, Jimmy had hitched on from Minneapolis to Buffalo, New York, and I hitched off after him and met him at his parent's house. He borrowed $50 from his dad, split it, we hitched back to Winnipeg, and then stayed there a week in a very cheap hotel – we saved our money to go to the cinema and see "A Hard Day's Night" – until I was flown north to decent food and life again. Then, all alone, Jimmy found that as an American he could not get work on the Canadian end of the DEW-line, and with $1.50 in his pocket, he hitched back to San Francisco, leaving poetry instead of money at every place he ate. When I invited him to Europe a year later, Jimmy said he had been across the United States four times; what else was there in the world to see?

I went back to San Francisco at the end of that summer, paid my debts to Jimmy, and found a job as a copy boy with the *San Francisco Examiner*. I also acquired a steady girlfriend, Carole Clift, with whom I learned – at last! – about sex. The whole 1960s generation thing was beginning to happen, and San Francisco was one of its key cities. We listened to Bob Dylan and Joan Baez and went to marches against the Vietnam War. I organised poetry meetings and played a weekly game of poker and thought, like everyone else of my age, that we were the centre of the world. I did not feel driven about anything, about work, about life, about right and wrong. I did not feel anything about the third world - was that a concept then? - and I certainly wasn't left-wing. If I was full of passion it was for Carole, and later for other girls there, and for poetry, and for friendships. I met two of my oldest friends at this time, Mike Winecoff and Jay Jones, both Americans, who were also copy boys. All us copy boys wanted to be writers, either Ernest Hemingway or Jack London, though F Scott Fitzgerald would do.

The *San Francisco Examiner* merged with the *Chronicle* in 1965, and because I had been doing a job editing the cartoon pages deemed well above the rate at which I was paid, I got a bonus of $1,500. Restless and now with some money, I decided to return to England, missing the Vietnam draft, as it happens, by just two weeks. I did spent a year wondering if I should go back and be drafted and find out what the experience of warfare was like. I knew little about the rights and wrongs of the Americans being there.

Back in Stafford where my parents lived, I spent £25 buying a 1937 Austin 7 which I called Alexa, after a girl I had been infatuated with in America. I spent the next two years in London, working sporadically, trying to be a writer. Jay Jones and Mike Winecoff – Mike with his wife Susan – came over to join me in a bed-sitter in West Kensington. We worked when we had to, otherwise we wrote, and I met a girl called Fiona Campbell, with whom I fell in love. She was a colonel's daughter; her father, Ian Campbell, came from an old Scottish family, upper-middle-class gentry. He had joined the Army, I remember him saying, "to travel and play polo".

In the middle of 1967 Fiona went to South Africa, her birthplace, to see what it was like, and I went to a stone cottage on the west coast of Ireland for three months, to learn how to write. During this period, I sent Fiona daily letters, in the middle of one asking her to marry me. A month later she accepted. I spent the summer months of 1968 showing Americans around

Europe, including the Paris demonstrations in May, closed museums by day, the streets of the Latin Quarter by night. Though I joined the students, sometimes besieged in the Sorbonne, I had no political thoughts at all, and my values, though affected by my generation – hey, I wanted to be tolerant of everything – remained untouched.

My first really big adventure was driving Alexa across Europe and half of Africa in that winter of 1968/9, intending to present the Austin 7 to Fiona. I drove 7,600 miles, including 18 days in December in the Sahara Desert when I crashed once – suffering from ptomaine poisoning – and ran out of water twice. I spent Christmas in Kano in northern Nigeria, in the middle of the war against Biafra, while a convoy grouped itself around my car. We drove through Cameroun, Chad and the Central African Republic, and after delays, into Zaire, (then and now again) called the Congo.

It was a period of some violence. There were still strong traces of white colonialism, only four years after Mike Hoare and his white commandos had put down the "Simba" rebellion and watched Mobutu get to power. The roads generally worked though they were deteriorating, and we stayed at missions every evening (Catholic missions, because they had beer and the Protestants didn't). For the last 2,000 miles of the drive I had only three working pistons, with no plug in the fourth piston, where the rings had gone. I did 900 miles without any brakes, lights, shock absorbers, starting handle and starting motor, and I was five weeks without any money, relying on two Swiss members of the safari to grub-stake me.

There was one memorable night when, invited by a Belgian former mercenary called Captain Gaston Bebronne to the consecration of a Congolese bishop, I ended the evening among four white men left standing, and drank for England; I can remember how luminous the hangover was. Later, in Mungbere, when I came to Mount Ruwenzori, 7,000 feet high in the country which now houses the Interahamwe (those lunatics still slaughtering each other and those around them), I had finally to abandon the drive; I was down to only two pistons that day.

Aside from running out of water in the Sahara, there were three possible near-death experiences, two in the Sahara. One was where a Land Rover driven by four young British boys left me in the worst part of the desert, hacked-off with forever pushing me out of sand-dunes, and I was surrounded by rather hostile Arabs, one of whom pulled a knife. I shouted at him in

English to stop being a bloody fool and put away the knife. It all happened a bit too quickly to get frightened; he later offered to get into my sleeping bag, but I declined. A day later I had a radiator leak and ran out of water, and went into a very detached state. But I found a well and haggled for five gallons from a passing Bedouin who seemed to think he was in charge of the water (I paid five cigarettes and two aspirin, a bargain really).

The third time was in the Congo when my radiator broke once more and I was waiting, reading *To Have and Have Not,* for the others to catch me. I looked up once and there, coming down the track, each carrying machetes, were six young native men. It would have been the work of 20 seconds to have hacked me up and robbed my vehicle; instead, they waved back when I got out to raise my hand, and all accepted cigarettes. We were squatted around the broken radiator when the rest of the safari turned up. It was only later that I thought I should have been much more fearful than I was. It was obviously not bravery, though, just ignorance.

I was driven out of the Congo by Arthur Lang and Werner Streiff, the two Swiss men who had grub-staked me, and paid back my debts to them in Kampala, Uganda, with money from articles I wrote for the *Irish Independent* about the journey. I used the rest of the money to fly to Johannesburg, where Fiona picked me up. There I worked for 6 months as a journalist for the *Johannesburg Sunday Times*, writing two articles a month for the *Irish Independent*. The South African Special Branch used to throw out six journalists and six priests a year under *Apartheid*, and they took exception to one of my articles for the Irish newspaper. On the night Fiona and I were writing our wedding invitations, there was a knock on the door and I was thrown out of the country.

Back in England I worked as Assistant Press Officer for the Liberal Party during the 1970 election – the Liberals were reduced to six seats – the while planning to join Peter Hain in his "Stop the Seventy Tour" of South African cricketers. Peter (now Foreign Office Minister and perhaps destined for the Cabinet) came to our wedding two days after the election; Fiona's mother, South African-born Peggy, nearly had a coronary when I introduced him to her as she was serving the champagne.

It was from here on that I started to acquire some conscious values. Before that, I had the instincts of a young white, insular Briton. I saw myself as British, rather than Irish, because I had been brought up in a British environment. My voice, when I came to hear it later in broadcasting, was English, but of an odd clipped sort. It seemed to have its roots in 1950's black and white films like "The Dambusters", "Reach for the Sky", "Angels One Five". Foreigners thought it very English; the English, especially if I became excited and started to speak in the iambic pentameters of the Irish, knew it was not, but they were not always sure where it came from. It was often a choice between South African and New Zealand.

I had a period between 1970 and 1972 as an active Young Liberal, standing against Peter Hain for the chairmanship of the NLYL, allegedly from the Left, but really from the counter-cultural 1960's wing of the Party. In Holland we would have been called *Kabouters*. Peter and I got the same number of Conference votes, but he thrashed me on the postal ballot. I cut my teeth in youth politics on the 1971 campaign against the Census, which I instigated, raising the difficult issue, back then, of privacy against encroachment by the State, and was rewarded with a Royal Commission on Privacy. Oxford Street was first closed to cars on December 18, 1971, because of action I organised against cars in cities; 44 of us were arrested that day, and it was not so frightening an experience. We later tried to close Piccadilly Circus using the same tactics, with Fiona as much in the thick of things as I was.

(She was once the front half of a Young Liberal cow outside the Albert Hall during the demonstrations that year against the Miss World competition. I remember a doleful French TV reporter asking if any of us could speak French to explain what was happening, and I pointed to the pantomime cow. He thought his boat had come in when Fiona whipped off the head, and, in perfect French and still with a girl's head – an MP's secretary – shoved up her bum at the back end of the costume, made a fiery speech in favour of women's rights. Giles put Auntie Vera in Fiona's place in a cartoon not long afterwards.)

Fiona and I were married 29 years, in 22 of which it was a real marriage, two of which it wasn't, and five during which we were separated before I took the initiative, after surviving the flight around the world, to get a divorce. We bought a large property in St Albans in 1971, first as a commune with another Young Liberal couple, Tony and Sue Rodgers, and then when they soon split, on our own. Our marriage nearly split itself after two years when Fiona had a public affair with a poet – I was struggling to get established at the time as a BBC local radio reporter – but we got past that. One factor for me in wanting to save the marriage was the arduous journey I had made to get to her in the first place. After a dreadful miscarriage on

Christmas Eve, 1973, our son James was born in 1975, and Jade in 1978. In 1974, I took up hang gliding, and it became an obsession for a few years.

Briefly, I worked much of the rest of my life as a journalist, 10 years with BBC Radio London, the last two as a current affairs programme editor, and 15 years in television. We moved to a big house in Bristol, and then another Bristol house, and I bought a second house in London when I found I could only get work there, and not in Bristol. Fiona became a bona fide feminist, getting close to what I call the hairy-handed five percent whose motive seems to be hatred of men, but she was not really attracted to that and moved back into working in the real world again, in marketing. The nearest I got to a proper job, a permanent post with a pension, was five years with TV-am from 1982 to 1987. I started as an editor, went through being an Industrial Reporter, and then became Financial Correspondent, with four live slots a day about City subjects. In 1990/91 I was Editor/Presenter (and founder) of *European Business Today*, a half-hour daily financial programme beamed into Japan, Europe and America. In 1994, as Editor of Euromoney TV, I might have made my fortune with the sale of modular financial programmes, but though contracts were signed with Kuwait TV for $750,000, they never paid the cheque. I went on for a while to become Editor of *Sky Business Sunday*, and later a reporter with *London Financial News*.

Fiona and I split while I was at Euromoney. It was her shout. I took the small *pied a terre* house we had bought in the East End of London, and a holiday home in southern France, while she had the big house near Archway.

During this whole period I gradually became more conservative. It seemed to be a natural process. I kept the instincts and experience of a Young Liberal, in the willingness to challenge established order if I thought I was right, but I also instinctively supported that order. In simple terms, I changed from reading the *Guardian* to reading the *Daily Telegraph*. Around about 1991, focussed on Will Carling's team at the Rugby World Championships, I started to see myself as English, rather than British, whatever my blood lines. I seem to be part of the general disentangling of Great Britain, the Union formed in 1707, that has been going on in the last few years.

My father died in 1986, and my mother in 1993, both in Dublin where they had retired. Each time, I went across for the burial. My father had always wanted to go and live in Australia, and even at the age of 74 with heart problems he was planning to do so some day. My mother just loved being back among her own sisters in Ireland.

After my mother's funeral, my daughter Jade went off to see some cousins and fell in love with Dublin; that afternoon she decided she wanted to go to Trinity College there, and did so. I went to Kilmainham Castle that fateful day, the central shrine to Irishness, and walked all the corridors and exhibits looking at everything. Kilmainham had been one of the centres of English power in Ireland for hundreds of years. I looked at the notes written by Irish rebels to their wives and lovers the night before they were to be executed, usually for murder of a British official. I read the tracts, declarations of independence, traced all the years of revolt up to 1921. We were shown around the prison cells of those arrested after the 1916 Easter Rising, and then taken outside to see the bullet marks where they had been lined up against a wall and shot.

During the afternoon I tested my feelings, waiting to hear, as it were, the call of blood to blood. Would that happen to me? There and then I made the decision I have lived with since, and expect to live with for the rest of my life.

I am an Englishman.

It is more than Lord Tebbit's "cricket test". It also implies a set of values, and an acceptance of history, that I am still discovering, and against which I judge my actions. It is not just a right, but a responsibility too.

Those early adventures gave me a taste for the game, and while much of my working life has been in a relatively straight line (for a journalist) every now and again I would leave that life and go into another one, quite different from normal. As a journalist, I am a spectator of other people doing things. As someone who wanted an adventure, I became a do-er myself.

Ten years to the day after setting off in my Austin 7 to drive across Africa, I fell out of the sky in my powered hang glider. My son James was only 3 years old at the time, and Jade six months old, and I was the sole bread-winner with a big house to support in St Albans. It did not stop me hang gliding – I went back after 14 weeks – but it did stop me taking many more risks during that period.

When I moved into TV-am in 1982 it seemed as if it was a permanent move, a place I would stay as long as the station existed (until 1992). As a hobby, I kept writing proposals for adventures, including one about a microlight flight from London to Sydney, Australia. By a series of chances, this idea came to the notice of the great Australian financier, Kerry Packer. I was summoned to the Savoy Hotel, driven there by Packer's protégé, Bruce Gyngell, my boss at TV-am. Packer bought the idea, for six weeks only, of backing me to fly a microlight – he had four of his own – from England to Australia, but then abandoned the project as "too expensive and too risky". It would have cost £100,000, a bill pushed to that level by his own demands. As it happened, that week he was reported to have lost £8.5 million in one of London's casinos; Packer is one of the biggest high-rollers in the world.

That summer I met a lot of powerful people through the live interviews I conducted on TV-am's "Money Matters", which I had founded. One of these powerful people was a newspaperman, David Brewerton, City Editor of *The Independent*, who introduced me to Tony Spalding, head of corporate affairs at a 140 year old company called Dalgety. Tony bought the idea of backing me to make that long microlight flight, but I had breakfast with Dalgety's CEO, Terry Pryce, as a test to try and persuade him to sponsor me. I had no idea how I was doing until Terry finally said, "We've been doing business since 1840 and always paid a dividend, but people think we're a trifle dull. This sounds exciting. Let's give it a whirl."

Standing outside TV-am 10 minutes later in a daze, waving Terry off in his chauffeur-driven Daimler, Tony elected to stay behind and talk to me. A tall man, he looked down at me kindly.

"For tax and financial reasons I have to pay you some money now," he said. "Would a cheque for £60,000 do?"

I described what happened on that adventure in detail in a book called *The Dalgety Flyer*, published in 1990 by Bloomsbury (Harry Potter's publisher). Briefly, I bought a 3-axis aircraft called a CFM Shadow, and clocked up 100 hours learning how to fly it, and making various cross-country flights to learn how to navigate. In the middle of this training I resigned from TV-am after an unfair spat with Bruce Gyngell, an action I regretted immediately, but now feel saved my life. The great stock market crash of October 19, 1987, would have so drawn me back into financial media that I would have neglected my training, and I had enough difficulties on the flight anyway, with the small amount of experience I did clock up.

I left London on December 2, 1987, chasing the ghost of Ross Smith, personal pilot to Lawrence of Arabia and the first man to fly England-Australia back in 1919, and had a series of bizarre adventures. In the Rhone Valley, in rotten winter fog, I twice attempted to fly out of the mountains and was caught in cloud with no blind-flying instruments, and could quite easily have ended up in pieces against a mountain. Flying to Crete in low cloud and increasing wind, I was forced to land on the island of Kythira where a strong cross-wind flipped me upside-down as I was taxiing in. My friend Mike Atkinson, a mechanic travelling by first-class ticket to Australia (with 30 stopovers, shadowing me), turned up a day later and laughed wildly at the wreckage of my aircraft. But during the next five days, flying out the aircraft's designer David Cook to help, Mike and David and I glued the aircraft back together again. It looked like the Portrait of Dorian Gray, having grown old suddenly, patched together with gaffer tape and araldite. I was quite nervous crossing the Mediterranean in such a cobbled-together machine.

In Akaba in Jordan I was, unknown to me at the time, given jet fuel, kerosene, rather than petrol, which killed the engine when I was at 5,000 feet trying to fly over some 6,000 feet mountains near the Dead Sea. I landed on a road 1,200 feet below sea level. Mike turned up by helicopter that night, we discovered what was wrong, found some good fuel and a day later I flew into Amman where I was summoned to meet King Hussein. He became a patron of the flight. Going out into the desert I had a lot of carburettor problems which I fixed myself, but then a succession of tanks of poor fuel forced me down three times in the Saudi Desert, thankfully without damage, though it was a close-run thing.

On Christmas Day, 1987, because of a blockage in one of my three fuel tanks, I was still 32 miles out over the Persian Gulf when the engine stopped. I ditched, was found by a search aeroplane, picked up by helicopter whose crew returned to their Christmas lunch while I had a cup of tea and phoned London. I told Tony Spalding I thought I could get the aircraft to fly again, if it had not sunk. The helicopter took me to Abu Dhabi where I met a little chap called Rachid Abad, dressed all in white, who told me I was under the patronage of Sheikh Zayed, whom I didn't know. Sheikh Zayed was a rich man, who then owned the bank, BCCI.

"I just need to find my friend Mike Atkinson," I said. I was irritable.

"No problem," said Rachid, and we jumped into his big Mercedes and drove around a few corners. There, suddenly, was Mike, walking in circles around my spare engine, which was so small he carried it as hand baggage.

"I'm sure she'll fly again, Mike," I called out. "But we've got to rescue her from the sea."

That evening Rachid whistled up a huge helicopter full of tough young soldiers, which carted Mike and me out on a compass course. There we found my little aircraft deep in the water, but still afloat. We jumped in to the sea and swam to the aircraft, while the helicopter flew away north where two tankers were being attacked by Iranian gunboats, and seven men were killed. Mike and I found my aircraft was being circled by a chap in a dinghy. I introduced myself, and waved at Mike, saying he was my friend.

"My name is Charlie Rogerson," said the man, "and I'm from Manchester. I am the diver on that boat," and he pointed to a large flat ship called the NMS 401.

We rescued the aircraft after an hour and a half more in the water, and before being escorted off to get dry clothes and have Christmas dinner of turkey and pudding with the ship's captain (who was a Christian), Mike looked the dripping aircraft over on the deck and came to the same conclusion I did, that it could fly again.

On Boxing Day, December 26, we drove the aircraft to an airfield, and worked on it for five days, swapping the spare engine for the wet one – they were known as "Sweetie Pie" and "The Gobbler", because the latter allegedly used more fuel than the former – I flew "The Gobbler" the rest of the way. On the test flight bits of air-streaming that Mike had improvised for the wing struts fell off in flight, and I thought I was going to die after the aircraft started to shake horribly at a thousand feet. But I got her down and we took off the experimental bits, and I flew on to Muscat.

After a day's failure because of a storm, I crossed the mouth of the Persian Gulf to Gwadar in Pakistan.

I had three days crossing India, following a forced landing when my fuel filter clogged up, when I became excessively frightened and suffered hallucinations. A nasty thing I called a *Djinn* appeared on the nose of the aircraft, and told me to jump. I was at 5,000 feet at the time, without a parachute, and it was touch and go for hours whether or not I would jump. It would have been very easy, just knock my seat-belt off, lift the flimsy canopy, and roll over. Lone yachtsmen suffer from the same syndrome. In my case it was caused by fatigue – I had been flying or repairing the aircraft for 34 days – claustrophobia in a cabin two-thirds the size of a coffin, vertigo, and plain old-fashioned cowardice.

I managed to banish the *Djinn* on the way down to Burma by thinking of a series of pretty girls and making love to them – in my mind, of course – which seemed to fascinate the creature, so it stopped scaring me. But he has never completely gone away, and from time to time, way down the corridors of my mind, I still hear him screaming. It is the fear of him that crops up in the Atlantic flight.

Back then in 1988, flying down the west coast of Malaysia, an earthing wire broke on the engine – just after a 50-hour service – and I was forced to land in a paddy field. Mike turned up the following day and we repaired the engine and I flew away down the peninsula, straight into monsoon weather which three times put me on the ground. The first time was on a muddy track in a plantation, where a helicopter came out to offer me a home for the night. The second time was to land on a road to ask the way, after the helicopter disappeared into the mist, flying far too fast for me. The third time was at the helicopter base after the helicopter itself "bounced" me, blowing my canopy in and nearly killing me (they said later they were so pleased to see me, which was not reciprocated).

I flew around monsoon weather all the way down the island of Sumatra and along Java and other Indonesian islands, mostly out to sea, finding my way back at the end of each day to try and find an airfield (there were no GPS's then). On the way from Kupang on Timor across the shark-infested Timor Sea to an island marked by an Australian pilot with a cross on my map, the wind changed direction. I found a drilling rig being towed by three tugs and a helicopter circling it which gave me a new course to steer, and in this way found the tiny Troughton Island where I landed safely. I made Darwin the following day.

South of Darwin, racing to Sydney for the Australian Bicentenary, I was 10 hours in the air one day, and landed at Tennant Creek in the dark, dodging thunderstorms which were really vicious, just in time for the second of three of the biggest earthquakes in the last 100 years of Australian history.

"Nothing happens here for years," said the very weary looking mayor, "then on one day we get three earthquakes and you turn up."

I spent the Bicentenary in Brisbane, having been warned off Sydney by the nervous aviation authorities, worried that I would be killed over Sydney Harbour as the whole RAAF flew by. On the way south the following day, landing on a golf course – hoping to meet Greg Norman, the Great White Shark, but it was the wrong golf course – I broke the front leg strut, weakened by the Kythira crash. After some minor adventures like re-building the propeller and having to cart the aircraft from one rain-filled ex-airfield to another by truck, I got to Sydney two days after that. It was 59 days after I had left London and was, for ten years, the longest, fastest microlight flight in the world. Terry Pryce, of Dalgety, was pleased, and backed me to fly around the

Outback (with my engineer Mike Atkinson driving underneath, accompanied by my organiser, Neil Hardiman, who went on to marry an Australian girl and settle there) to write a book about the flight. Terry said a few months later he *would* be interested in backing me to fly around the world in a microlight, but the financial predator Robert Holmes A'Court bought 10% of Dalgety ("just to see what will happen") and what happened was that the Dalgety board panicked and removed Terry.

Back in England no one in the microlight community was impressed by my flight to Sydney. For years I traipsed from one potential sponsorship prospect to another, trying to stir up interest in a flight around the world. In the meantime, as always, I had small adventures, what I called "wheezettes" as opposed to "wheezes", which were the real thing. In 1976, still early days in hang gliding, I had established a world record for a two-man hang-glider drop from a balloon with a friend, Graham Driscoll. He bummed cigarettes off me all the way up to 13,770 feet, and the drop, dangling 20 feet below the balloon, was so exciting that when we landed I could not stand still for 90 minutes, working out the adrenaline.

The following year the same balloon pilot, Philip Hutchins, agreed to cart me to 20,000 feet, solo, under his balloon, to try and be the first person to fly the English Channel by hang glider. A friend, Ken Messenger, was in a second hang glider, dangling off a second balloon flown by a terrific Tory squire called David Liddiard. On the way up Liddiard burned so much gas he leaned over at 5,000 feet and said, "If I say GO, then GO, because I'm coming straight after you." David's safety device at the top of the balloon was burned off and Ken carted it all the way across the Channel. They got to 18,000 feet over the coast before Ken dropped, and both he and Liddiard made it safely. But my balloon pilot, Philip, was worried about having enough fuel to cross the Channel himself, and started going down at 14,500 feet, still a mile and a half short of the coast, and shouting at me that I could make it from there. I dropped off anyway and tried for France, but failed to make it. Philip got across, having started with six bottles of gas, and still had two and a half full bottles left after landing. Fiona, who had arranged the sponsorship for this event, was quite pithy in her comments.

After ninety minutes swimming to France I was picked up by a Russian ship called the *Kargopol*, whose crew threw large jam-jars of vodka down my throat every time I moved from one place to another (the sea to the dinghy, the dinghy to the ship, the sauna bath to the ship's bridge). By the time I phoned Fiona at 7.30 in the morning, I was quite cheerful. French newspapermen were later impressed, or so they said, by my *sang-froid*. My daughter Jade was born nine months later.

One of the best of the wheezettes was flying out of Heathrow Airport on August 25, 1994, the 75th anniversary of the start of the first international scheduled air service. The original service was begun out of Hounslow on August 25, 1919, and I gathered together 22 other microlight pilots to fly 16 journalists to Paris. The weather had been dreadful, 600-foot cloud-base and lashing rain, and 22 of us got off (one declined). Only 16 of us got through to Le Bourget in Paris the following afternoon, and only 7 of the journalists; no one was injured, there was just a large attrition rate with bottle problems. More women landed in Paris than had taken off from London. We were followed by a coach with our dinner jackets, and little black dresses for the girls, and the whole event was enlivened by being sponsorsed by Famous Grouse Scotch Whisky; we had eight cases, and each pilot carried two bottles. Those who took part in the event remember most of what happened to this day.

The adventure that changed my life was the flight around the world in 1998. By then I was separated from Fiona and living in a little terraced house in Bethnal Green in East London, working for the *London Financial News*, a specialist City newspaper. I interviewed a man called Dallas MacGilivray for a column I wrote on hobbies of City people, about his hobby of scuba-diving. In a discussion afterwards, I asked if he knew anyone who might be interested in sponsoring a microlight flight around the world in 80 days? Dallas introduced me to Paul Loach, then chief executive of the Liechtenstein Global Trust, who was captivated, and Paul in turn introduced me to Prince Philipp of Liechtenstein, whose family owned LGT. I went out to Switzerland to make a presentation on May 6th, 1997, and the following day heard I had won backing, and would I put together the project?

Because of doubts about my own fitness at the age of 55 to get around the world in 80 days hard flying, I planned the world flight in a flex-wing machine with a partner, a co-pilot called Keith Reynolds. He was a microlight instructor, and a man I had known 20 years since coaching him on the British hang gliding team in America. I bought a Pegasus Quantum 912, like the Atlantic-flight Mainair Blade a flexwing, and we made a number of flights together to learn about our flying styles, to Corsica, to Liechtenstein, and across the North Sea in winter to Berlin. Just before we left on the big flight, friends of Richard Branson of Virgin Airways, a famous adventurer, offered a million dollar prize if we would wait so a Branson team could race us around the world. This was a proposition I turned down (as did Dallas, Keith was not involved in the decision); who wanted the chance to be second around the world?

On March 24, 1998, Keith and I set off from Brooklands in south west London, and had a number of adventures together. These included being bounced ten times by a Mig 21 in Syria, trying to get through to Amman in Jordan, where we were to be guests of King Hussein. The Mig 21 did not fire at us, but it was a close-run thing. In the Saudi Desert our engine blew up seven times, five with Keith flying it, and then when we replaced it, twice with me. We discovered that the extra fuel we were carrying had blocked the air-flow to the radiator, over-heating the engine, so Keith moved the radiator in Dhahran, tie-wrapping it to one of the legs of the aircraft. Our first test-flight, because of hassles from Saudi bureaucrats, was over 300 miles of Persian Gulf, which we completed successfully.

Temperatures in India were dreadful, above 114F even in April. I was physically ill some of the time. We had lost three days in the Saudi Desert, changing engines, gained day one back in a brilliant flight from Calcutta to Mandalay in Burma, lost another day in Laos, and then lost five days in Hanoi, Vietnam, while the Chinese debated whether we could fly in. When we did fly on from Nanning to Macau, with Keith at the control-bar, much of the flight was completed in a white-out condition, just on instruments. But because the aircraft was pitch-stable, it was nothing like as dangerous as it would have been in a 3-axis conventional aircraft.

We had two days delay in South Korea waiting for the Japanese to allow us in, and then eight days in Japan waiting for the Russians to say yes to our entry, only to find, when they did say yes and we finally flew in, they would not let us fly out of the city of Yuzhno-Sakhalinsk. It took 18 days of negotiations, partially in London, some of it our embassy in Moscow, and some of it by me in Yuzhno-Sakhalinsk to get permission to fly on. By this time Keith had brooded about the Branson million-dollar offer, and told me he had to be out of the country before his visa expired. He was alarmed at the fierce tenacity of my fight with the Russians to fly on, risking imprisonment by saying I would stay if our visas expired, as the authorities had threatened not to renew; Keith wanted to be out of the country rather than fight. His reasons, though, were hardly noble ones.

"If this flight fails," he told me one morning, "I can go back now to London, pick up the phone to Virgin and, with my experience, be lead pilot to Richard Branson."

When I did get permission to continue, the proviso was that I was forced to take a Russian navigator with me across 5,200 kilometres of bleakest Siberia to Nome, Alaska. I asked Keith, whom I was paying £800/week plus expenses, to take an airliner to Alaska and wait for me, but when he got there, he saw it in his best interests to fly home, abandoning the flight to leave me on my own. If, on my own, I failed, Keith would still have a chance to be the first man to fly a microlight around the world. Simply put, he took a bet that, without him, I would fail.

I flew across Siberia with the chief navigator for Far East Russia, Peter Petrov, in the back, and again, had adventures. It was very cold. Once, landing to avoid a storm, I broke a few bits on the wing, and was turned half-over by the wind. We pushed the aircraft back on to its wheels and I took off from a track on my own, asking Peter to find a car to get himself to Magadan. I said I would meet him there the following day, where I replaced the bent hang-point on the aircraft (the wing-keel was bent 4 inches, but I only discovered that back in England). Peter and I crossed the Bering Sea buried in cloud, flying on instruments and covered in ice, but got to Nome, Alaska, safely. From there, I flew on my own down to San Francisco, across to New York, and then across the Atlantic via Baffin Island, Greenland, Iceland and the Faroes Islands, the first man ever to make a west-east crossing of the Atlantic by microlight.

Many of the stages were completed in dreadful weather, surrounded by cloud and turbulence. The crossing from Greenland to Iceland, in particular, was harrowing, where I spent a period of three hours "beyond fear", but I completed it safely. I arrived back home after 120 days, in what was then the fastest open-cockpit single-engined flight around the world, beating the record of 175 days set back in 1924 by four American aviators in two biplanes called Douglas World Cruisers (Colin Bodill beat my speed record two years later, doing the same flight in 99 days).

I won all the awards it was possible for an Englishman to win in aviation for that flight, including the Britannia Trophy, once won by Sir John Alcock (but not, oddly, Sir Arthur Whitten Brown, or later, Amy Johnson), and also the Segrave Trophy which *was* won once by Amy Johnson. It had a big effect on my life. Like the Australia flight, I had completed it successfully, but at a tremendous cost, especially in wear and tear, fighting bureaucrats. Breaking down the 121 days I was on that flight (I had two June 11ths, flying east through the date line), 71 of them were spent flying, actually going somewhere. On 6 days I was grounded by bad weather, or turned back because the weather stopped me making my goal. The remainder of the 35 days I was fighting officials, 5 days against the Chinese, 2 days the Japanese, 26 days the Russians, and 2 days fighting the Danes. The latter queried whether I was really a microlight with all the fuel I had on board, but after a terrific fuss then threw up their hands:

"If Brian Milton wants to kill himself, what business is it of ours?". Too bloody right.

I spent 405 hours in the air on that flight, some of it with Keith Reynolds but we did not talk much, and Peter Petrov and I had language problems. Otherwise I was on my own, turning over thoughts in my mind, hour after hour. It left me with firm opinions on values, which were stripped of other people's influences or any type of political correctness. I had also become accustomed to fighting officialdom, which I saw as bent on stopping genuine enterprise.

The easiest way to summarise my values is in Kipling's great poem, "If". Not long after I had returned home from the world flight I heard it discussed on BBC Radio 4's *Today* programme. Possibly because of schedule changes during my flight, I found I had consciously to resist throwing the radio out of the window a dozen times a morning at the opinions I heard expressed there. The discussion on "If" took the biscuit. The poem easily won a poll as Britain's favourite, to the obvious rage and disgust of the *Today* team; in a discussion, Dame Sue Macgregor called it "derisory". For the life of me, I could not understand this, except perhaps the last line, "you'll be a man, my son" (Ms Macgregor has a reputation as a feminist, though I don't suppose she would see herself as one of the hairy-handed five percent that hated men). I could not find a line in Kipling's poem with which I disagreed, and saw nothing *derisory* in it at all. As for men wanting to be men, to have a code of behaviour against which to measure themselves, I felt we have always needed that. I certainly did:

IF

If you can keep your head when all about you
Are losing theirs and blaming it on you,
If you can trust yourself when all men doubt you.
But make allowance for their doubting too;
If you can wait and not be tired by waiting,
Or being lied about, don't deal in lies,
Or being hated, don't give way to hating,
And yet don't look too good, nor talk too wise:

If you can dream- and not make dreams your master
If you can think- and not make thoughts your aim
If you can meet with Triumph and Disaster
And treat those two impostors just the same;
If you can bear to hear the truth you've spoken
Twisted by knaves to make a trap for fools.
Or watch the things you gave our life to, broken,
And stoop to build 'em up with worn-out tools:

If you can make one heap of all your winnings
And risk it on one turn of pitch-and-toss,
And lose, and start again at your beginnings
And never breathe a word about your loss;
If you can force your heart and nerve and sinew
To serve your turn long after they are gone,
And so hold on when there is nothing in you
Except the Will which says to them: 'Hold on!'

If you can talk to crowds and keep your virtue,
Or walk with Kings – nor lose the common touch,
If neither foes nor loving friends can hurt you,
If all men count with you, but none too much;
If you can fill the unforgiving minute
With sixty seconds' worth of distance run,
Yours is the Earth and everything that's in it,
And – which is more – you'll be a Man, my son!

It is a simple way of summing up my values, which I brought into the Atlantic flight. All the adventures I have had have included tests of Kipling's propositions. The *Today* programme team brought in an alleged poet called Adrian Henry and a woman whose name escapes me, as a platform to slag off "If", and each produced some piffling effort which was offered instead of the nation's favourite. I have come to accept this episode as yet another measure of how alienated I am from official voices in my own country, and it underlined the urgency of the search I wanted to make for real and lasting values on the Atlantic flight. I was determined that, aside from the physical business of flying, a debate should go on about values. Central to this debate, it emerged, was my correspondence with Stephen Lewis, a man I count my best friend, but at other levels the debate went on with friends, pilots or otherwise. On all previous adventures, especially when I was young, I had been accustomed to being on my own among strangers. But in the Internet-age, when communication by e-mail is so easy, and it costs virtually nothing to send letters, I lived in the middle of a constant toing and froing of ideas.

As fuel for the debate, I took six books with me on the Atlantic flight. If you have never spent down-time on an adventure, be assured that this is where things normally go wrong. When you are in the thick of it, battling gales, struggling overland from one place to another, then your attention is focused on staying alive. But when you cannot fly or bureaucrats are holding you up, that is when you confront all the various doubts inside you, and become prey to red herrings, errant thoughts, and risk losing the plot. I believe the decisions Keith Reynolds made on the world flight, especially in Yuzhno-Sakhalinsk and later in Anchorage, were directly affected by the fact that he had no book to distract his mind from the problems we faced. He had no games either, and every morning after breakfast he retired to his hotel room, faced with the prospect of four white walls and a television set with programmes in Russian. A young girl, Lena, with whom he had a relationship, thought she could bonk him morning, noon and night, and this would keep him sane and happy, but it does not work like that.

On my previous adventures, driving an Austin 7 across Africa, or on the flight to Australia, I had always sought some distraction from reality. On the Dalgety Flight I read *"Winged Victory"* by V.M.Yeates three times in 1987/8, and read the same book five times on the world flight in 1998. Without it, I could have gone completely mad with frustration.

On the Atlantic flight I faced a possible six weeks in St John's, Newfoundland, every day checking the weather forecast, and making decisions about it. If the answer was not to fly, as for many days was likely, I had the rest of the day to fill. I expected to check the aircraft over a hundred times, and there was St John's to explore, to photograph and video. I could look for places where Alcock and Brown visited, and find anyone who remembered their departure in 1919. But I wanted to avoid the frame of mind that I think pushed Keith into making the disastrous decisions he made.

I was also envious at the ease at which Englishmen had once slipped into a mode of behaviour I deemed courageous, and which is now so hard to discover. In the Boer War, for example, in a terribly bitter battle against the Afrikaners, the latter said, however much they hated the British, they never found one who was a coward. The historian James Morris has a lovely quote, about an English officer carried wounded from some battle murmuring, "I'm only a sportsman, y'know". This is an attitude of mind that fascinates me, and which I sought to achieve myself ahead of an ordeal beyond any other I had faced. However other people had judged my behaviour, and the Segrave Trophy carries the words *Imagination, Courage, Initiative*, I myself had doubts about where I would find the will-power and determination to see things through. Was I capable of putting the whole adventure together and bringing it to a successful conclusion? In the past, I had done so (though I counted the drive across Africa as a failure, in that I did not get the Austin 7 down to Johannesburg). *Pace* Sue Macgregor and the rest of her ilk at home, I needed to discover a set of values which would sustain me. They would have to be true values, as I thought Kipling's were, because they would be tested at the extremes of physical behaviour that I saw ahead of me on my Atlantic flight.

The six books I decided to bring with me were the result of weeks of thought. First was *The Last Place on Earth,* by Ronald Huntford, an account of the race to the South Pole by Scott and Amundsen. Scott had always been a hero to me, albeit a remote one. I knew about him from history lessons at school (I bet he is not taught to children nowadays), and I wanted to know more about him. His motives had been traduced and his blunders magnified, and especially his patriotism, his idea of England, had been ridiculed. I wanted to make up my own mind about this.

The second book was Edmund Blunden's *Undertones of War,* said to be one of the finest autobiographies to come out of the First World War. I had read most of the WW1 classics, Siegfried Sassoon's *Memoirs of a Fox-Hunting Man*, Robert Graves' *Goodbye to All That* (of course), some of the poems of Rupert Brooke and Wilfred Owen, *Sagittarius Rising* by Cecil Lewis, and the best of them all, *The Middle Parts of Fortune* by Frederic Manning. But Blunden had had as difficult a war as anyone on the Somme, at Ypres and Passchendaele. The WW1 poets, the best of them, were fighters, as poets should be (could one say that about Adrian Henry? Ho ho), and not woofters. I had come to the conclusion that England, as apart from Britain, had been wounded fatally in the First World War, and it was one of my tasks to try and determine why. I hoped Blunden would help.

The third was a small book of poems called *Flame of the Forest* collected by Wilfred Russell, honorary uncle to my former wife, Fiona Campbell. Wilfred, known to Fiona as Uncle Pomp, was still alive when I left for New York. He had gone to India after Cambridge in 1935 as a merchant adventurer, but so fell in love with the country that he entered politics there, sitting as a Congress Party MP before the last world war, and hob-nobbing with Gandhi and Nehru. He went through the war as a flyer in the RAF, and left India in 1965; he was, for a long time, treasurer to Leonard Cheshire's Homes. I knew him in 1966/8 when he lived in Eaton Square; I once found him listening to the Beatles album, "Revolver" with all those Indian influences on it. His collection of poetry included works by Englishmen and by Indians, most of them unknown but obviously appreciated, and some of his own poetry. I determined to dip into it in faraway Newfoundland and see which poems echoed in my mind.

The fourth book was a collection of Rudyard Kipling's poems, selected by T.S.Eliot. It was as much to do with Eliot's selection as Kipling's poems. James Morris, in his terrific – and in my house, dog-eared – trilogy, "Pax Britannica", wrote that Kipling was the one true artistic genius to come out of the British Second Empire between the period 1837 and 1965, and I found his poetry as moving as ever.

The fifth book was a prose version of Homer's *The Odyssey*. I had been a long time getting around to reading this. Nothing in English high culture in the last 160 years could really be understood without having read *The Odyssey*. It was the first great adventure story in western culture and the basis for English education throughout the nineteenth century. All the allusions made by authors of that period, and many of them later, are lost unless I know the context.

The sixth book was a biography of George Leigh Mallory, whose body was discovered on Everest two years before my flight, and 76 years after he had disappeared in 1924 trying to reach the peak of Everest. *The Wildest Dream* had a nude Mallory as its front cover (he loved being photographed without his kecks), and was written by Peter and Leni Gillman. The book had been praised by the great climber, Joe Simpson. Mallory was always a hero of mine, and he was a particularly English type of hero. I wanted to know how and why.

Most of the events on the Atlantic attempt are threaded through with reaction to the values I found in these books.

6

Sponsorship

Ever since I came back from the world flight in 1998 I had been in occasional touch with Paul Loach, the man who had agreed my sponsorship with GT Global. The company, of which he had been chief executive, had been bought by Amvescap for $1.3 billion and, though Paul had lost his job, GT's owner, the Princely Family of Liechtenstein, had adequately compensated him for getting such a good price. Paul had no need to work again, and for a year experimented with being a rich and leisured man, not a life-style that he had been accustomed to from birth. He had begun his career in financial services in 1975 with the investment bank, NM Rothschild, and specialised in small and medium-sized companies. In 1981, he co-founded Throgmorton Investment Management, and two years after that company was acquired by the Framlington Group in 1986, Paul was made Group Chief Executive. He joined GT Management in 1994 as boss of their European operations to begin with, but was later appointed to lead the whole group, which is when I met him. After leaving GT, he wanted breathing space.

During this period I put him up for membership of the Reform Club, and we had lunch or dinner from time to time. He is an energetic and charismatic man, restless and intellectually curious, with a long background in Labour Party politics, although this had rather faded. He had also come to admire my friend, Stephen Lewis, who seconded his application to the Reform. Paul was a regular guest at Stephen's political lunches at the Reform, where some of the Great and the Good were other guests.

Though Paul had been in at the beginning of the world flight, which would not have happened without his support, the fact that he was not there at the end probably weighed with him. If I put up another adventure and he judged that it was significant and had a chance of success, one of the reasons he might be attracted to it was that he could be there at the end as well as the beginning. In City terms, Paul felt he had at least one more cycle in him, another business career, and when the rootless life of a rich man did not prove satisfying Paul joined up with two other men who had also, in John Buchan's terms, "made their pile".

One was Tony Canning, who had spent 25 years as an international "angel" investor in London and New York. He had become a specialist in advising companies on their relations with shareholders and the investing institutions, and a strategic adviser on fund raising and stock market floatations. The other was Rollo Clifford, scion of an old English Catholic family; the Clifford in the original secret CABAL in the seventeenth century was one of Rollo Clifford's ancestors. He was originally a metal broker, but had become a specialist in the early stages of emerging high-tech companies, a founder shareholder, for example, in Bookham Technologies. Rollo had once sailed the Atlantic in a replica of the 1851 yacht *America* which had started the America's Cup Yacht Race. Canning and Clifford co-founded Lion Capital partners in 1998, Paul Loach joined them a year later. Tony Canning was Chief Executive.

Despite the bear market, Lion Capital Partners had done well. They drew from a pool of investors in the City of London, and in four cities in the United States, Washington DC, Baltimore, Boston and New York. Though, by City terms and the money they had handled themselves in earlier careers, the funds were small, £50 million, they had turned this into £95 million in two years, and laid seed for the next bull market. One of their specialities was investing in emerging technology in medicine. This made the involvement with the Artificial Heart Fund more attractive.

Between March and April, cutting my budget back to suit the size of a company that was much smaller than GT Global, I made my case to Lion Capital Partners to back one of the adventures. They were not interested in the Coney Run, but they were in the Atlantic. I secured two budgets, an operating budget to make the flight happen, and a much smaller budget to get the raw material to video the flight. I had not then secured a commission from television for any documentary, but if no video was shot then there would be no documentary anyway. This second budget was at virtual cost, but it did include the funding to raise Liam Abramson's wages by another £300/week.

It emerged that the three partners were not that interested in immediate publicity from the flight, though that was welcome. They wanted it to succeed and would then exploit it fully. I discovered much later that the sponsorship was much more personal than that; rather than involve, formally, Lion Capital Partners, whose non-executive directors were dubious about it, the three men underwrote the costs individually.

I know I face being accused of repeating those immortal words of Mandy Rice-Davies, "he would say that, wouldn't he?" but I do want to say that whatever physical courage projects like mine demand, the corporate courage required to back them is much more rare. The aviation circle that I am in, the New Aviation, is almost completely detached from Mainstream Aviation. Either it does not generate sufficient profit, or as these things are measured, it is not sufficiently admirable, to arouse the sympathy, interest and money available to our bigger but more cautious forerunner. We are tolerated but not admired. As a result we have no constituency, as, say, climbers have with the long-established Alpine Club or yachtsmen, with Britain's long involvement with the sea, to call upon for help. When you look at the companies Sir Chay Blythe has enticed into yacht-racing around the world, you know that there is a shared history of the same activity – sailing – between the powerful and the poor, in which they all share the same values and admire the same qualities. In the New Aviation, we have come to depend on chance to find the right people who respond to the dreams we spin. They are few and far between.

To give you an example, in 1996 I got into a bun-fight over sponsorship with a City company, in which I convinced a forceful man within that company, Malcolm Callaghan, now a friend, that backing me to fly around the world would be a good thing (this was before GT Global had said yes). Malcolm and I rehearsed all the arguments about why it was worth his company, which wanted a higher profile, backing my venture. But I appeared a little late in the game, when some people within the company had already set their heart on another exciting venture, Formula One motor racing. In the internal debate which followed, in which I was involved only on the side lines, calling out moves for Malcolm, it came down to spending one million pounds (according to the London *Times*; the *Financial Times* said £3 million) to buy nine inches of space on either side of the racing helmets of Jacques Villeneuve and Heinz-Harald Frentzen, both drivers for the Rothmans Williams F1 motor-racing team. The alternative was spending just over a third of a million pounds on my operating budget, with another two thirds of a million spent marketing my flight. This was the year when, after a period of dominance, Frank Williams had lost his iron grip on Formula One racing, and both

Ferrari and Maclaren were coming through fast (I believe Maclaren won that year, 1998). This could easily have been predicted, even by an amateur like me; all the commentators were also chronicling the change.

I wrote a paper for Malcolm saying that his company was in danger of joining a long line of sponsors, some of whom (Rothmans) would be paying up to £20m, leaving his own company at the bottom of the pecking order. Whatever value the sponsorship had as a venue to take clients, lured by the glamour of motor-racing, they would soon see where the company ranked in the internal sponsorship pecking order, and react accordingly. Who wanted the last five minutes at the end of the day with two racing stars fulfilling their glamorous duties to the smallest sponsor of the team?

And who wanted, I wrote, to back a team destined to come at least second, if not third or worse?

In the committee of three which made the final decision, power rested, not with Malcolm, but with a then-powerful woman. She opted, inevitably, to take the motor-racing option. Matters turned out as predicted, the space on the side of the helmet was not often seen, and half-way through the season the company cancelled the sponsorship. That then-powerful woman is now working in the same job with another City company; I cannot guess whether she would make the same decision again.

I still lost, of course, and it was worth noting why.

The adventures I am attracted to are out of the ordinary, and essentially naked. There is no hiding place within them. If I fail, it is terrifically naked, and my sponsor must fear the risk of being tarred with the same brush of failure, even if every possible effort is made to succeed. In motor-racing, by contrast, when Ayrton Senna died, an obvious and catastrophic failure, those sponsoring him did not suffer. People were sympathetic, and commiserated. In their defence, Senna's sponsors could point to a whole sheaf of other sponsors, just like them, big important companies with clout in the world, which also took the same risks as those backing Senna. There was comfort in numbers, even if most of those sponsors backed losers. The "glamour" overcame the coming second or worse.

If no one lost their job buying IBM, who needs corporate courage?

With the world flight in 1998, as with the Australian flight in 1987/8, and now with the Atlantic flight in 2001, any sponsor was absolutely exposed. To my mind, such sponsors had much greater corporate courage than those making the easy decision to get involved in the glamorous group-sponsored events like motor-racing and global yachting. Corporate courage is rarer than physical courage. We all can find within ourselves some measure of physical courage. It is one of the *manly* qualities – there's a word seldom used these days – that men have been encouraged to discover within themselves since time began. But corporate courage is the ability to make the decision that wiser souls, those whose judgement is considered "sound" (an English word often meaning "acceptably mediocre"), suck their teeth at.

It was always easier with an unusual project to say "no thanks", to opt for the safer option, to hide within the box of what other people believe was sensible. Those who say yes to such a product are really out of the ordinary.

If these views are true, and I believe they are, this made the decision by Terry Pryce of Dalgety to back my flight to Australia, and Paul Loach, now at Lion Capital Partners, to back, not just the world flight, but also the Atlantic flight, all the more courageous. With Terry, for example, I knew when I was wrecked on a Greek island and was sticking the aircraft back together, or when I was pulling it out of the Persian Gulf on Christmas Day, 1987 after it had been six hours in the sea, that there were gentlemen on his company's board who would have used such an event to hurt him. They had stayed quiet, or murmured discreetly, when he had backed me in the first place. It was an imperative with me to get the aircraft back into the air again, and complete the flight to Australia, which after a lot more troubles and in the teeth of great hostility and contempt (at the time) from the British microlight community, I did. I knew that Terry's back was exposed, and that I had a responsibility to protect it.

When Terry turned up to greet me in Sydney he was the epitome of a Hemingway hero, exhibiting "grace under pressure", and exciting the most profound admiration in me. He said then that the £100,000 in sponsorship money was the best the company had ever spent. At the drop of a hat, I would have gone over the top of a First World War trench for him. The fact that within a year those forces within Dalgety had mustered enough clout to get him, and that he was removed from his position, was neither here nor there. It is instructive to ask, where is Dalgety now? Before Terry's corporate assassination, it had existed as a company for nearly 150 years.

I felt the same way, though in different circumstances, about Paul Loach. The ultimate decision to back the world flight came from Prince Phillip of Liechtenstein, but the prince had made the decision under Paul's guidance.

Paul was always the back-stop, and during a difficult period before I left on that flight, it was Paul who dispersed mediocre and frightened forces that could in other circumstances have destroyed it.

I am not quite sure what either Terry Pryce or Paul Loach, if they ever meet, would see in each other, and whether they would become friends. I only know that each have that quality of being different from others, and the courage to back their judgement. I had written in *Global Flyer's* dedication "I am grateful for the stylish way you backed this flight, and I hope you feel that you got value for it. I tried never to let you down, and I do not believe I did so." It is always an awesome responsibility, no matter how often I asked for it, and I felt it keenly as the Atlantic attempt developed.

The sponsorship made a difference in my approach to the Atlantic flight. I could afford a week in France test-flying the aircraft, just getting flying experience on it in its legal Permit-to-Fly state. I need to do this because all my previous experience had been on Pegasus machines. We launched the project at the Science Museum in west London on March 15th, displaying my little Flyer under the original Vickers Vimy that Sir John Alcock had flown across the Atlantic. The venue was tight, but it made a good photograph; there was a moderate amount of media interest. We also displayed the Flyer at an adventure sports exhibition. I spent whatever time I could – still planning to do the Coney Run – up at Plaistow Farm, near St Albans, where I kept the Flyer, getting as much air-time as I could.

Later that month I flew across to Kidlington Airfield near Oxford and took Nikki King's star heart patient, Peter Houghton, up for a flight in front of local television cameras. Peter, in his early sixties, was completely reliant on his artificial heart to keep him alive, and was obviously full of trepidation at his first-ever flight in my microlight. He was, though, game for it, and once into the air it was obvious he was not going to be killed and he enjoyed it. He has since proposed that I fly him around all the islands in Britain in the year 2002; island-collecting is a sort of hobby of his.

Mainair had commissioned two aluminium Atlantic fuel tanks from a company called Docking at Silverstone, who had gained their expertise in Formula 1 Racing. These took time to construct, so I blew off for a week across France, flying in quite rough conditions, heading for Corsica where friends – Brian and Doreen Winterflood – would put me up for two days. The first day down from Le Touquet on the French coast to Sarlat/Domme, near where I had a holiday home, was very rough flying. The wind rose close to gale force, and there were big patches of rain through which I flew. I spent 7 hours in the air, clearing the cob-webs and feeling pleased at how the Flyer handled, and how I had coped myself. I intended to fly on the following day via Marseilles and Nice to Corsica, but found, thankfully before take-off, that a *Mistral* was whistling down the Rhone Valley with 60 mph winds that would have trashed me. That *Mistral* blew for the next three days, after which I headed north to Carrouges in Normandy, a village where Malcolm Callaghan lived. I had met Malcolm originally to write a story about him; he had gone out in France intending to buy a barn to house a 1934 Lea Francis car, and instead had bought a whole village, in which he now lived. It was there I stayed the Easter weekend.

Again, the flying was rough, hour after hour being slung around the sky, and hardly any other aircraft were in the air. It was satisfying to me to find that, at 58, and in so physical a flying activity, I had evolved methods that enabled me to fly for quite long hours without tiring myself unduly. I took Malcolm's son, Tim, along the invasion beaches at low level, about 150 feet, over the Easter weekend, and returned home the following via Cherbourg and Southampton, 90 miles over the sea, the longest such flight I had made since returning on the world flight in July, 1998.

The Blade was slower than the Quantum by about 2/3 mph, but it was more comfortable. I thought it would be slightly stiffer in roll, but there turned out to be no significant difference. It was a very reassuring aircraft, and even in rough turbulence I felt safe. I had psychological limits in my mind about the altitude I could fly at, and found on that flight I was able to lift them and fly higher than I usually did. I tried testing everything possible, including the wing cameras which I had transferred from the GT Global Flyer, and using a diary camera to record the flight. Amongst the innovations were carrying music disks to while away the hours, experimenting with Pavarotti, the Blues Brothers and Little Richard. They were not suitable. I decided I wanted music I could sing along to, rather than just listen.

These were typical notes I made to myself about the flight:
1. *Must learn to change tanks in mid-air. Mirror must be fitted on spat.*
2. *Wing and keel cameras do not work well. Why?*
3. *Fix the turn in the wing, now left-hand. Can I have an in-air trimmer?*
4. *The sound from the intercom to the video is still very poor.*

5. Must secure CD player/disk wallet better. Practice changing disks. Need spare batteries to be able to change in flight.

6. Why is the highest EGT (exhaust gas temperature) so close to 800C on 4,000 revs?

7. Must place the Hi-8 video recorder in a more accessible place.

8. The electric gloves don't work. Why? Suspect the cigar lighter plug. Try hard-wiring in a direct loom, otherwise send back to manufacturer to correct.

9. Diary camera still not right. Picture is too narrow. How can I better it?

10. Helmet face mask needs a lock (now fitted, nicked from GT Global helmet).

11. Suffer badly from cold, despite 2 flying suits (one thin) plus GT Global jacket. I need an electric waistcoat, but would it work with a survival suit? I think not.

12. How much will my flying speed be degraded by the big tank? The Tim Callaghan effect.

13. Radio reception is quite poor. Why? I have all-new gear. I don't like the new Icom A-22E. Swap for an old one?

14. I must use chest camera audio linked to intercom, for imaginative shots and pieces to camera, as well as external shots.

15. Nerve myself to test toilet facilities, and in survival suit.

My height fears, those psychological altitude limits in my mind, are notorious within the British microlighting community. They arrived in force that day in India when a *Djinn* appeared on the nose of my aircraft and told me to jump, but they had been latent for years before that. Flying hang gliders is exciting, but if you have any imagination it is easy to get worried about the one piece of webbing that attaches you to the hang-point, or to look at the swages on the rigging and wonder if they were put on late on a Friday evening? I used to have problems when hang gliding with my feet in a stirrup harness, outside the hammock in which my body was slung, imagining the feet in my flying boots would drop off at 2,000 feet and tumble separately to the ground.

That fall out of the sky in 1978 removed any blind faith I may have had in the technology of rag-wings. No matter how much reassurance I was given, and I could read all the technical specifications as well as anyone, at bottom the bird-brain buried within my human brain was always nervous. I had to be careful how I allowed my mind to work, or it would travel down corridors where, well, bandersnatches lurked, just waiting to leap out and consume me with fears. It has become increasingly obvious as I get older that I am in a race between the deterioration of my nerves, and the achievements I dream of making. As a young man it is easy to be brave, but getting older gives you experience. I have lost a number of friends who, in other circumstances, should have out-lived me.

Sometimes, in flight, I get a vivid picture of every single foot of air there is between the bottom of my spine, the three inches of air to the keel of the trike, and then through the skirt and all those tumbling feet to the ground. I might be thinking of some flying task, and drift off into a day-dream, and these fears will rush at me, and I must grapple with them.

I am not, naturally, courageous. Whatever risky enterprise I enter, I suffer failure a thousands times before I am able to actually get to the enterprise. I am relieved to find – so far – that the physical process of making something happen also forces the fear back into a quiet corner of my mind, where I leave it alone. I suspect that I am not alone in this, that it is commonplace even among some of the men I count as heroes, but it is also a subject not much discussed. There is a great deal of good to be said for the stiff upper lip, with not sharing fears and just sticking it through the way we used to do. But if I was genuine about examining values in making the Atlantic flight, then I had to discuss, honestly, what was going on inside me. Those flying fears were real, they will always be with me. They crop up throughout the account of this flight.

7

Technical Preparations

The Atlantic tanks were set to be completed in the middle of May. I expected to have to ship them to America and fit them after doing the Coney Run. But when Paul confirmed that Lion Capital Partners were going to sponsor the flight, Liam Abramson made a very strong case that I should postpone Coney.

"You won't have enough time to do both," he said, forcefully, after a meeting with Paul on April 3rd. "You will be spread too thinly to make either flight successful."

It was difficult for me to stop wearing blinkers, especially as the year 2001 was the 80th anniversary year for the Coney flight. But Liam made a strong case, and convinced me. This process meant constantly changing plans about when I would arrive in America and, at the same time, we were dithering about David Gleave's assurances that we would get an Antonov 124 to give me and the aircraft a lift. It would have saved so much hassle of packing and re-packing had he done so.

I expected to get to New York by the middle of May, and leave on the first leg of the flight, perhaps in two legs via Halifax, Nova Scotia to St Johns, Newfoundland, between May 28 and June 1. I was not paranoid about getting to St John's in one hop, a flight of 1,151 miles. Halifax was about half way, and it all depended on the wind.

I was getting advice on the peculiarities of ditching in a microlight. David Bremner, Editor of *Microlight Flying*, wrote:

> *… I'm sure you'll have seen this already, but I couldn't help thinking about a recent incident in Sweden, when a pilot had an engine failure in a flexwing over shallow water. Contrary to expectation, the trike surfed relatively stably on the water surface as it slowed down. It sank right way up, but what would*

have killed him if the water was any deeper was the VERY strong tendency for the wing to pitch down as it descended through the water. This meant that the bar pinned him to the seat. As he was only in about 10ft of water, he survived to tell the tale, but I pass this on in case you haven't heard it to help you formulate an escape strategy in extremis …

I did not test-fly the aircraft into the water to test this tendency, but I thought that the peculiar size of my fuel tank would tend to push the bar away from me if I ditched. Another pilot, Andy Buchan, had been on all my smaller adventures, including both Bleriot crossings of the Channel, and the Heathrow-Le Bourget flight. Andy was concerned about the heated clothing I needed:

> *… it might be worthwhile calculating the electrical drain on the battery with everything switched on. I had a look at the 912 data. The alternator puts out 20A at 5000 RPM which may give you a realistic 15A to use on consumables. Also, on the 912 Quantum (not sure about the Blade) the supply from the regulator is fused at 15A:*
>
> *Assume a current drain at 12V: a heated bar will take 2 amps, and a Widder heated vest 3 amps. I think the Widder 'chaps', which heat the top of your legs, use 3 amps as well. That leaves 7amps. A GPS will use 1 amp or more? Radio and others communications, 1 amp? Other things? Toaster? Jaccuzi?*
>
> *Have you heard of Ted Simon? He rode around the world a few years back on a Triumph 500. He is now revisiting people and places on an R80GS BMW, and has been using electric clothing. He experienced battery overload with a 20 amp alternator, but he also has GPS, lights, and recharges his laptop and phone from the bike, which may be where the problem comes from …*

Andy continued the theme a few days later, in a discussion about exhaust gas temperatures (EGT). I wanted to lean off the engine, but the only measure I had about how far to lean it off was to monitor the EGT. It should not, according to Jim Cunliffe, go above 800 degrees C, but it was regularly around 795, so how could I lean off without pushing the EGT into the danger area? Andy queried my figures:

> *… Maximum EGTs on a Pegasus 912 Quantum manual are 925C, way above the figure quoted for a Blade. On the Flydat there is a warning limit at 880C, with the alarm going off at 900C.*

My personal experience with the 912 is that the max EGT differs between engines but is at around 4400rpm and can be up to 825C on a standard engine. If I have an engine running much below this I would be happy to lower the needle jet to lean the mid-range (and therefore get better fuel economy). At higher power settings the engine will be on the main jet and the EGT will drop considerably.

Fuel burn ... my figures on my 912 Quantum with needles lowered one notch, measured over a trip to Sweden last year were as follows:

Carried load approx 150kg (me plus camping gear, inc fuel)

Indicated Air Speed: 63mph

RPM: 4150 (approx 50% max power)

Fuel burn: 9 litres / hr

Rotax manual figures give:

5800rpm 100% power 24L/hr (hold for less than 5 mins)

5500 96% power 23 L/hr (max continuous power)

5000 75% power 16 L/hr

4150 50% power 9 L/hr (my figure)

It is unlikely you can get 10L/hr with the load carried at 65MPH.

With the load carried in your machine (estimate around 600kg at take off including fuel?) you will be at around 5500rpm for maybe one hour to reach 8000ft. After that I guess you will be at around 5000rpm, giving 16L/hr. But with altitude you can lean off the mixture, in this case it would have to be the main jet, so leaning the needle will not help at this rev range.

Average 16L/hr, 400 litres, 25hrs duration best.

1950 miles, 25hrs airtime = 80mph groundspeed needed – I think this agrees with what you said.

+15mph tailwind needed with 65mph airspeed. But do check the accuracy of your air speed indicator. On our Swedish trip, Simon Reeve had a Mainair Blade, and his ASI read 70mph, cruising alongside my Quantum showing 65 mph.

ALSO You will have to fly at around 50 – 55mph to get a decent climb rate for the first hour.

CONCLUSION: I think you need an average 20mph tailwind!

I wondered whether he had allowed for a decreased fuel-burn as the load lightened. Andy replied that he had tried to even out the figures, which were approximate. He thought I would get the 10L/hour at 65mph that I wanted only when I had a fuel load of less than 70L. He recommended getting a system to lean the air/fuel mixture at height, and ensure I had a better estimate of the maximum EGTs that would indicate the leaning-out did not damage the engine. He thought I needed to have search and rescue services on standby for the last 100 miles of the flight.

I worried about falling asleep on the flight, and looked for a simple way of coping. It took time to find the practical solution, though the theory had been there for some time. I wanted to have an instrument that would wake me if I fell below a certain altitude. Over the Atlantic, there was nothing I could hit, and if I did doze off, so long as I did not descend then I was OK. This might seem alarming to some people, but it should work well in practice. After investigating GPS's and electronic altimeters and getting quotes of £1,000 for experimental work, I found the best free-fall parachute alarm, a product called Pro-Track, and talked to the manufacturers, Larsen and Brusgaard in Denmark. They asked some intelligent questions, and then sent me two little instruments, about the size of a matchbox, one of which I kept in reserve, the other I attached to the face-guard of my helmet. When switched on, if I descended below a certain height, the alarm would go off.

Good communications were vital, especially as I wanted to be able to get through on the radio, but also plug a CD player into my ear-phones, and record any thoughts I had to a face-video camera. I went to Lynx, who had done all the communications for the film "Fly Away Home", and were the best-established of the microlight radio links makers. Not only did I get reliable standard gear, but Lynx were also able to get me the equipment to audio-link into the Hi-8 camera, something I had not been able to do on the world flight.

Paul Loach insisted I did flight tests in England before I left for the USA, carrying a full load, either of fuel or of water of the same weight. As sometimes happened, I was blinkered about the capability of the aircraft, and tended to believe what I was told by Mainair, but Paul was right to insist. On May 11th I drove up to the Mainair factory in Rochdale, Lancashire, and saw the Atlantic tank installed for the first time. I had not really appreciated how gross it would be, and for a while I was in a slight state of shock. It was certainly "in yer face" about the amount of fuel I was carrying. Testing took place later that day at the big airfield at Warton, near Preston, test base of some of BAe's most advanced aircraft.

These are the weight and other figures we worked with.

The empty weight of the aircraft was 172 kgs. There were two Atlantic tanks. The biggest, tank 1, was calculated to carry 372 litres of fuel (74.36 imp gallons, 92.95 US gallons). Tank 2, the slipper tank, was accurately measured at 44 litres (9.68 imp, 12.1 US). Tank 1 fed the slipper tank, which fed the engine. Once switched on, before take-off, they did not need any more switching, which was a relief, because when I got tired I might forget to turn some vital switches. The only switching was to the separate reserve tank 3 at the back of the aircraft, capable of carrying 22 litres of petrol. We filled the reserve tank with petrol, and then started filling the main tanks with water. If it did not work, and I crashed, then I wanted to be surrounded by water instead of fuel.

The AUW – All Up Weight – including me, but not carrying my photographic gear, was 607.9kgs, or 1,336 lbs. That was 0.55 of a ton. The wing had already been tested, and not destroyed, beyond 2 tons in weight, which meant they were capable, on paper, of taking the gross load. To avoid having the big tank 1 bottoming out on the rear trike struts, Jim Cunliffe had blocked off the rear suspension. We put 50 psi air pressure into the tyres.

Before testing began, two deep indentations had to be made halfway up the tank, so as not to rub against the seat frame. Two or three leaks were plugged by extra welding.

I did the test flights, and these were my comments at the time:

"We rigged the wing, then married it to the empty trike, connected up the two new tanks, and half-filled them with water with a load roughly equal to the 230 litres of fuel I had carried on the world flight (fuel plus Keith Reynolds). I taxied out and tested this by climbing to 20/30 feet and holding my height while we looked at the wing to see if there was any distortion. There was none. The aircraft handled much like any other heavily loaded trike, nothing out of the ordinary. Jim Cunliffe, who chased me down the runway by van, saw no reason not to go immediately for a full load. I taxied in and waited in the cockpit while, for what seemed a very long time, water was poured into the new tank system. I recorded my impressions:

"Now you have to treat this as any other flight. In other words, fly it. Don't start thinking about all sorts of other things. You just must think about it as it is, just a flight. So when you get into the air you should think about being in the air and steering it right and all the other stuff ... I can't really go around corners fast (back-tracking) because just pushing out on this bar is really difficult ... temperatures are perfectly OK... I must test *these hot mitts (supplied by Andy Buchan ... they turned out to be the dog's bollocks, terrific) ... right! we're off, the real thing! ... up to 40 miles an hour, 40 miles an hour now, 45, push out the bar a little bit, won't climb, climbs ... holding her off, holding nice and steady, but, heavy, much heavier, still she's holding OK, take off some acceleration here ... nice and stately, she doesn't want to move a lot, I don't want to be coming down too fast, so I'm back down and I'm doing 65 miles an hour now and holding nice and steady. Now there's not very much of a crosswind and it isn't really very heavy, but I obviously cannot bang this thing on the ground, at all ... she feels like she could fly hands-off, not that I'm going to try it. Don't know what distortion there is in the wing (glanced right and left) there doesn't appear to be any distortion at all. I'm still holding down the centre line. It's bumpier up this end of the runway. I must be aware of my revs all the time, what revs have I got? 4480 and I'm holding on 4480 and I'm starting to come down, take the revs off, hold off, hold off, hold off, hold off ... not as good a landing as I did last time but a perfectly reasonable one just the same ... "*

Jim and I talked before the third run. We agreed that I should not flare out when landing, but fly it into the ground gently. He confirmed there was no distortion in the wing in any way, and was delighted by this observation. He worried about landing at the far end, where there was more turbulence, and I said I would land halfway down the runway where I wasn't being pushed around by the wind. After all, the intention was only to take off with this gross load; it was not to land with it. This was the second commentary, about the third and final flight ...

"... 30 ... 35 ... 40, 45, push the bar out, 50 ... 5,200 revs and we're off ... we're off at 62 miles an hour, and I just want to let back the revs a wee bit, just sort of hold her there, see what she's like, revs at 4,500 revs, she's maintaining at that. I just want to take those revs off and come in nice and gently ... that's nice and gently so I haven't frightened Jim ... ."

At the end of three test flights, they were deemed a success. There was no distortion in the fabric wing. The aircraft handled quite heavily on the ground, and it was very stately in the air, though there was little turbulence. But in general it was very good and handled well. The key thing for me was that I could get 4,480 revs and maintain height. That was below the 4,500 rev level at which I crossed the Atlantic on the world flight, where I had got 11 litres to the hour. The other good news was that I was doing 65 mph, and that meant with just 15 mph wind behind me I might get across in 24 hours. At that latitude I could expect a much stronger wind at height, without danger.

That was not beyond the wit of man or even the wit of me, and made me feel rather good. In all, terrific news. We had a very good aircraft.

It was the last time she flew in England. Jim Cunliffe took her back to Rochdale and started to pack her up to be shipped to America. I went home to London and booked my own ticket, and began keeping a detailed diary for every day thereafter. The account that follows is derived from that diary.

8

American Preparations

I spent the last few days before leaving for America on May 18th not really believing what was happening to me. The previous Sunday, May 13th, I had a farewell lunch with Moira Thomson, her sister Julie and Julie's girlfriend, Barrie. It was not as wrecking as meals with Moira usually were. We spent a lot of time looking at photographs, with Moira, who had lost about 20 pounds in weight and was looking terrific, constantly pointing at pictures and saying, "look, I'm not fat there".

On Monday, Valerie Thompson, at one time one of the best traders at Salomon Brothers, came by. I fed her, and we talked and dreamed for half the evening.

Tuesday was my daughter Jade's 23rd birthday. She phoned from Dublin and we talked about France that summer, and her trip to Tahiti to see her mother. Jade had a little weep about being so old, all of 23 years. I was not terrifically sympathetic, though I did think life more difficult for 23-year olds than when I was 23. Young people were more adrift from values; I thought this was why Jade had latched on to learning history as if she had been dying of thirst. My son James was the same way once, but his reading of history had made him quite right-wing.

Tuesday evening was my traditional farewell dinner with Stephen Lewis, who was to become, by e-mail, my closest confidant on the Atlantic flight. He had dined me before the flight to Australia in 1987, and before the world flight in 1998. This time Stephen took me to Simpson's on the Strand for smoked salmon and rare roast beef, and, abstemious for us, only two bottles of red wine. We disagreed, a rare thing, over the idea of England, of which I thought more than he did. It was an idea whose quality, under the pressure of a flight like this, I wanted to examine during the long nervous waiting period in Newfoundland. I felt the idea of *England* had been traduced and deliberately misrepresented in the last few decades, a necessity if we were to be subsumed into continental Europe. But I also thought that the way *England* was used in the first world war had dealt it a blow in all those terrible innocent deaths, from which it had hardly recovered, even now. The Rupert Brooke poem was a classic example, "If I should die think only this of me, that there's some corner of a foreign field that is forever, England …"

On Wednesday, Helen Dudley came around for what I thought would be my last dinner with her. She had been my beautiful muse on the world flight, about which I wrote in *Global Flyer*. I was curious to see if she would emerge with the same role on the Atlantic flight. She worked in marketing in the City, but was a leading amateur actress, which is how I had met her. She now had a regular boyfriend, Neil Murphy, which she had not on the world flight. Would it be thoughts of her that would sustain me when things got difficult? Or would I cast around for someone else to play the muse? Helen had taken it as a task to find me music to while away the long hours over the Atlantic, and chose the songs of my father's generation, inspired choices which, without her decisions, I would never have made. They included Flanagan and Allen's *Underneath the Arches*, a collection of Noel Coward songs sung by himself including my favourite, *Don't Let's be Beastly to the Germans*, which was extremely difficult to sing in key. Another Helen choice was Gracie Fields singing *Sally*, and *I took me harp to a party.*

After a cottage pie and peas and bottle of red wine, Helen and I listened to extracts from most of these songs. I was very taken with Gracie Fields. Growing up after the War, I had a residual memory of the songs of Gracie Fields's successor, Vera Lynn, and Dame Vera was, in fact, the first person I ever interviewed as a television reporter with TV-am. But Gracie was big during and after the Depression years in the 1930s, and there was an absolutely English quality to all she sang that was a revelation to me. I looked forward to singing along with her to cheer myself up through the looming terrors of an Atlantic night.

That evening Helen gave me back the amethyst (which I later mis-identified as an opal) that I had brought back as her present from Evensk in Siberia on the world flight, and charged me with its safe return from the flight.

Thursday I spent rushing around, belatedly getting my car through the MoT, trying to find the car insurance, and settling all my bills, including an overdue one with Mainair. I agreed a price, £1,500, to get the Lion Atlantic Flyer shipped to Caldwell Airfield in New Jersey, and paid £1,050 to get insurance cover for the whole adventure, including a policy providing $400,000 air/sea rescue coverage in case it was needed. I chose this policy more to shove two fingers up the nose of whinging interviewers who raised questions about the potential cost I might be to taxpayers if things went wrong, than with any belief that rescue services could get to me in time if I ditched. On the flight itself, I would be far north of the shipping lanes and not easy to get to.

I finally managed to get my car taxed on Friday morning, 15 minutes before the taxi arrived to take me to Victoria Station. At Gatwick, Adrian Whitmarsh, of Premier Aviation, who had done so much to get me through the customs rites sending the Flyer to America, met me for a cup of tea and a chat. He remarked that if he had known me before the world flight, he was certain I would not have had those troubles with the Russians. But I thought that whatever had been brewing in my then-partner, Keith Reynolds, would have found another outlet, and it was as well Keith abandoned the flight in Russia as elsewhere.

Ironically, considering the way Richard Branson's involvement in the world flight in 1998 nearly wrecked it, I flew to America on a Virgin flight. I sent a note to the captain, Phil Greenwood, and sat in the cockpit as the 747 cruised over a cloud-shrouded Newfoundland at 38,000 feet, looking down at good conditions and wondering what my return flight would be like. Phil told me there was 800 foot cloud base over Newfoundland, and a north wind blowing, but much of the Atlantic from Ireland until 200 miles from St John's looked perfect for my flight, including a west wind *(as it happens, it was the last possible good day for more than six weeks)*. Phil wrote in the message book I carried with me, "Keep the wind on the tail, the Emerald Isle on the nose, and look after the motor".

Otherwise, I carefully read my way through the first 40 pages of Homer's *Odyssey*. It was hard sorting out which characters were gods, and which mere humans. Until I was 19, I had owned only one book, a present from an early girlfriend called Valerie, a collection of poetry by Thomas Gray, including "Elegy written in a country churchyard". I had been trying to catch up ever since then. My children have had books since their cot years.

Getting to Caldwell Airfield, my base in New Jersey, was a hassle. I had to drag my luggage on to a monorail train and halfway across Newark, then find a bus, argue with the car hire company who wanted me to change the cheap vehicle I had booked for a limo, and then find my way by a roundabout route, with lots of mis-directions, to a hotel.

That evening I had the best meal for some time in America, a country which, for all its riches, was pretty rotten on the food-taste front. I ate Carpaccio with a vegetable base, and chicken with blood orange and asparagus, plus a bottle of quite reasonable French wine. But I discovered the wine waiter did not know the difference between a *vin de table* and *appellation* wines, confirming all the French ideas about barbarism in America. I read Edmund Blunden's *"Undertones of War"*. He was far too self-consciously a poet. What did this line mean?

"Man is a splendid creature, wherever possible." Hokum.

I resolved to spend the weekend looking at the shopping mall that occupied Roosevelt Field, where in 1927, Lindbergh took off on his flight to Paris. I needed to find a decent weather forecaster and a short route to the airfield. It was a delight, though, to be at ease with e-mail and the Internet at local phone prices.

In my room the following morning, I made a comparison between two of my adventures, the journey by 1937 Austin 7 across Africa in 1968/9 to marry Fiona Campbell, and the coming Atlantic flight. There was a terrific contrast. To film the coming flight I had a video recorder strapped to my knee, and a junction box to choose between a camera on the nose looking down at me, and a second camera on the wing looking across. I had a diary video camera on the front strut, with a fish-eye lens, and a fourth hand-held video camera in a chest pocket for general shots. All of these had back-up batteries, charging units, leads, along with video stock. For stills photographic work I had two Olympus water-proof cameras, one of which I had carried on the world flight and which I cherished. I also carried film stock for these cameras, about 30 un-used rolls.

On the Africa drive? A box Brownie. When I looked at the poor picture material I brought back from Africa, about 30 snaps, compared with the 2,500 I took on the world flight, that was a big difference.

To record the flight in words I had a Toshiba *Libretto* computer, the same one sent to me in northern Japan on the world flight, and which went across Siberia and the Atlantic in 1998. I had become accustomed to the smaller keyboard; it helped that spelling mistakes were marked with red lines. The games on this little computer stopped me going mad in Russia, and I saw them having the same calming effect in Newfoundland *(little did I know then how necessary that was going to be)*. It was through that computer that I e-mailed all my material back to Liam Abramson in London, for him to enter on the web-site. Even in 1998 this had all been double-Dutch to me, and I had sent back material by air-mail on floppy disks.

For back-up and daily notes, I was becoming accustomed to using the graffiti language of a Palm Pilot, which also had a fold-up keyboard to attach to it, and a charging unit. I had the same four-plug adapter from the world flight, and a bag full of connections to tap into the local electricity supply for the US, Canada, Ireland and also France. I hated not being able to use my appliances.

On the Africa drive across the Sahara and down through the Congo, by comparison, I had carried on the seat beside me a large, heavy 1947 Olympia 9 typewriter which I called Brunahilde, and on which I evolved the typing style I had never got out of, banging the keys hard. I had also carried carbon paper to ensure I had copies of all I wrote; the subsequent book about that journey, called *Alexa*, had never been submitted until now for publication.

In Africa, my entertainment had been the collected works of Nietzsche, which I dipped into but never finished. I smoked then, and could still remember the wonderful pleasure of a long slow cigarette at the end of the day. I had not smoked since the fall out of the sky in November, 1978, which induced in me a determination to mark the luck that I was still alive by making some form of sacrifice. That sacrifice was smoking.

To entertain me, now a more experienced traveller, I had the six books I described earlier. I was finding Edmund Blunden heavy going, and did not see why he had the status of being a Penguin Modern Classic, but Homer's *Odyssey* became easier to read as I understood the conventions.

I also had a CD player and a folder full of CDs, and a small tape-player, which went with the heavy course of four tapes and a BBC book on how to learn French. I resolved to send this back separately from Newfoundland, but was determined, like the 19th century ship-board travellers to India, to improve my mind by learning how to speak French better.

As for navigation, back in 1968 I had just two maps, one of which, a Michelin road map covering north Africa down to the Congo, became rather tatty. The AA had provided me with an old-fashioned guide, drafted before Africa became independent and started the long slide into chaos and corruption, which made travelling then rather civilised.

(Comparing the distances I travelled in 1968 with driving in Africa in 2001, it was faster then. In my 1937 Austin 7 Ruby I regularly covered more than 100 miles/day. If you do 80 miles today in modern vehicles, that is considered good going).

On the Atlantic flight I had two maps covering the journey from New York, via Halifax in Nova Scotia to St Johns, Newfoundland. They were million-to-one scale, and showed the terrain; most of my flying would be coastal anyway. Obviously, I had no map for the long journey from St Johns to Shannon in Ireland; just seeing the Irish coast would be quite enough. I needed an aviation map of Ireland for the journey to Paris, but once crossing England and then, via Le Havre to Paris, I had half-million scale maps for this journey. I carried these maps, and intended to use them in a wide-open cockpit, so I had a wide map-holder velcro'd to my knees.

My primary navigation was by means of GPS – Global Positioning System – and I had three of them. One, a Skyforce 2, went around the world in 1998. Of the five GPSs on that flight, one disappeared at the same time as my Russian navigator Peter Petrov, a second was sold, a third was stolen and a fourth was lost. I decided to work with just the simplest GPSs as back-up, and bought a basic Garmin 12, and a Garmin GPS II Plus; they were both pre-programmed with the lat/longs of the whole flight.

There was all the extra equipment concerned with flying that a car driver did not have to think about. I had two ICOM radios, and a full Lynx communicating system, enabling me to use all the above in flight. I also carried three torches, all with strings on to ensure they did not fall into the pusher propeller. I did transport a food box in 1968, with tins of beans and ham; this time I planned to have pockets of chocolate and fruit bars and other reward food. I also had a large jar of Marmite.

In 1968 I leapt out of the car three times a day for a pee. For the Atlantic flight I had a tube strapped to my willy, and hoped to pioneer my own version of an in-flight toilet system. The former world microlight champion, Richard Meredith-Hardy, had told me before I left that he had long ago perfected a method of peeing in the air, but he never went into details. I remember looking at him and wondering if he just slung his willy over the side? And how did Amy Johnson do it?

In 1968 I had three T-shirts, and my daily clothing was a pair of jean shorts, shoes (without socks), and a symbolic pair of goggles that I wore around my neck on driving (as compared to repairing) days, so I could recognise where photos were taken. I did carry a couple of shirts, one tie, a pair of jeans, and one good suit that always needed pressing and was ruined by the journey. I looked around my New Jersey hotel room at three sweaters and three T-shirts, all branded with *Lion Capital Atlantic Challenge*, six pairs of socks and shreddies (underpants), four flying suits, a heated waistcoat and a second unheated waistcoat, gloves and moon boots.

Did all this equipment change the essential nature of the adventure? No, it just meant I had a better record of it, but the quality of that record, especially the written word, depended, as it did on the African drive, on how much anyone else was drawn into my adventure, and I hoped, inspired by it to achieve their own dreams.

In the evening I went out, carrying four beers – BYOB, bring your own bottle – and dined at a local Pizzeria, the Deli Santi, watching the woman who ran it spend an hour telling her 17-year old son that he must sleep more regular hours instead of coming home at 3 o'clock in the morning.

Some hope.

On Sunday, I drove out to where Charles Lindbergh had taken off from on Long Island, Roosevelt Field, formerly Curtiss Field in 1927, to see if I could take off from there too. It took an hour and a half to find the "Cradle of Aviation" Museum in a wind-blown area surrounded by rotting concrete in the middle of four old hangars that obviously dated from near the beginning of the twentieth century. I thought that, with difficulty, I could get off the old tarmac in front of the museum, perhaps dodging telegraph poles, but it would not be a pleasant prospect.

Driving around the former airfield, now full of shiny and slightly forbidding new company buildings, I finally found the Roosevelt Field shopping centre that Liam had been negotiating with from London. There was a large car park in front of the store, shared with Macy's, and with a slight kink of a few degrees after take-off it made a perfectly feasible take-off area, even with the 40 US gallon load I planned to take off with. That was 145 litres, about 30 litres more than I had carried on the world flight. Solo, this was a third of what the wing had the capacity to carry.

Back at Macdan Aviation I showed the receptionist, Emily McDonald, the video that had preceded the world flight. She had no idea what a microlight was. It was curious, watching Americans watching a video cut and shaped in England. Almost all the shots in my video were of at least 3 seconds duration, and the story developed in a logical linear way. This was by contrast with the fake excitement Americans constantly strive to generate on television, each story sounding as if it was going to be the Second Coming, visual shots lasting less than 2 seconds, everything zappy and, to my eyes, right over the top. Looking at the way stories are developed in American television, their style was quite different to the way I was comfortable with. Would that change the way I shot this particular story? I came to think I should look for more shots of an event developing than I had planned for.

In the afternoon, reading, Edmund Blunden got better as the fighting on the Somme became the subject of his musings. I ate a take-away Wendy's hamburger, drank a few Miller Lite beers, and my brain went into limbo again.

I was impatient to get my hands on the Flyer and into a decent flying state within a couple of days. Without an aircraft, I was just a tourist. Woke up in the middle of the night with a vivid vision of how tired I would be, approaching Shannon.

At 12.30 Monday, May 21, I got a phone call from Dee Egan, the Rock-It agent, that the Flyer had cleared customs, and would be trucked to Caldwell by 3pm. It was such a relief. Feeling happy after a good roast beef sandwich at the Deli Santi, whose meals confounded my low opinion of American food, I drove through rain to Macdan Aviation where Guyon Nelson showed me the three big cases which held my aircraft. The packing was a work of art, and when I cut the wrapping off the trike I found detailed instructions on how to put it together. I spent the day slowly following instructions, and heaping up a huge pile of packing material.

Some of the engineers with Macdan remembered me being in the same hangar three years earlier on the world flight, and I answered all the usual questions, starting with fuel capacity. There was a detached quality to their reaction which I noticed in all Americans, as if they were cut off from the reality of what I wanted to do, and the questions had nothing to do with my own fears about the flight.

The early re-building was easy, lifting the trike and attaching the first suspension legs for the rear wheels. But it took the attention of two of the best Macdan engineers, Keith Bruther and Dave Cababe, an hour of sweating to get the other four connections made. I examined the new bag made for the dinghy with some curiosity, wondering how it fitted on to the trike. I felt surprisingly tired after toiling away for just four hours.

Messages piled up in the address book I carried with me, to remember names for later. Adrian Whitmarsh wrote: "Stop and think, act on gut reaction and fly straight and true. See you in LBG". Liam Abramson, my organiser: "Our doubts are traitors and make us lose the good we oft might win, by fearing to attempt". Now Michael Jacobson, an engineer there: "Fly safe, drive fast, take chances." I thought their comments were as much about them as me.

I ended the day with the Flyer's wheels on, and the small 44 litre belly tank attached, and was working my way through the intercom wiring, trying to remember what I had agreed with Mainair's Jim Cunliffe. I half unpacked the huge main tank, looked at it with trepidation and hoped I did not end up, when I had installed it, with a couple of bolts and fittings left over.

Dined again in Deli Santi, to eat the local version of a hot dog and watch the US version of "Who Wants to be a Millionaire?" The girl behind the counter, Nicole, daughter of the owner, was working her way through college, studying that cod subject, sociology. As the TV programme changed to one about Anne Frank, she said she had also done a course on Genocide, "you know, about the Jews, American Indians, the Irish and so on."

The Irish?

I was almost driven to start an argument about exactly *when* genocide was committed on the Irish, as I had heard American "academics" had produced such a subject. Why were so many people looking to become victims? Did the Irish "case" date back to the potato famines of 1845 and 1847, despite the concept of genocide only evolving in the late 1940s? How did the London Parliament, particularly feisty during the 1840s with a full complement of 80 Irish MPs, go along quietly with this "genocide"? Where was the policy evolved? Did it have the same status as US Government representatives later that century handing blankets infected with small-pox to Native Americans (they use to be called Red Indians)? Was it morally the same as Vietnam's My Lai?

I had to balance an urge to have a go at Nicole's degree, and the fact that her Dad served up good grub. The grub won. Why should I rock the boat? It might have been better had I done so, because in the sleepless hours before dawn, I was involved in an argument with myself, putting pros and cons. On the other hand, it could have been even more intense. I woke up suddenly with a vision of the way the dinghy was attached to the trike. Looking out of the window, I felt the local weather was terrible, full of low cloud and a threat of thunderstorms.

On Tuesday, after only two hours sleep, and hours of restless dozing, I drove myself down to a good breakfast, cereal, toast and marmite, and American tea, and was at Caldwell at 0900. For the next 9 hours, without a break, I worked to get the Flyer together. I had never built a Mainair aircraft up from packaging, and inevitably there were mistakes. There were detailed notes from Jim Cunliffe, and I had heard from other sources that he was worried about me. I forced myself to check and check again, and spoke out loud, quietly, the better to understand what I was doing.

The engineers at Mac Dan were kindness itself, and seemed to volunteer in shifts, when they were not servicing their own aircraft, to come across to help me. The wing went together well, except for a mistake that is, theoretically, impossible, having the outside leading edge of one wing 180 degrees out of true. That was corrected, and as soon as the wing was up, joining the other different wings in the hangar, I felt I belonged there as a flyer. Before that, I was just a Limey stranger slaving over a weird piece of equipment in the corner. People came to admire my wing, touch it, look inside it to see how beautiful it was and how brilliantly it fitted together.

I followed instructions strictly in getting the wing married to the trike, finally unpacked the giant fuel tank, and with the help of an engineer, Phil May, got it into the trike. There were twenty anxious minutes checking there was no chafing between one piece of metal and another, and brief visions of wearing a hole in the fuel tank 800 miles from nowhere and watching life dribble away. But there was a logic to it fitting together, and even though some bits of metal were too close together, I felt that when fuel was fully loaded, the tank would settle deeper on to the keel and open up safe gaps between one piece of metal and another. Getting the big hose fitted between the main and slipper tanks caused Phil May to sweat a lot, but oddly, no swearing. I later heard caustic comment from one of his colleagues as Phil turned on some music to work by, because it was classical and not pop. Why can't an engineer be a cultured man?

I spent the afternoon getting the wing cameras fitted, and all the wiring for communications and power sources for the three GPSs. Why did everyone laugh at the thought of three GPSs, mandatory for the Atlantic flight? To fit the tip-camera I drilled a simple hole right at the end of the wing, millimetres away from the sail, and after experiments found I could get a good inclusive shot with the narrow-angle camera.

To the keel I fitted an extension sticking out the front like a probe, rather than at the back looking forward as I had it on the world flight, because the main tank blocked out any interesting view. I attached the wide-angle camera to the probe, capturing a shot that would give the viewer a profound sense of the loneliness of the flight. I resolved to use the free camera I kept in my chest pocket to continually take shots looking forward, to show what I was looking at, framed between the rigging, even if it was boring.

The second GPS was attached halfway up the front strut. This was not just convenient, it was also slightly vain. With a GPS on my knee, viewers were going to get lots of shots of the top of my head as I short-sightedly tried to find the navigation line to follow. With the front strut camera I was forced to look up, as if to the stars, which was a better shot, but more "heroic". I pasted a *"Lion Capital Atlantic Challenge"* poster on the big tank by the side of my head, and found that the diary-camera, in recording all my thoughts, observations and inanities throughout the flight, had a shot that just worked without distortion. If I was going to make this flight work, I wanted to record it better than I had on the world flight.

By the end of the day, aside from an untidy heap of packing, the Flyer looked ready for a test-flight. It had rained all day, sometimes heavily, and inside the heated hangar it was comfortable putting the aircraft together. Jim Cunliffe sent me a note saying I should not take chances:

> *"At our first meeting you asked us to make a Blade with a tank large enough to fly Alcock and Brown's route across the Atlantic, St Johns to Shannon, in 31 hours, one take off and one landing. No problem. Now you are flying Lindbergh's route from New York to Le Bourget in Paris with a minimum of three take-offs and landings and maybe 65 hours flying, plus possible press flights. You need to fly as little as possible to reduce the risk of tank damage caused by vibrations, landing shocks and so on. Remember that you have no suspension (blocked off to stop the main tank bottoming-out on the rear wheel struts) and every bump is going through the airframe and tank. Be very careful with her."*

Back at the hotel I discovered that Roosevelt Field mall were not interested in me repeating the take-off from Lindbergh's old airfield. I forced myself to the swimming pool, which, though small, was satisfying, and induced a small feeling of self-righteousness because I was exercising (was this a subliminal response to all those hysterical advertisements on US television about getting fit?).

At my favourite pizza place, Nicole, charming in that young innocent American way, showed me, unbid, her latest college grades. She had achieved an "A" in "Racism and Sexism", which I found quite horrifying, thinking of my own daughter, Jade, also in her third year at university, studying English and History. Was victimhood so institutionalised in America that they now had college courses in it?

Listening to Nicole talking – I ate while she bustled around keeping the restaurant tidy – I was struck by how right-wing, in the traditional sense, her attitudes were, despite the rubbish that was being stuffed into her head in college. She wanted all the usual things, a job, marriage, children, but she also felt bringing children into the world where guns were carried at high schools and drugs were so common was something she did not want to do. Her family had emigrated from Italy when she was 4 years old, and had worked hard, and were still obviously working hard and honestly to build their restaurant. It was empty when I judged, from the quality of the food and service and prices, it should have been heaving with people. Was it the location? They needed, in my opinion, to make one more move. Nicole's father, a nice genial hard-working man, came out to say hello, and told me the cult series about the Mafia, "The Sopranos", was shot locally. Did we have that in England? Really! On mainstream television? Wow! They only had it on cable.

Nicole thought of herself as the X-generation but also expressed a deep sense of dissatisfaction at the emptiness of life. She seemed to think that my generation (the Beatles generation) was impossibly glamorous, as were the generations, measured in decades like the '70's and '80's, that followed. She worried that there was so much money sloshing around that values were meaningless.

I thought all this sounded hopeful. There were echoes of what I had heard from my own children and, if it was difficult for them to find goals and meaning, then they would sooner or later re-examine some of the social values taught them by the current generation running things and go back to basics. The problem they would have was flaws in the tools we were giving them, in the way we educated them and taught them to think, that they would bring to this task.

I drank root beer, went to bed at 9.30 pm, took a sleeping pill, and woke at 6 am on May 23rd feeling good after unbroken sleep. Maybe they *would* work the night before I set out on the big flight to Shannon? I checked my e-mails, and was re-assured by Liam about my travelling arrangements once I set off:

> *David Gleave has received all the final paper work from Canada and is now putting the finishing touches to the whole thing. It's all looking good but the one rule that we can't break is that you will have to file a flight plan when you fly from New York to Halifax and then another flight plan from Halifax to St Johns. David is meeting with City Airport (in London) this afternoon so we should know more about that later.*

Despite the appalling weather on Wednesday morning, low cloud and drizzle, I was at Caldwell airfield by 0930 and re-checked everything. There did not seem to be anything else to add, aside from equipment not essential to the flight, just the recording of it or for my own comfort. I filled the reserve tank with 5 US gallons of gasoline. We had a debate on exactly how many litres were in a US gallon, and some old-timer on the phone was adamant that it was 3.785 litres = 1 US gallon, so that was what I worked at.

As I was gathering my gear, putting on a flying suit, finding my helmet and earphones and gloves, there was some excitement among the engineers. It was not at the prospect of the microlight flying, though they were curious about that. It was over the tiny Sony digital video recorder I was using to record the flight. This was the latest tecky gadget, and Americans were fascinated by gadgets. It attracted ooohhs and aaahhhs that, in another era, the flight itself might have drawn.

I did not feel nervous about getting into the air with the big tanks, but we took things carefully, Phil May pushing me backwards out on to the rainy tarmac where I started the engine. It took time to burst into life. I ran the engine a short while, happily, and then put on my flying clothes and began adding cameras and lenses and fired up the three GPSs and prepared to fly her for the first time in America. A small crowd gathered when I radioed the tower, asking for permission to taxi. A special VFR flight was agreed, that is, at my own discretion, because cloud base was officially just 600 feet, and in fact, just over 300 feet. When the engine was warm, oil about 50 degrees centigrade, I taxied past the tower.

"What the heck is that?" exclaimed the air traffic controller.

I laughed and told him it was an English microlight aircraft, and I wanted to see if it would fly straight. He was dubious it would even fly, but gave me permission to line up, after checking that no one from any other airfield was flying in. With such a light load she took off quickly, and the first real difference was that the control bar, normally ten inches from my chest, was just 2 inches away. It felt odd, because I could not pull on speed without the bar hitting my chest. And because of the bulk of the monstrous tank behind me, which looked like a small garden shed shoved down my trousers, she felt ponderous. I reasoned after a few moments that the reserve tank being full, and the slipper tank under my legs being empty, was affecting the attitude of the trike in the air; when I took on a fuller load, the bar would move away from my chest.

The two wing cameras, one on the nose looking down, one on the right wing looking at the aircraft, worked well. I flew cautiously around a circuit, feeling low enough to pull the top leaves off the trees, landed carefully, with no suspension, taxiing in to applause. About twenty minutes later I did a second test flight, this time with all cameras working, again scraping along the bottom of cloudbase and anxious to keep the field in view, and was pleased with the results. The pictures looked stunning.

I spent the afternoon trying to work out how to get a 72-hour weather forecast. The FAA, Federal Aviation Authority, only released 24-hour forecasts. At a pinch, I could perhaps get a 48-hour forecast, but nothing beyond that. The Weather Bureau, which had charts going out to 120 hours, actually had the information, but was not authorised to give it to pilots, except through the FAA. In all cases they seemed to be worried about being sued for telling me something that might turn out to be wrong. I found bureaucrats in the United States quite as pleasant as bureaucrats in Russia, but suffering under the same constraints. They knew about the system; they just could not buck it. As it happens, this worked for Canada in spades.

Two oddities in the day. Talking over lunch with the engineers, I could not believe it when one of them said that, for all the beer advertisements you see on television, in none of them will you see a person actually drinking the beer. They can beam at it, wave it around, look as if drinking it is better than sex, but actually getting down to imbibing the stuff was forbidden. It was one of the little strands of Puritanism that laced through the American public character.

The other oddity was that, even three years after leaving Russia, I still had an odd love affair with plastic bags. One was given to me with the new battery, the bag big enough to contain all my dirty laundry, and I fell upon the previous plastic bag, which I knew was inadequate, and happily replaced it with the new one. This would, in another person, be an action of no consequence; with me, it was a source of delight. I still vividly remember on the world flight buying chocolate and other goodies at Beaver Creek in the Yukon

Territory, and instead of gloating over the sweeties, I gloated over the bag they were put in. I had been in Russia only seven days earlier.

Liam e-mailed to tell me he was having trouble getting the GPS tracker to work in England. With this tracker, anyone in the world on the Internet could follow the flight, minute to minute. More to the point, if I fell into the water, Liam would at least know where I was last in a dry state.

In passing, I was very happy, as happy as I had been flying into Rhodes on the world flight, and as one gets from time to time on adventures like this. There were big matters ahead, I had done – I thought – all my preparations, and I was intensely curious to see whether they would all work.

On Thursday I discovered that my base, Caldwell, was the airfield where John F Kennedy Junior took off from on his last fatal flight to Hyannis Port, Massachusetts. I also visited the Statue of Liberty.

In his e-mail that morning, Liam took me to task for interfering with matters about organising the departure that were rightfully his area of expertise. He had pulled me up sharply, for example, when earlier in the week I had contacted Roosevelt Field shopping centre on my own initiative, when he had been conducting delicate negotiations of his own. He had felt that I had rather ruined the strength of his hand, so I received a rebuke for my impatience:

> *Just a little pep talk. I fully realise that as the flight draws nearer and nearer, things are bound to get more and more real. I also realise that you have been sitting in the US for the last week just waiting for things to start happening. Rest assured we are all behind you and all are working very hard over here to make sure that your flight is safe, legal and enjoyable. Relax and smile; this is meant to be fun, isn't it?*

The weather began to break in the late morning, the sun came through, temperatures rose, and I felt I should make another test flight, this time following Highway 3 to the Hudson River, directly opposite the Empire State Building, turn right and down to New York Harbour.

As ever with something new, I went into a nervous state, examining and re-examining the route and my own feelings. Did I need to do this? Yes, I did. Why? Because you needed as much experience of flying out of New York as you can get. Yes, but why today? Because it was possible, and what were you going to do anyway?

I found an aviation map of the area, colour photo-copied it, and wrote down six radio frequencies I needed. I was still adding equipment to the Lion Atlantic Flyer, including an electric waistcoat which I wanted to test. If it worked, did I really need four flying suits? On the other hand, if it failed halfway across the Atlantic, might I not freeze to death?

By 1.30 I was ready to go. The two wing cameras seemed to work well, and I had bought an extra battery for the Hi-8 recorder, giving me six hours total recording life, more than adequate. I fitted the diary camera, and put a second little digital video camera into my chest pocket, worrying that I had no secure points on my flying suit to which to attach the leads securing the cameras. I remained very fearful of dropping anything into the pusher propeller.

Cautiously, I warmed up the engine and taxied out, with a map of the area stuffed down one of my pockets (I had left my map case at the hotel, so by the end of the flight the map looked like a well-used hankie). I took off and climbed, heading east, and wondered why I could not immediately see the fabulous New York sky-line. My speed was down in the 40's, I was being bumped around, and having to cope with the control bar virtually pinning me in the seat. I would like to have concentrated on the flying, but I was required to talk to one ground station after another. The more it became obvious I was an unusual aircraft, the less anyone wanted to speak to me. I kept being passed on to someone else, so I recalled little about the first ten miles, because all I was doing was gabbling.

When I was able to gather my thoughts and really look around, I was at 900 feet, being bumped up often to above 1,200 feet by thermals, nothing very rough but feisty, and nowhere that I could see to land if anything went wrong. There were six airfields within 15 miles of me, so that was a comfort. The Manhattan skyline loomed out of the misty distance, and I found myself heading directly at the Empire State Building. In the constant change of frequencies, I ended up with one covering the Hudson River, which appeared to be pilots talking to each other, just saying if they were heading north or south, their height, whether they were on the New York or New Jersey side of the river, and where they were relative to George Washington Bridge. A helicopter flew right over me as I reached the river, and a couple of minutes later said hello, informing the other pilots that either a parachute or a hang glider was wandering down the river. I soon came to be referred to as "that hang glider" as in "watch out for that hang glider, guys".

Some of my brain cells began to register enjoyment at the tremendous view as I turned right and headed down-river towards the statue of Liberty. The shots on the wing cameras were brilliant, but the diary camera soon began to register it was running out of either power or tape. I also found that in the turbulence, which was nothing out of the ordinary, I was reluctant to let the control bar go and get sufficient shots with the chest-camera. This had to be overcome if I was to record the big flight.

The view at 800 feet was just terrific, and though the radio traffic was heavy, I saw few aircraft. I flew to the right of the Statue of Liberty, and circled it twice with it on my left, and then headed back up-river, into wind, being bumped around. Because of the big tank at my back, I had less room than in a normal microlight, and I experimented with how to get comfortable for the hours I was going to spend in the air. Shoving my feet into the well of the nose pod, under the pedals, enabled me to stretch a bit, but I reasoned that, from time to time, I would have to undo my safety belt, and hoist myself up into a standing position to keep my blood circulating. This might also allow me to stick a leg out, either side, and waggle it around in the wind, an action that would have done much to alleviate the madness that attacked me on my CFM Shadow flight from England to Australia in 1987/8.

At the Empire State building, I turned left, put Caldwell into my GPS, and bumbled along, still below 1,000 feet for another 16 miles, trying without success to radio Caldwell. There was a hill in the way of radio transmissions, and I only picked up the airfield 5 miles away. The landing was smooth, and conformed to all Jim Cunliffe's strict admonitions to be "very, very careful". The experience did nothing to encourage me to look forward to doing that flight again, except that next time I would keep heading east out into the Atlantic Ocean, and then along Long Island heading for Nova Scotia. It would be a relief to turn off the radio and tune into Gracie Fields.

Ate again at Deli Santi, and it was from Nicole Santi that I discovered Caldwell was where JFK Junior set off on his last, fatal flight. I remembered – who did not who was alive then? – the death of his father in 1963, ten days after I had arrived in the United States. I also remembered the child's poignant salute and felt, as many Americans did, some sympathy with the flawed and doomed Kennedy family, however much they were blood enemies of my own country. Flying along the coast of Long Island I knew I would wonder exactly how he was feeling on his own flight, as it gradually dawned on him that he was out of his depth in the conditions. I resolved to choose the right conditions for my own flight, because the current 26 mph easterly was certainly not a goer.

On Friday, May 25 I tidied up the Flyer. On the Statue of Liberty flight I had been concerned that no one picked up signals from my transponder, a device carried by aircraft which identifies them on radar with a number. When asked by air traffic control (ATC) to "squawk 0360", a pilot entered those four numbers into the transponder, turned it on, and on the radar screen his little dot had a number next to it, which officials could track. But when I squawked, nothing happened on the tracking radar. This would be alarming to the authorities, because microlights did not show up well, or even at all, on radar.

I had actually bought my transponder at Caldwell airfield on the world flight three years earlier, and transferred it from the GT Global Flyer to the Lion Atlantic Flyer. It did not seem to work, and one of the MacDan engineers, Terry Good, set down to find out why. It turned out the connections were not brilliant, and we had fun trying to extend our arms into the front of the pod to dismantle various aerial fixtures. After an hour's work Terry found the fault and fixed it, which was a terrific relief. The easiest way to piss off mainstream aviation when you were flying in controlled air-space was to have a duff transponder. I gave Terry one of the very few baseball caps we had produced, and promised him a copy of *"Global Flyer"*.

My world flight had been the subject of a separate chapter in a new Chris Bonington book, *"Quest for Adventure"*. It was a pleasant surprise to me to discover that, not only had Terry Good owned a copy, which he brought in for me to sign, but Phil May, another helpful man, also had a copy. I had not appreciated how big a readership Bonington had achieved with his books, especially in America.

Liam's stickers turned up, along with more English tea-bags (I did not like American tea). I isolated bits and pieces I had brought to America and decided not to take them, despatching them home with a cameraman called Barrie Bayes, or in a separate parcel. The big question was, did I keep all four flying suits, or return two of them? Using the electric waistcoat, I found myself comfortable with just one suit, so a second could be in reserve. So long as the waistcoat worked, I was fine. But what if, 900 miles into the flight and darkness coming on, a fuse blew in the waistcoat?

Checking weather forecasts, I finally began to see the chance of a break in what television stations were calling "this dreary weather". Until Monday, May 28th, it looked like rain and some thunderstorms. But on Tuesday the weather was forecast to change, with the persistent east wind swinging south and later south-west, the direction I wanted. It was too far ahead to predict what would happen in seven days time, but it looked good, the only downside being a cold front predicted about a hundred miles from Halifax, with north east winds behind the front. I thought I might get to Nova Scotia in good time, and have a struggle over the last 100 miles. If that was the way it was, so be it. Until I got away and actually into the flight, I would be more full of doubts than I should be.

I was nearing the end of Edmund Blunden's "Undertones of War", and was glad I had persisted in reading it. Blunden had a terrible war, in that he was surrounded for years by the horror and violence of the trenches around Ypres, Passchendaele and the Somme. But he also coped with it, and survived it, wonderfully, and I was full of admiration for that. The elliptical way he dealt with this dreadful experience probably worked very well with those who also experienced that horror, and in 1930, when he wrote the book, there were millions who had. But for me, with no experience of what he went through, the book did not work as well as for those others.

There were, though, passages that jumped out. One was an incident in late 1916 on the Somme, walking between a support trench called Stafford, and Maple Copse where some big guns were sited:

> *"A German battery at close range made beautiful groups around Kenward and myself one day, and the interested faces looking on from Stafford Trench had the pleasure of seeing us refuse to quicken our pace. As we expected to receive the next salvo on our persons, we felt that running would be a little tedious. I looked down and saw a shrapnel helmet, with blood and hair in it."*

It was not just the wonderful understatement of that passage that was so moving, it was the attitude of mind. It was an attitude I aspired to, and often felt incapable of achieving. In reading Blunden's autobiography it became apparent, time after time, that he and his fellow soldiers accepted the chance and immediacy of their own deaths. But they also determined to impose an honourable code of behaviour upon themselves, and on their companions. He was merciless about cowardice, and would have none of the modern compassion for those shot running away. I thought that code of behaviour, so strongly imposed and so wide-spread, accounted for why we were then able to cope with such horror. The lack of such a code nowadays meant we ran off to councillors at the slightest trauma. Imagine being able to have sued the Government in those days for the effect of war upon you?

Blunden, born in 1896, died in 1974, seemed to use his poetry as a way of coming to terms with what he experienced. It worked for him, and perhaps for his generation. I could see why that generation judged it a classic. It may have lost its power because the values that were naturally assumed then were not common to us any more. As we cut ourselves off from our own history, by ignoring the teaching of it, those values die, or at least weaken. I felt firmly on the other side of the chasm in this split, on Blunden's side, and I was glad my children, both keen on history, were on the same side. It did make it hard to communicate to anyone else, though.

I was cheered up by a lovely e-mail correspondence with my witty and attractive friend, Moira Thomson, ("look, I'm not fat there") who commented that my collecting of plastic bags, a leftover from my period in Russia, was at least as odd as the hobby of my organiser, Liam, who collected postcards from airfields. Moira claimed to collect hangovers, and we fell to discussing the quality of individual items in her collection.

On Saturday I saw "Pearl Harbour", technically brilliant, but as far as the story went, banal. It was interesting to see Hollywood portraying the British as heroes, though it played as if we were holding the fort until the Americans came in. On Sunday, no one turned up to the press conference launching the flight. A British reporter, Molly Watson, New York stringer for the London Evening Standard, said I should not have chosen Memorial Day weekend.

Also on Sunday I went back to reading Homer's *Odyssey*, getting to the point where Odysseus, the hero, has escaped the clutches of the nymph Calypso, she having held him for seven years as a lover. He had spent his nights in her bed, doing what she wanted of him, and days sitting by the shore crying for his wife Penelope. After a harrowing voyage across the sea, Odysseus tells his story to King Alcinous, having been washed up naked on the shore of the land of the Phaeacians in front of the lovely Nausicaa, the daughter of Alcinous. From everyone's reaction to him, including Nausicaa, Odysseus appeared to have the same effect on women that Mel Gibson does in films. They fancy him rotten. But Odysseus was so manly that chaps were full of respect as well, though he had to demonstrate his manliness – by hurling a discus further than anyone, for example – from time to time.

There were aspects of the story, which was getting really exciting, that puzzled me. After the Siege of Troy, wandering the eastern Mediterranean with his warriors, Odysseus comes upon the home of a giant Cyclops, a one-eyed race. Odysseus gets in among the sheep and goats of the Cyclops, eating them without that fellow's permission, and when the Cyclops does turn up Odysseus demands to be treated hospitably. I could quite understand why the Cyclops demurs and, upset at their bad manners, starts eating Odysseus's companions. What I did not understand was why Odysseus thought he was in the right being so rude to the Cyclops, and then kills him?

There was another incident in which Odysseus sacks a town, puts it to the fire, kills all the men there, and divides the spoils and chattels, including the women, among his crew. But not everyone in the town is killed, and the survivors gather a large army of their fellows from other towns and attack Odysseus. He seemed outraged that this should happen to him, and again, I wondered, what did he expect?

Odysseus went on to tell the story of the ghosts he met in Hades, including the ghost of his own mum, who had died of a broken heart at the continued disappearance of her only son, himself. He had a lot to answer for, that Odysseus.

The *Evening Standard*'s Molly Watson asked me, if the flight was cancelled, would I feel any sense of relief? She referred to all the fears she had ahead of a point-to-point horse race in which she was a rider. If the race was cancelled, she said she always felt, deep down, a small sense of relief that she did not have to go through the risks she had imposed upon herself. I told her that I would be devastated if my flight was stopped. Who would have wanted to be anywhere else in the world right then? In truth, I was very happy. I could compare my situation to Odysseus, in that life for me could quickly become nasty, brutish and short, and the way I would survive would be by my own wit and aspirations to courage. But for all our attempts to deny this in the way we have built society, with insurance and stability and our deep desire to avoid risk, that was how life had always been.

On Monday, May 28th, I found a helicopter company to transport Barrie Bayes, the cameraman arriving from England to film my departure from New York. I wanted shots like the previous departure, against the New York skyline. I also bought power food bars, similar to those eaten by marathon runners.

In the afternoon I divided my effects into two piles, deciding which would come with me to St Johns, and which went back home. Everything was considered, down even to electric plugs. I sent back one of my flying suits, retaining two from the world flight, and deciding to trust the electric waistcoat to keep my upper body warm during the big flight. I kept a thick pair of gloves, and a pair of chamois gloves. It gave me a sense of satisfaction to look at the heap going home and knowing I would not have to add it to my heavily over-loaded microlight.

In the e-mails sent by Liam, I had hotels and hangars booked in Nova Scotia and Newfoundland. Liam found me a kindred spirit in St Johns, booking me into the same hotel as Peter Bray, who was training to paddle a kayak across the Atlantic, starting out at the end of June or the beginning of July. Bray was, of course, an Englishman.

Ate dinner at a steak house, absorbed in the latest twists and turns in the *Odyssey*. Our hero has returned to Ithaca, artificially aged by his patroness, the goddess Pallas Athene. She disguised him as a tatty beggar and he joined the household of his own pig-keeper, who did not recognise him, to plot his revenge against all the suitors hoping to marry his faithful wife Penelope, and meanwhile eating him out of house and home. Odysseus has started to test the loyalty of his former subjects to see who was on his side, and who was not. Meanwhile, Athene has rushed off to find Telemachus, the son of Odysseus, and persuade him to return to Ithaca and join his father, without exactly telling him that his father is alive.

Looking at the half moon on the drive home, I could see few stars – we were too near New York – but I did think there would be enough light for night-flying. I separated my own regular doubts as they emerged, and tackled them individually. Nothing would be resolved until I was up there, face to face with those doubts, dealing with them hour by hour.

On Tuesday, Liam sent me details of where I was to stay on my flight through to St Johns:

> *Last piece of the puzzle. Shell Aero Centre at St Johns International will provide you with hangar space at C$20 a day. That's a reduction from C$150. They are expecting you, just ask at the tower and you will be directed. Spoke to St John's Flight Services and they are OK with you flying in so long as you file a flight plan. So your route from NY to St John's via Halifax is now cleared and approved.*

I did a final check on the Flyer. It looked neat and clean, much better put together than the GT Global Flyer, essentially because of Mainair's involvement. The wiring was neater, the way the instruments fitted, the fuel flows. I did not get the feeling I sometimes had with the Global Flyer that I was sitting in a heap, surrounded by goodies, among which I had to move carefully in case one went over the side into the propeller. I would still have to think about every major move in the cockpit, such as undoing my safety belt and sliding my back up the sheer face of the fuel tank to allow my blood to circulate from time to time, but there was much less to disturb in the Blade than I had in the Quantum.

In the afternoon I hacked through rotten traffic to pick up the cameraman, Barrie Bayes. He brought the GPS tracker Liam and Jay Madhvani had been testing in England, which would enable Liam to plot the Flyer's course over the Atlantic, so those who tuned into the web site could also follow my progress. It sent out location signals every five minutes, each signal costing 15 pence, or £1.80/hour. It made it possible for those tracking these signals to work out what my flying speed was, and from that make an exact estimate of my time of arrival in Ireland.

There was a terrific thunderstorm while we were looking at the Flyer, winds of 50 mph, all the outside aircraft tied down, hangar doors closed, noise and lightning for half an hour.

I bought a cheap map-light to illuminate the dashboard during the night flight; I had three torches tied to my life-jacket for just such a purpose, but the dash-light did the job hands-off. The Flyer needed fuel; I planned to put in 156 litres in all, and then she was ready to go. I was, too.

Back at the hotel, Barrie looked over the video pictures I had already taken, and approved them. I had wanted an opinion on the nose-camera pointing back at me, and the resulting shots, and also a view on the diary camera, which only really worked through a fish-eye lens. Was the shot acceptable? I had a better sound system on this aircraft than the last one, so in-air comments without buzzing and static could be recorded. I saw these as a vital record on the big flight, because I expected to go through so many states of mind over the 24 to 30 hours that I would forget, later, where I had been. If I transcribed what I had recorded, it might be boring as television, but edited for the book it would at least be a stab at the truth.

I told Barrie I had booked him a helicopter, and he remarked irritably that he had not brought the small camera he needed for helicopter shots. He had done this, he said, on Liam's advice that there would be no such shots required. I e-mailed Liam to ask why he had told Barrie this, and Liam denied flatly anything of the sort. He had, he wrote testily, relied totally on Barrie's professional judgement. Liam went on sharply:

> So far, I have not made any major decisions without consulting you first. Give me the respect of your trust that I wouldn't start now. Please believe me that, while you may be relatively isolated over there, everyone over here is working very hard to make sure your flight goes well and we are all – Charles Langley (of the London Evening Standard), David Gleave, Nikki King, John Sewel, Jay Madhvani, Chris Finnigan, myself and countless others – doing nothing but "thinking things through first, and covering all eventualities."

By the time we turned up at the pizzeria in the evening, it was 1.30am in Barrie's body clock so we had a quiet meal. Back in my room I watched five minutes of *"Fatal Attraction"* until I discovered that one of Michael Douglas's screen children wanted a rabbit as a pet; I knew from a previous half-look at the film what happened to that rabbit, so I turned it off and crashed out. The alternative on television was yet another of Mel Gibson's efforts at emulating Josef Goebbels, a film called *"Braveheart"*, expressing once again Hollywood's perverted view of history, and with the same motives as Goebbels had. Gibson may have more charm than Goebbels, so his lies about history were more easily swallowed (though that was a moot point; was Mel Gibson more charming than Josef Goebbels? Goebbels was able to score with lots of women despite a club foot, and he needed charm as well as power for that; one wonders how Gibson would score with a club foot?).

I found I could not watch.

Depressing.

It came of taking history personally.

On my last full day in America, there was some media interest in my leaving. NBC TV wanted to cover it live from a helicopter, so much of the day was spent making arrangements for that to happen.

Otherwise Phil May, one of the engineers at Mac Dan Aviation, did a real engineer's job on the GPS tracker, fitting it to an extension of the keel with nothing between the tracker and the satellites above. I also secured the navigation GPS's to the aircraft, tidied up the wiring, adjusted the cameras, and filed the flight plan. There was nothing else to do.

As I looked around my hotel room, all that was left were my few clothes, those surviving the great shake-out and which would go the distance with me. My little pile of books lost the autobiography of Edmund Blunden – I could not read his harrowing but detached accounts of the Somme fighting so soon after the first reading – and I alternated between the Anglo-Indian poetry of Wilfred Russell, and Homer's *Odyssey*.

MacDan Aviation had been wonderful hosts. Nothing was too much for them. I paid the petrol bill, about $156, but they waived charges for accommodating the Flyer, and for all the bits and pieces and time and concern they gave me getting the project together. Phil May told me he had tracked down on the Internet a copy of the first book I ever had published, *The Dalgety Flyer*, about the microlight flight to Australia in 1987/8, and he bought it second hand for $55. Another deeply touching moment. Once upon a time they were considering remaindering that book.

Part of me remained detached from what was going on. When we poured in the fuel, and I shook the aircraft to ensure I could see the gasoline through the sight-tube, I thought that 156 litres was more than I had ever carried (the test load was of water), and yet it hardly registered on the gauge. I knew I had at least another 250 litres capacity in the main tank, and told myself not to be fearful if all trace of fuel disappeared from the sight-gauge. I intended to track my consumption on a fuel-flow meter, and if that ran out, the 20 litres I had in reserve would enable me to make a decision whether or not to head for the nearest land and look for a road or airfield. On the big flight, of course, I would head south to the shipping lanes, like Harry Hawker did in 1919, and look for a ship. He landed beside one. I fancied my chances, with my slow speed, of landing on one.

Paul Loach, of Lion Capital Partners

Jim Cunliffe of Mainair, with Flyer

Simple cockpit layout

Liam Abramson, before resignation

Dr Carl Hallam, advised on diet

David Gleave

Stephen Lewis, Guru
Valerie Thompson in background

Julian Parr – own value system

Helen Dudley, still a Muse

Moira Thomson, "collects hangovers"

Adrian Whitechurch, the man who said "Go"

John Hunt, engineering adviser

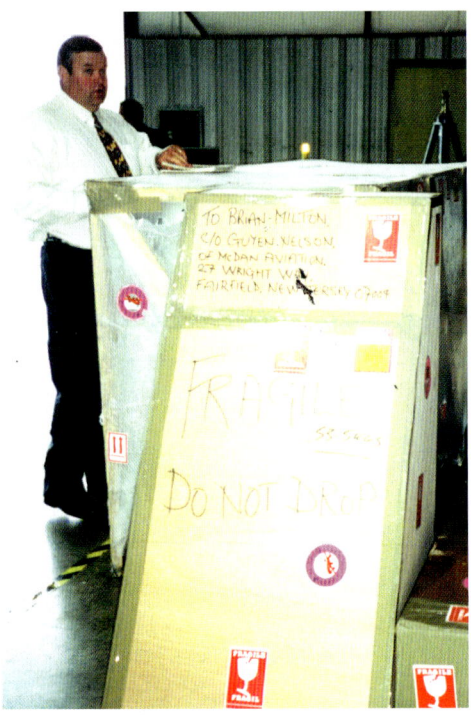

Guyon Nelson of MacDan Aviation, NJ

Author in MacDan hangar, NJ, with re-built Flyer

Ready to leave New York

A view never to be seen again

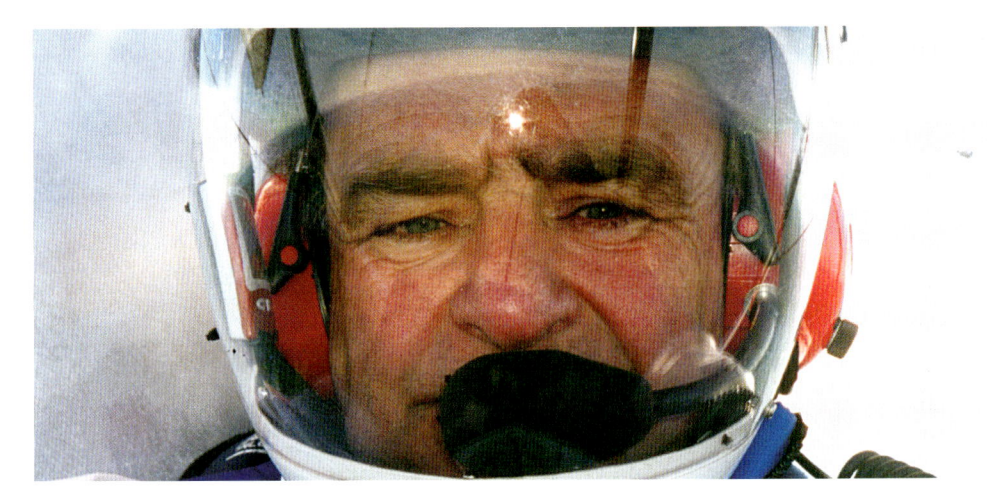

In-flight after rain, New York to Yarmouth

Stephenville hangar, getting legal again

Yvonne and Katrina Dennis

l-to-r: Al Skinner, Dr Terry Dennis, Sean Sheppard, Author

Schoolchildren at Baie D'Espoire

Ed Lavalle owned the secret Stephenville hangar

Emily and Don Cooper, Grand Falls, Windsor

Wrecked Flyer

Author five minutes after crash

9

New York to Newfoundland

On the night before my departure from New York, I slept badly. I had gone to bed at 10 o'clock, but fears played on my mind without any rational reason. At 1.30am I woke up with the words of "Don't Let's be Beastly to the Germans" playing in my head, and spent the next three hours and 30 minutes, half awake, half asleep. Lindbergh went through the same experience.

Barrie Bayes was with his camera gear at the hotel entrance, where I paid the hotel bills, about $1,600 that did not appear on my original budget, which had to come out of contingencies or extra bits pared off elsewhere.

There was an odd sense of relief that I was off, because of the terms of the deal with Lion Capital Partners, which were that I was liable to pay all the sponsorship money back if I did not get the aircraft to the start line in New York in working condition. Having done that, it was one less worry for me to have to think about.

I drove Barrie to Caldwell and set about packing, tying one long black bag to the left leg of the trike, and my computer bag full of bits and pieces to the right leg. I felt a sense of satisfaction at having so little left to put in, but made the mistake of putting my trainers in the cockpit; later in the day they restricted my movements and stopped me exercising.

A lady producer turned up from NBC and we tested a cell phone on which they hoped to interview me live in the middle of the Hudson River. I went to the loo to fit the pee bladder, and stuffed it into one of the flying suit pockets. The invaluable lead to my electric waistcoat came out of the same hole in my flying suit. It looked as if you could plug me into a cigar-lighter and I would pee at the turn of a switch.

Very wound up, I did a couple of comments to camera, and then found my Skyforce GPS would not pick up any satellites. It *had* to be the aerial. Barrie rushed across to fiddle with it, and it worked. I would have been lost without it.

At 0745 I took off, following Highway 3 to New York. Barrie was far away in his chase helicopter, a mile or more much of the time, which I could not understand. If his shots did not work I would have to get the off-cuts from NBC and others for the documentary, but I had spent so much money getting him there; what was he doing? In New York Harbour I pottered around until 9 am, circling over the water between the World Trade Centre and the Statue of Liberty and generally trying to do what I was asked by the television helicopters. At all times Barrie stayed a long way away, though once I heard a request to get close to the Statue and circle tighter, which I tried to do.

Then I set off for Nova Scotia, following the route taken by John F Kennedy Jr and his wife, Caroline, on their last fatal flight. This took me under JFK Airport air space at 500 feet and along the bottom of Long Island. I was shocked at the northerly component in the wind, and was often down below 60mph, and even into the 40's. Then, for hours, it was turbulent, real gorilla-grip stuff, hanging on to the bar in animal country. I had the strongest woopsee I had had for years near Providence, Rhode Island.

All the time I conducted a debate with myself whether to land and get more fuel, but decided against it over a small field called Hansen, near the coast. Rather than follow the coast past Boston, the safest route, I blatted straight across the Gulf of Maine because I wanted to avoid the turbulence. Once well out over the sea, conditions calmed down. There was a journey of 4 hours, 230 miles, which was mostly smooth. I kept running thoughts deliberately through my mind to banish all the usual height fears that grew, and stayed at 2,000 feet.

At the coast of Nova Scotia there was a dramatic change in the weather, with a much stronger westerly wind and piled-up cloud. My tail component became 30 mph, giving me a really cracking pace towards Halifax, but it also took me into a weather front. Rain and cloud descended until my vision was obscured and I was not very high above the endless forests that characterise Nova Scotia. Barrie, waiting for me in Halifax, said later that cloud was down to the ground there. After 9 hours flying I decided to turn around just 100 miles from Halifax and hacked back to the coast again, and was down to 19 mph over the ground before finding the airfield at Yarmouth.

Virtually every person I met there asked me for money. It was not just the usual waitress and hotel staff. I apparently incurred charges just by being alive. I drew out C$500 – the Canadian dollar was then worth just less than 50 British pence, so it was not as damaging as it might have been – and constantly paid it out.

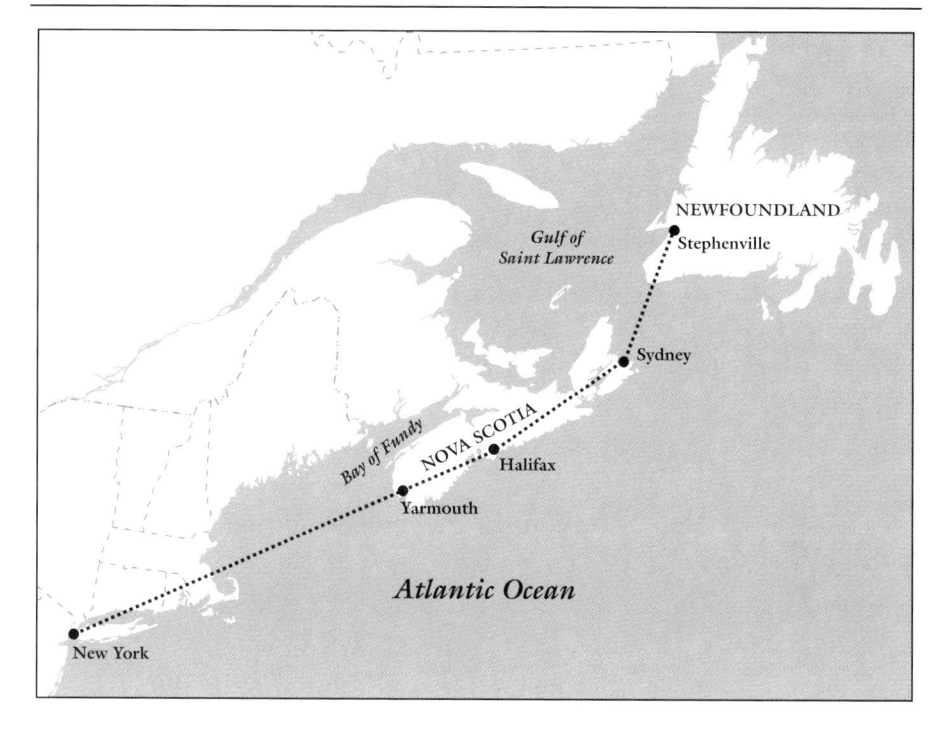

Maritime States

Oddly, I felt ready for another 10-hour flight after landing, despite four hours of turbulence at the beginning and an hour at the end of the flight which would have taxed anybody, even Colin Bodill. But when I sat down to eat I felt sleepy. I had existed during the whole day on one fruit bar, and ate just half a pizza that evening.

    I seemed to have got into a state of mind where everything was exalted. I was becoming hyper-critical of what was happening, at the same time, turning off parts of my mind. It was as if I was a machine waiting to burst into action, and meanwhile I carried on the usual machine tasks, videoing the flight, steering the aircraft, leaving the main part of my mind detached from what was going on. On landing, I came out of this state. In ten hours in the air I had not needed to pee, though I was all ready for the operation. As soon as I landed, of course, I headed off to pee, opting to tear off the conveen rather than use it. It was an odd sense of aesthetics. None of this was complying with the wholly sensible advice about diet from Dr Carl Hallam. I agreed with his advice, but it was difficult to force myself to comply with it.

Though I had wanted to make Halifax in one day, I thought nothing was lost by landing short. I could get to the capital of Nova Scotia the following day, June 1st, a journey of just 150 miles, and on to St John's the day after, a Saturday. But it did put paid to a possible claim for one of the ten longest non-stop distances ever flown in a microlight, at 612 miles, if I had made it to Halifax in one go. Colin Bodill beat this on one leg of his world flight, and of course, Guy Delage's superb 26-hour flight of 1,313 miles over the South Atlantic was still the world record.

Most of my flight had been at 2,000 feet. I used 113 litres in 10 hours, which was not bad. I was not able to find a point at which leaning the fuel mixture drove up the exhaust gas temperatures.

Tea in Yarmouth tasted as if it was made from swimming pool water.

On Friday, June 1, I woke feeling stiff, after another night with little sleep. I could not work out why. I phoned Liam to say I was OK. He said the media were demanding to know why I had landed short, and I explained about the weather. Despite 10 hours in the air, I was surprised at how fit I felt. Yet I had woken at 2am, and read, opening the biography of George Leigh Mallory. I slept later and woke at 7am, late for me. I had expected the weather would be poor, but skies were clear though it was windy. The wind turned out to be from the north and up to 19 knots, which meant I had a head-wind component on the way to Halifax. After a Continental breakfast, I took a taxi to the airport, met a few journalists and other flyers, and paid hangar dues, C$75 a night, the minimum rate, then I put the aircraft together and taxied off in the fresh wind to put in 50 litres of fuel.

Despite the hassle with the wind I got away at noon, climbing into the stiff breeze, turning on course and discovering I had to hack my way east, bounced around by wind and thermals. I settled between 2,000 and 3,000 feet, looking down on a big highway not marked on my map, and tried falling into a frame of mind to allow time to pass. Surprisingly, when I tried listening to Gracie Fields, the Clog song, it didn't work. I thought I might have to settle for Noel Coward. The words of his song, "Don't let's be beastly to the Germans", written and sung long before we knew we had won the war, keep turning up at odd times in my heads, so I began to learn them. It passed the time. It was difficult to get the tune right, because it was so complicated. The song had lovely lyrics, really witty, and with light strong defiant values from a different era from the one we lived in now.

Forty miles out I was able to pick up Halifax Radio, and alternated between filming with wing cameras, diary camera and the chest camera, the last of which was a struggle that I expected to produce some amusing pictures. After nearly three hours I landed, straight into the arms of Transport Canada, and struggled for hours to meet their requirements.

The worst words you could hear on a flight like mine were "he isn't going anywhere." I overheard those words after the four officials pounced on me, demanding to look at my paperwork. I was taken to a private office and someone in Monkton, head office for Transport Canada, said he had never heard of my flight until it appeared on NBC. This official, a nice-sounding chap called Bob Lavers, said I had no Canadian paperwork, and that because I was not an aircraft or a parachute, I was therefore flying an Ultralight – as the Americans define it – which had to weigh 248 pounds. In any case, flying such an aircraft, I needed formal permission to fly into Canada. Had I got that specific permission? I told him that, so far as I knew, I had. Liam had handled all permissions, and delegated Canada to an experienced British expert on officialdom, David Gleave, whose card described him as a Chief ATC Investigator for a company called Aviation Hazards.

The Canadians told me that they had heard of David Gleave, but had no paperwork from him since April!

It was after that I heard those fatal words, "he isn't going anywhere".

I phoned Liam to outline the problem. He was dismissive, and did not think it was a serious one, but went off to phone David Gleave. He came back in a state of shock, without a straight answer out of Gleave. Liam said he felt partially responsible for this situation. I told him he was totally responsible, that it was his job to clear it up, and he should do so. I decided to withhold judgement, but feared that all bureaucratic problems were serious, because some legal way had to be found through regulations.

It was frightening to be held up in this way, even before getting to St Johns.

Later, my aircraft in a hangar and staying at the same bed and breakfast as Bayes, Liam phoned again and told me he had talked to Transport Canada and I now had permission to fly on to St Johns. Despite Liam's optimism, it was not as simple as that. Bob Lavers phoned again, and told me I had to have official validation of entering the country, along with proof of a Permit to Fly, and registration documents. I did not have the latter, but I did have the former, so I faxed those to another official called Claude Daigle in New Brunswick. It would cost C$100, but if that was all I had to pay to get out of this hole, it would be worth it. I was not full of optimism.

Even then, the weather for flying the following day did not look brilliant, but I would rather have had the worst weather I can imagine than fall into a bureaucratic hole. Fog was forecast for St Johns, said to be having the worst Spring for some years.

On Saturday morning, June 2nd, I started a long wait by the phone at 7 o'clock my time, 10 o'clock Liam's time, for Claude to e-mail me permission to fly on. Claude had gone in to work on his day off, a Saturday, at that early time to pick up Liam's fax, but nothing was there. Liam told me when I phoned an hour later that he had not received my e-mail about sending such a fax, dispatched the previous evening. I sent another immediately, which he received a few minutes later – I have no explanation for why e-mails go astray, who knows what cyberspace is really about? – and finally Liam got things moving.

I spent hours playing games on the computer, trying to calm my agitated mind, while Barrie Bayes joined Judy and Winston, our hosts at the B&B, and two other guests, bemoaning the state of the modern world. It was a conversation that would have gladdened the heart of any conservative. I cannot remember how many different groups – the young, immigrants, asylum seekers – came in for criticism. I listened but did not join in.

In these situations, which I had been in on adventures ever since driving across Africa in my Austin 7 in 1968, I needed to divert my mind or explode. The energy that drove me to create such adventures had to find an outlet when frustrations arose. I tried to pretend I was not furious, but fury coursed through my body and I resorted to the sort of displacement activities that animals do when caged. If there was room, I paced up and down for hours, working off the energy that would go in other circumstances towards bopping someone on the nose. It would not have been helpful doing that, though nineteenth century Englishmen were always doing it, at least in *Boy's Own* stories.

Every phone call from Liam was some relief, but cut off from a telephone or forced to use one through the operator at ruinous prices, I finally decided to get all my gear and myself to the airport. Meanwhile, Barrie depressed me further by telling me that the shots he took in New York Harbour were no good. Barrie said I had not obeyed his instructions, which was true, but even if I had heard his instructions, I was harassed by local TV stations. Surely, filming my flight, he was supposed to follow me, not me follow him? But instead of forcefully telling me, through his pilot, what was happening, he hovered around three miles away and tried to get shots like that. They did not work. How could they? I had followed the flight path I had agreed with him, and, brutally, it produced nothing. I thought I could save the situation by begging for pictures from the US TV companies, having had a positive response from one of them, and these would cover my departure from New York if a documentary was made. Barrie did at least get pictures of the take-off from Caldwell, but when I flew into Halifax, because the airport manager apparently ratted on a deal, he failed to get the landing shots. It did not improve my temper.

Judy's husband Winston, who suffered from a heart condition and had the black humour of someone facing the early prospect of dying, drove us to the airfield. There were no Transport Canada officials there, but I broke the log jam when Winston lent me his phone and I managed to track down Bob Lavers, and then Claude Daigle. Claude went into his office for a second time, found Liam's fax, asked for a number to fax his authorisation to, and when I found one, he cleared me to go on, six hours after I had expected to get such permission. The delay meant St Johns was not on for that day, even if the weather had allowed it, which was doubtful.

I had got into this situation, I now realised bitterly, by relying on David Gleave, who had seemed to be at the centre of the British aviation establishment. He appeared enthusiastic about the flight, always helpful, and he was extremely plausible. He undertook three jobs, all volunteered, none of them forced on him. One was to find me an Antonov 124 to transport me and the Flyer to America. The second was to get me to fly off one of its wings, to publicise the flight. The third was to clear me through Canada's aviation officials. In the weeks leading up to the flight, Liam and I at first relied on what we were told, that the Antonov was a distinct possibility in the right time frame, that the company owning the Antonovs would be delighted with the publicity resulting from a wing take-off, and that Canadian officials were all squared away about the flight.

When it became clear that if we had relied on the Antonov promises I would still be in England, I made other arrangements. But Liam believed Gleave's promises on Canada were good ones, and, by proxy, so did I. After all, Gleave was a client of Liam's brother, John, a lawyer. At one time Gleave raised the possibility that I might fund a trip to Canada and back for him, just to clear up some loose ends. But when we got to the heart of the matter that Friday evening, it transpired that Gleave had, indeed, raised the issue of clearing me through Canada's aviation laws more than a month ago. He had promised the authorities he would meet all their queries by sending through the appropriate paperwork, which would have included, of course, my Permit to Fly.

After that, said the Canadians, nothing had happened.

They had not heard from Gleave for the previous four weeks. Liam told me that evening he would drive down to Gleave's workplace on Monday to get any paperwork and letters that passed between Gleave and the Canadian authorities. I hoped we would not have any more wearing hassles like that again.

I refuelled the Flyer with 50 litres, to add to the 50 litres I thought were already in the main tanks (I could not get the hang of the ELBA fuel gauge at that time) and gradually put all her equipment on to her. The heated bar grips, which, when working, were so brilliant, were no longer operating because the grips were not fixed to the control bar, and the exertion of flying in turbulence gave me the strength to push the grips up and down the bar. The way they were installed this was fatal to them, and I had torn the wiring from one of them. I started to worry that my hands would freeze out in the cold Atlantic.

The weather forecast for flying to St Johns was poor, but I could at least break the 559 mile journey by flying 200 miles to the end of Cape Breton Island and a town called Sydney, the last airfield before Newfoundland, where fog was now reported all over the island. I took off at 2pm, climbed into a half-tailwind on my right beam, and within three minutes, my ears were assaulted by a terrible noise in the ear-phones. It was howling, crackling, and sounding like a gigantic washing machine, and I might have landed to find out what was wrong. But it had been a hassle getting out of Halifax International, not a wilful hassle, just that I had been mixed up with big airliners and I did not want to go back and experience that again. I flew north-east to a town called Truro, and then along the north coast of Nova Scotia with that dreadful noise in my ears. For much of the time I kept the volume turned off, so I could not hear myself speak, or sing, and I could not actually play the Noel Coward songs I had lined up on the CD player.

Bashed around by thermals, including one vicious one that nearly tore the bar from my hands, I flew in this mute condition, which allowed my latent height fears to come into play. I tried all the usual ways I had developed of countering this. Why my friend, the beautiful Helen Dudley played a part in resolving these fears remained a mystery, one I still do not want to explore because it may remove her effectiveness. The counter measures worked, enough that I flew safely and did not land and, forsaking flying forever, take up the priesthood (not that I believe in God anyway). The small cumulus clouds gradually disappeared, and the afternoon developed into bright, sunny, brilliant weather, with mist and fog at the far edges, but a clear route through to Sydney.

I crossed 35 miles of sea, an inlet where I could have turned right and remained over land, but I went over the sea, relieved to stop the thermals banging me around. Although my arms and hands sometimes felt like they would seize up, they didn't. It was just something to overcome.

Passing Port Hawkesbury, which marked the start of Cape Breton Island, I radioed a position report, and was touched when ATC asked me if I would fly overhead. When I said I was 20 miles to the north, they replied that they would charge me no landing fee. I stayed in contact with them, not speaking much, for an hour. Once, a small aircraft flew over me, 500 feet above, and reported he had seen "a hang glider".

It was around this time that, looking at my instruments, I saw the *Flydat* panel go down. This recorded my engine revs, exhaust gas temperatures, cylinder head temperatures, oil pressure and temperature, and how long the engine had been running. As I adjusted the mixture, lean or rich, according to the EGTs, I immediately ran rich again (I had stacks of fuel), to avoid any potential damage to the engine, and decided it did not merit finding a nearer airfield than Sydney. It was also around this time that, driven half mad by the howling in my ears, I fiddled with everything on the cockpit floor, and moving one of the Lynx sound cables to the intercom, the noise stopped! This cable, which I should have plugged into the CD player, had been shorting on something, and that had caused the noise. I did a lot of singing after that, cheerful once more. It was still impossible to duplicate Noel Coward, at least for me.

I landed at Sydney after 3 hours 45 minutes flying, into smooth and beautiful conditions, and straight into a hangar. John Reilly, who fuels up aircraft at the airport, looked after me, also guiding me to a B&B called Becky's. He found me a hire car at C$38.00/day, a wonderful rate, considering one taxi trip in Halifax cost C$33.00. Becky's daughter in law, Charlene Oliver, settled me in comfortably and I immediately did a laundry, wash and dry, so I was clean again. I had learned on all my previous adventures that being clean kept my morale high, and it was a top priority for me.

Dinner was three hot dogs, four beers, and my nose stuffed into the biography of George Leigh Mallory. I was struggling to come to terms with all the homosexual characters that surrounded him at Cambridge. He seemed to have had just one physical affair, a single bonk, although a lot more snogging and face-touching with James Strachey, one of the notorious Bloomsbury Set on the edges of which Mallory hovered. It was, apparently, something he did not want to repeat. Girls were starting to turn up in his life.

I remember hoping when I got on to Scott of the Antarctic, that I did not have to struggle with stories about *his* homosexual side.

I woke up late on Sunday morning because I had set the alarm clock wrong, looked out of the window and saw perfect conditions, so I washed, shaved, bolted breakfast, and drove to the airport. Had the forecast been wrong? Shouldn't I be in the air? What was I doing sleeping when I should have been flying? Vikki Smith at ATC told me immediately that, however perfect the weather was at Sydney, it was rotten in St Johns, with no prospect that day, and the following day, of getting there. I would not get VFR clearance. As I had found on the world flight, being stuffed by weather was a lot better than being stuffed by officials.

I spent the morning repairing the Flyer, replacing fuses on the Flydat and the heated mitts. Three drag racers, Gary Pozzebon, Tom Aucein, and Sheldon Shepherd, the latter with a face like a grizzled mediaeval knight, were building a giant portable commentating platform around the shell of an old bus. Amazingly, they had the fuses I needed to repair my aircraft. Gary telephoned his son and drove him out of bed to turn up at the hangar to help me. Listening to their voices, all born and bred in Nova Scotia (or Cape Breton Island), I was convinced they had Irish backgrounds. Gary was of Italian stock, Tom of French, Sheldon of Scottish, and yet there was a distinct Irish rhythm to their speech, their intonations were Irish, even the phrasing was Irish. As I had found on the Dalgety Flight in the Australian Outback, on the world flight in the Yukon Territory, and now in Nova Scotia, I was aware of the great and vigorous movement of people out of our islands and across the world in the last thousand years. I was at home there, as I was at home in the Outback and the Yukon, surrounded by people who were just like me, of my stock and my history and my values.

I was not happy with the pictures I was getting from the wing cameras. They were full of ripples, and I spent the afternoon finding out why. I also explored Sydney. One thing leapt at an English eye; there were no black people, no Indians, no Chinese. If there was an ethnic minority it was French, but you could not tell they were French until they spoke. It was like England forty years ago, but I was also reminded of George McFly's adventure in "Back to the

Future", spirited back to 1956. The closure of the local coal mines meant there were a lot of people on welfare, but there were cars everywhere, neat lawns and wooden houses, and a sort of deep drawling kindness to everyone I met.

Weather is everything in Nova Scotia, because that is where it goes to die. Low pressure areas were forced up into the region by a combination of land and water, and hung around Maritime Canada until they faded away, to be replaced by another. The one in the area I was looking at stretched back to the Great Lakes. The local feeling was that the weather was getting worse. The previous winter was a bad one, and there had been no real Spring. I could not choose any other year to make this flight, but it was not a great year. The wind that blew me to Sydney came from the south east, and the banks of fog out over the sea crept in overnight.

I wanted to fly direct to St Johns, straight across 200 miles of sea, and over a leftover relic of the wars of 250 years ago, the island of St Pierre, still French territory, and into the capital of Newfoundland from the west and south. One alternative was to carry on going north, about 180 miles to a former US air force base called Stephenville, and then a flight of 160 miles over high ground and perhaps through a valley to Gander, and south from there to St Johns, another flight above 100 miles.

"That's the way the airlines have been doing it this year," said a weather lady in Halifax. Maybe it would be the way I had to do it?

In the intense discussions I had with myself, I felt at ease, rather than the usual feeling I had in such situations, a nagging discontent, with doubts about my own commitment and courage. Was I doing everything I could to get to St Johns? The answer was yes. Did it matter if I was two or three days late? No, it did not. Didn't I expect there to be a long patient wait, as there was for Harry Hawker and John Alcock and those other intrepid flyers in 1919? Yes, I did.

They did not have my complications, convincing the Canadians that, however claggy it was around St Johns, 200 miles out, if I chose the day right there would be a good healthy 1,700 mile westerly waiting to carry me home. But I expected to come to that fight later. I especially wanted to settle in at St Johns because I knew that Liam had found a B&B and hangarage. I planned to hire my own car, and also looked forward to meeting Peter Bray, preparing to kayak across the Atlantic. Who was he? Where did he come from? How was he planning to carry his supplies? How long would it take him? How could he sleep in bad weather? Just think of the palavers of going to the loo. If my journey was a bit out of the ordinary, then his was more so.

Meanwhile, Liam visited David Gleave that Monday, June 4th, to pick up the paperwork and put together the – belated – case to the Canadians, assuring them I had taken all sensible precautions about the flight. He e-mailed me afterwards:

> *Please can you let me know the details of what GPS's you are carrying, the make, models, etc. Also, your VOR (a radio beacon finder, of which I had two in my Icom radios), is it part of one of your GPS's or a separate unit? Thanks. Making headway here. DG (Gleave) is a difficult man to deal with but I am putting all my forceful man-management skills to use (as you well know I can!).*

I compiled a list of my equipment to see that it fitted with their paperwork, an exercise slightly different from the actual precautions I was taking. I did not think that an Atlantic flight by microlight was really any huge technical thing. It would come down to the human involved in it – me – and my capacity to hold it together, through all the hours of daylight and a full night, and then the most dangerous hours, when I think I have won through and make that one silly mistake that kills it all off. Lindbergh and Alcock took their engines to the limits of the day; but there are almost no limits to my own engine. We had all the technological marvels of the age, but what we don't ever know are our own limits. When you looked at what we did with those marvels, the movie "Pearl Harbour" being the latest example of our technological brilliance and banal production, we could plumb the depths. I did not want my flight to be banal, and felt that Liam, who was not an experienced flyer, needed all the help he could get in putting my case.

Later that day, Liam e-mailed me again, apologising for communicating by dribs and drabs, but engaged in work vital to the flight:

> *I have just spoken to Bob Lavers and told him that I will be sending the (safety case) document to him tomorrow. I will then have a conference call with him and his boss, Marty (Pumpstead), where we will thrash out all the problems and see how we can move forward. I'll keep you posted. Just for the record, if I had handled this Canadian thing myself from the beginning, it would have been done by now!*

I had two days down-time, checking the weather forecast in the morning and the evening. I used that time to learn more about where I was. Becky Oliver ran the B&B with her husband Cyril, a tough old fireman who rejoiced in the nickname

"Lulu" (he used to call chickens Lulu when he was a child), and she directed me to the local university. Becky had four children, the eldest a sergeant in the RCMP, the Royal Canadian Mounted Police, a job and a title which still carried enormous prestige. This was evident in a print hanging in the hall (next to one showing Diana, Princess of Hearts) featuring a tall, lean iron-man Mountie, his face a picture of 19th century British determination and rectitude. He was riding his horse, which was also suitably heroic, and looking down on two rather noble looking native Canadians (they used to be called Red Indians), building a canoe.

The Olivers were a moon-shining family, with a tradition of running a still to make illicit liquor. Lulu's father distilled moonshine for 18 years, and Lulu himself lost a car to the Mounties when he was a young man, after they raided one of his stills in the woods. Now their son was a Mountie himself.

"You'd arrest your own mother if you caught me speeding," said Becky to her son.

"Of course, I would," he replied. "You shouldn't be breaking the law".

It was quite moving that such an attitude should survive into modern days. She was, of course, rather proud of his reply.

In my biography of the mountaineer George Leigh Mallory, George, like his whole generation, is heading towards the First World War, and seems to be developing an interest in girls. He wrote to one, so innocently, saying his previous experience of "friendship" was with men, "friendship" being the cover at the time for an exploration of homosexuality. I wondered how modern women would feel at being approached by a chap who said a similar thing? Curious? Challenged?

When I was much younger I had met the last man who saw Mallory alive. His name was Noel Odell, and he was at the final camp on Everest in 1924. He looked up through a telescope that fatal day, when the clouds parted to show Mallory and his young companion, Irvine, "climbing strongly for the top". Odell, then a Fellow of a Cambridge college, said of Mallory that "the homosexuals made a thing of him", which could be why his reputation has lasted so long. At the time, I was a BBC Radio reporter, and Odell felt I was to be trusted with this information. A few years later, when I worked for independent television, TV-am, I went back to see if I could get him to speak on camera about Mallory. Odell rejected me out of hand. It wasn't television itself he objected to. He took against me because I worked for *breakfast* television, which he thought an abomination, and felt was undermining the moral fibre of England. Who was to say he wasn't right?

Monday morning, June 4th, the 39th anniversary of being chopped from RAF Cranwell, was leisurely. The weather deteriorated, rain sweeping in, wind increasing in strength to gusts of 60 mph. I pottered around writing notes, and reading more of Mallory's biography. His role in the birth of rock-climbing in North Wales appeared to be a secure one, because of the routes he pioneered there, and he also had a part in the way the philosophical basis of climbing evolved. They seemed to go through exactly the same stage in 1912 with fatal accidents, five in one year to the core group, as we went through in hang gliding in 1978. As a result of changes, things became a lot safer. The reputation of mountaineering improved, while that of hang gliding did not, sadly.

Media interest stirred in the flight. A local newspaper reporter, Sharon Montgomery, finally tracked me down and I drove out to the hangar to show her the Flyer. She spent 20 minutes scrabbling around the hangar floor, experimenting with photographic angles, the while telling me how she loved adventures but had never been further in her life than Prince Edward Island, which is near by Nova Scotia. Apparently, the Flyer was "awesome".

I learned something about Cape Breton Island. Right at the top, back in 1497, the explorers John and Sebastian Cabot landed at Cape North. Across the water 12 miles from the largest town on the island, Sydney, was Englishtown, the first permanent settlement, with something called Giant MacAskill's grave, and the first Jesuit mission locally.

I had flown in over a big sea-lake called Bras d'Or, at the bottom of which was Baddeck, the site of the Alexander Graham Bell Museum. It was also the location of "the first flight in the British Empire" (not a boast you would hear elsewhere today), the Silver Dart in February, 1909. That was about five months before Louis Bleriot flew across the English Channel.

Tablehead, another small town nearby, was the site of the first transatlantic submarine cable in North America, and the island also housed the Marconi Station, first transoceanic wireless station in North America.

Sydney itself had the Cossit House Museum, a building dating back to 1787. Glace Bay had its Miner's Museum, and just down the coast was Port Morien, site of the first coal mine in North America. A curiosity was a local holiday, set for a week away, called Davis Day. It was not a holiday celebrated in the rest of Canada, or even Nova Scotia, just this small corner of Cape Breton Island. The holiday was to remember a miner called Davis, shot dead by police during disturbances over a strike. Both the big mine and the steel works, which provided the bulk of employment locally, had closed in the last five years.

Dinner with Becky and her daughter in law, Charlene Oliver, who was six months pregnant and very pretty, was terrific. Becky worked as a waitress in the local casino, full of OAPs gambling away their pensions on slot machines. Charlene ran a local ladies clothes shop, but she was also a judo brown belt, and instructed in the subject for just 40 English pence an hour. I brought a couple of bottles of wine to the table, Charlene had no French ideas about drinking and pregnancy, so Becky joined me in denting one bottle and half-denting another. We talked about all the subjects under the sun, but chiefly about how similar our customs were, and the nuances of our language.

Just before bed the phone rang, and a sharp voice demanded to know who was going to rescue me if I fell in to the water. It belonged to Bert Rose in Iqaluit, now capital of Innuit-land (they used to be known as Eskimos). Bert had been a kind host in 1998 on my world flight when I went through his city, a place where he had had enormous influence in choosing all the teachers in the region for the previous 30 years. On that flight he had followed my progress on the Internet, about which I knew practically nothing at all then. Now he found me again. There was nothing within a thousand miles of Iqaluit that Bert did not have some sort of a handle on. It was lovely to hear him; apparently, he read my *Global Flyer* book a number of times.

I had to check in to Search and Rescue services and promise to let them know when I was going. There was no threat to the flight in this. They were reassured by the knowledge that they could follow me on the GPS Tracker.

On Tuesday, June 5th I did a few interviews with journalists, two for newspapers, one for television. I saw the result that evening. Aside from saying I had a 60HP motor (it was 80HP) it was accurate, and relied a lot on my own comments, rather than summarising them wrongly. I was in and out of the car all day, finding a bolt to secure one of the GPS's, or looking to bind together my microphones so that they did not get tangled the cockpit. Becky and Lulu Oliver fed me lunch, chicken sandwich and salad, and fielded various phone calls, as journalists wound themselves up for the story. There was a certain air of disbelief in what I was doing, then a wave of support.

I washed everything, including my one pair of jeans, walking around all afternoon in a thin flying suit, aware I had nothing else between me and immodesty, the same state I was in after coming out of Russia to Nome, Alaska.

Part of me felt like a gunfighter preparing for a long show-down. I looked at all my equipment, weighed it in my hands, wondered whether I needed it or not, and kept discarding items. The long black bag I strapped to one of the rear legs may actually have been affecting the flying characteristics, turning the aircraft to the left, and I planned to test this theory in the remaining flights I had left before the big one.

An option ahead of me the following day, June 6th, was to head north east to Stephenville. I would really speed my way there with a following wind, and once overland, valley-fly my way through indifferent weather to Gander, either to wait until St Johns was clear, or nipping south to finally reach my goal. It was about 100 miles longer than a direct route, but thought to be safer.

Meanwhile, I was running into Canadian regulations all time. Despite hundreds of hours of bad weather flying on various adventures, including cloud and night-time flying, I had no paper IFR qualifications – an instrument rating – and that meant, technically, I could be banned from flying in many of the conditions I had safely flown in. I foresaw a real difficulty in the Atlantic, where I might not persuade the authorities I could leave on the big flight because they were fearful of the first 150 miles climbing above fog banks, whereas after that, I would argue, the weather could be brilliant for a crossing. Alcock and Brown never had such problems.

Liam spent 50 minutes on a conference phone call to Canada, trying to repair the damage done by Gleave's fantastical delays. It was Liam's main job to get me through the permission process, and he plugged away at it doggedly. It should have been done weeks ago, but it was no use being upset about that; we had to sort it out from where it was.

I kept trying, despite all the practical hassles of making the flight work, to reach a particular state of mind, within which I would be able to complete the Atlantic flight. In reading about the Everest mountaineer George Leigh Mallory, I came across some of his more exalted and famous writings, but I was not happy that they expressed what I was looking for. He had not gone into the First World War yet, or discovered Everest; he had barely discovered women, but he had at least done that, falling in love with a girl called Ruth.

I remembered my admiration for Edmund Blunden's walk through almost certain death in a shell barrage on the Somme. I did not feel able to do that, but oddly, I could see my gay friend Julian Parr doing exactly the same thing as Blunden, even singing and dancing in defiance, and for the same reasons.

Julian had worked out his own value system which did for him, but not for me, though I was always fascinated by how he kept it all together and by how coherent he made it look to the outside eye. It helped that he had spent two years as *Agence France Presse* correspondent in Afghanistan, so he knew what it was like to come under fire, as I did not.

Stephen Lewis and I exchanged constant notes on this subject of values. His insight was greater and more articulate than mine, though I hoped that the closer I got to danger, the more truths I would find. I believed I was on the Atlantic flight because I wanted to force myself to the edge, to see what values mattered and what did not. I felt it was at those edges that my temporary companion on the world flight, Keith Reynolds, never having been there before, betrayed every tenet of the code of honour I was brought up with. It was a code I sensed more easily in people older than me, than among the young, though some of the latter, my children among them, were actively searching for such codes. The codes came easily to Wilfred Russell, for example, as I hoped to discover and understand through the poetry he chose. They also came easier to Tony Iveson, Chairman of Bomber Command Association who, when he was 21, had been a Battle of Britain fighter pilot, and at 25, still younger than my son James, had made 27 sorties with 617 "Dambuster" Squadron, including all three against the German battleship, *Tirpitz*. Both these men were over 80.

Stephen sent me an e-mail which had a deep effect on me:

> "There was an interesting programme on Channel 4 on Saturday morning. The Australian cricket team, on their way to England, stopped off at Gallipoli. After their visit, they were interviewed. There were, surprisingly, no Mel Gibson anti-British tirades, only an appreciation of the courage of the Anzacs who took part, pride in being an Australian and inspiration to co-operate to pull off a good team result for Australia. The idea of the English team going to the Somme or Passchendaele as part of their preparations or expressing any pride in what their forefathers had done is so incongruous as to be unimaginable. Why do we not live in a country where our young men still have a core of decency? I put it down to the half-baked republican and socialist teachers in the comprehensives. And they want more pay!
>
> "Believe it or not, they showed 'In Which We Serve' on BBC2 at the weekend. It was as powerful as ever, and contains subtleties that are easily missed on a cursory viewing. When I was a boy, I used to regard Noel

> *Coward as a figure of fun but I have since come round to the view that he was the British literary genius of the 20th-century, almost as good as Virgil. The peroration to the film where the narrator talks of the pride the British will always take in the Royal Navy even though values will change, though doubtful as a statement of truth in the light of the current situation, is so artful in its sonorous phrases and balanced sentence-structure as to send one's spirits soaring. I was reading the words of the Coward song ("Don't let's be beastly to the Germans") on your web site. The rhythms are fiendishly complex, yet the stresses invariably fall at the most telling satirical points. Brilliant!"*

Gallipoli had been an invasion of the "soft under-belly of Europe" through Turkey in 1915, planned by Winston Churchill, who was haunted the rest of his life by its failure. Anzacs, that is, Australian and New Zealand Army Corps forces, lost 8,000 men there in an operation now thought inept. It was a coming of age for Australia, and there is a whole modern generation who blamed the British for it, even – Mel Gibson again in his self-appointed role as an Australian Goebbels – suggesting that we deliberately killed Australians to spare our own men. In this victim culture, it was quite forgotten that we lost half as many men again as the Anzacs at Gallipoli, including thousands from Ulster, and none of the Australians at the time had the sick ideas that later infected views of that battle. Reading Ross Smith, for example, the flyer whose ghost I chased to Australia and who fought in Gallipoli, Smith thought of himself as British, as of course, he was, just an Englishman who had spent a few generations under another sun.

I felt the work on my own mind, preparing it for the ordeal ahead, would really start in St Johns. I was not really at the start line, though in one sense, that had been New York. I looked forward then to reading an account of the life of Scott of the Antarctic, a biography that sought to rubbish this once-iconic British hero. I also had the rest of Homer's *Odyssey* to finish.

On Wednesday, June 6th, it was foggy on Cape Breton island when Lulu Oliver made breakfast of bacon, eggs, toast, orange juice and tea. We read an article in the local newspaper about my flight. Afterwards, I was outside videoing the foggy conditions when a motorist drew up, stopped, walked over to talk to me for five minutes, and then offered me a donation! I asked him to contact the web site and give the money direct to AHF, the Artificial Heart Fund, but I was deeply touched by his gesture.

At the airport I checked the weather forecast, still no good for St Johns which was fogged in, and the wind was not brilliant either for the alternative, Gander, in the middle of Newfoundland. But there was a "short" trip of 180 miles, most of it over the sea, to get me on to the island itself, if I chose to land at Stephenville, a small town I later discovered was sustained by work at a giant paper mill. I filed a flight plan to Gander, via Stephenville, setting my take off time at 1115.

Three television cameramen turned up to cover the departure, with inevitable delays, each trying to carve out a piece of the story in a different way. It was odd how media interest had only started in Canada after I had been there a few days. I was later trailed across the sea with requests from air traffic controllers to "take down this telephone number", for a reporter in faraway Toronto. As I was often in the thick of doing something else, I had to force myself to laugh and comply.

I re-fuelled, adding 80 litres, watching the petrol rise on the sight gauge to 156 litres, easily enough for 12 hours flying, and I also had 20 litres in reserve. Rushing from ATC, to hire car to commissionaire to hangar worked me into a sweat, which I added to by slowly struggling into two thick flying suits. Finally, I was pushed out of the hangar with everything on board, started the engine, warmed up, taxied for take-off, and had a message via ATC, from Liam, to push in the plug of the GPS Tracker (it was not registering back in England). As I did so, I noticed the *Flydat* had failed again!

John Hunt had been worrying away at this problem back in England. Why had it failed the first time, on the way from Halifax? I had replaced the fuse, but this did not address the initial problem. He thought power from the engine had strong surges, judging from his reading of the GPS Tracker, and that needed fixing. Should I taxi in and try to fix it there and then? If I did, I knew I would not get away from the comforts of Sydney for another day, and who knew how bad the weather could turn? What risk was I taking?

The answer was, I would not know anything about how the engine was behaving. I put the leaning switch to "rich", and decided I had easily enough fuel to get to Gander, and all the time in the world at St Johns to fix it. Prudent or not, I made the decision to take off and sort things out later. In passing, the fuel flow meter seemed to stop working in sympathy, but I could always fly by listening to the engine, and making judgements about the revs by seeing if I was climbing or not.

Take-off was easy, with a climbing turn to 1,200 feet while I tinkered with cameras and settled down, then I headed north-west out over the town, and noted with delight that I had a weak following wind. This took my speed to more than 60mph over the water, rising to an average later of 67mph. Only two miles from the shore a thin bank of cloud was spread across the sea, and the further north I went, the thicker and more brooding this bank became.

There was never a way of predicting when I get attacked by height-fears. On this flight there were a couple of serious attacks. They stemmed from my own imagination, the utter awareness of every single foot of air between my back and the sea, and an urgent drive to lessen this, even if by doing so I was taken down into the killing clouds. I climbed to 3,000 feet, and later to 4,000 feet, each time eyeing the cloud blanket uneasily, and each time struggling to overcome these fears. At one attack I did a voice-piece to camera, in which part of my mind was aware that the short, clipped sentences were nothing to do with being some 1950's RAF film character, and all to do with maintaining a sane face. I occupied myself with anything as a distraction. The thoughtful 5-minute process, always nervous about dropping anything, of changing a tape in one of the cameras, served that fear-challenging process. As on the flight across India in 1988, I had constantly to discipline my mind not to go down various corridors where these fears lurked. I knew they were there, but they were not always there, and I had to resist the curiosity I would get to find out, once more, where they were. I was so relieved on some days to find they were not there at all. They had really started with my tumble out of the sky in 1978, but the experience over India in ten years later had formalised it.

All my navigation was by GPS. Above me, the sky was a washed blue, with wispy high-level clouds. Below me, I had occasional glimpses of the sea through holes, but then these closed up and I was left looking at various cloud layers and resolving not to be caught by them. The Flyer, when I let the bar go, did not take a straight line, but turned either right or left at its own volition, so it was impossible to tune out the turn. I found myself fiddling with something – the chest camera, for example, talking to it or taking shots of the wing – and looking at my GPS to see myself flying at ninety degrees to my intended course. This was not catastrophic, I told myself, because I might end up three miles off course, but in nearly 2,000 miles, who cared? It just was not a tight flying technique. But who was watching me for that?

After two hours I saw by the GPS that I was coming up to land, and over to the west I could see land and sea. I was not happy about staying above cloud over land (nasty things might appear as you descend through cloud over land), and descended to the left in thinning cloud to see if there was a bottom under which I could fly. There wasn't, so I climbed again and punted off towards Stephenville, ready at any time to dive to the left where I could see the ground, but knowing that I had to turn right at some time to head for Gander. The cloud broke up, some of it into big nasty lumps which, when I flew near them, tried to suck me in. At one time I was on tickover with the bar right in, which should have meant descending at 700 feet/minute, and I was still maintaining height, sustained there by cloud-suck.

The land over which I flew had roads and small hamlets, and was mountainous and covered in brush and shrub. I rose to 4,000 feet and then dodged beneath more cloud coming in from my right, where it looked seriously mountainous and covered with rain, and watched the coastline come back to meet me as I closed with the airfield at Stephenville. The girl in ATC was formal and incurious, but passed on a reporter's query as I turned east to set off for Gander. She seemed to have no perception of what it was like, wrestling in my tiny machine (but why should she?). About ten minutes later, approaching the mountains at just 35 mph ground speed into a strengthening breeze, and facing a line of rain from one horizon to the other, thick and dark and altogether unfriendly, I decided it was one risk too many. I made the fatal decision to fly back to Stephenville and stay the night.

The ATC girl said there was no prospect of hangarage, and winds on the ground were blowing 20 knots. I asked again, and she said, reluctantly, that she would "ask around". I came in to a gingerly landing, still with quite a heavy load of fuel on board, about 120 litres, and without springs I did not want to dent the under-carriage. I talked to myself out loud the whole way down.

Fighting to keep control in the fresh wind, I taxied off the runway and closed my flight plan with Gander. The ATC girl let me taxi off in the wrong direction. It was only when I asked where I should be going that she told me to make a 180 degree turn and taxi – downwind! – to a BP petrol station on the big airfield. When I struggled to get there, she told me to ask inside about hangarage.

"I cannot get out of this aircraft in these conditions," I replied irritably by radio, "because the wind will blow my aircraft away."

For ten minutes I sat there, presumably being watched in silence while I strained my arms one way or the other, before some lovely firemen directed me, first to their own building, and then a quarter of a mile away to a big old Nissen hut, once a hangar for the latest US fighter aircraft, now with a 20 foot wide entrance. There, with men holding both wings, I managed to get out and we pushed and pulled for ten minutes to get the Flyer to safety. Among those helping were the airport manager, William MacNeil, airport commissionare Kevin Dollard, and two fire fighters, Brian O'Quinn and his boss, Denis Burke. I was deeply grateful for their help.

Sean Sheppard, advertising manager with the local newspaper, *"The Georgian"*, saw me into the airport hotel as guest of his company. I rewarded him by eating and crashing out, so that when he called later, I was half asleep. I did not have a great night's sleep.

Weather prospects the following day, June 7th, a Thursday, were poor. Looking out of the window, I could see one of those skies with thin grey clouds everywhere, mild-looking, but with easterly winds – I wanted to head east – of more than 20 mph. The weather services said there was no chance of making St Johns. Even the IFR boys (Instrument Flight Rules) were having a bad time, and had been for days.

"You can get these situations here," said the weather man. "We get a persistent easterly and it lasts for weeks. It brings the fog in off the sea."

He said it was not uncommon that people heading for St Johns landed at Gander, 120 miles away, and took a taxi to their destination. I could not, of course, do that. It turned into another down-time day. I resolved to change the fuse yet again on the *Flydat*, and see if I could determine what was wrong.

Radio interviews and interviews by phone with newspaper journalists were becoming part of my daily life. I had three before breakfast. On the radio I heard that Tony Blair had won another landslide victory with a majority of at least 100. Helen phoned to say Hague had resigned. That was sad. Hague was a brave man, but that was not a quality that counted for much in politics right now. The fact that his voice grated had more effect on the voters than the quality of the man. Truly the actor was king.

I heard later that the *Daily Mail*, in London, on election day, had carried a half page article on my flight, quoting Liam at length. Certainly, no attempt was made to contact me. But, why on election day?

I had no chance that day of making either Gander or St Johns. Cloud was down to the hills, and a strong, sometimes 25 mph, easterly wind was blowing. I resolved to discover what was wrong with the Flyer, and to find my glasses which I had misplaced. I walked between airport building and hotel four times before the glasses turned up at reception, then went down to double-check the weather locally. I found myself in the company of the girl who had talked me in and left me at the mercy of the strong winds on Wednesday, Sherri Alexander. It emerged that she had no idea what a microlight was, never having seen one before, and she had not realised how much peril I had been in when I landed. We pottered around, looking at forecasts for various airfields, trying to find a glimmer of hope, without success. One of Sherri's colleagues turned up, Jack Tilley, and he was pessimistic about Friday, too, saying it might work at the weekend, getting into St Johns.

Denis Burke, the local fire chief, opened up the makeshift hangar where the Flyer had been put the previous evening, and various local men came up to look, sit in her, and be photographed. I changed the fuse again on the *Flydat*, so it worked again. There were suggestions from home as to why it was not working. John Hunt thought there may have been a surge of power which blew the fuse, that I might have loaded the electrical system with too many gadgets. Another suggestion was the wiring was loose. I tugged at it gently, and could find nothing wobbly. Denis brought in a local electrical expert who was also the pastor, a man called Keith Soebe, who checked all the wiring, painstakingly. He said there was nothing wrong with it, and if there was a fault it was in the regulator itself (this controls the electrical power generated by the engine, on its way to the battery). I started the engine, and with Denis holding the front strut and my foot firmly on the brake, ran it at full power for minutes to see if I could get another surge of power and break the fuse again. Keith monitored the event with a voltmeter. Everything behaved itself.

"If there's a fault, it's probably in the regulator," said Keith, "and you'll need to replace that".

I decided I could live with one more risky test from Stephenville to St Johns, where losing the *Flydat* was not the end of the world. The checking of the wiring, tugging it to see if there was anything loose, may have cured the problem. It nagged me that I might be over-loading the electrical system. The biggest load came from the electric waistcoat, which was not turned on when the Flydat broke last time; I could not do the flight in any comfort without that waistcoat. It was hard to believe I had flown around the world three years earlier without one. I asked Keith how much I owed him, but Denis had already squared him away.

"The hunting season starts in September, and I'll make sure Keith gets a bag of moose meat for today's work", he said.

So there was some poor moose out there right now, chewing away at the grass, not knowing that it was going to "donate" a few pounds of meat to fix my aircraft.

Back at the hotel, my host, Sean Sheppard turned up and gave me a tour of Stephenville. It had been a USAF base from 1942, part of the ferry route across the Atlantic, its lease purchased by the Americans as part-exchange for 50 clapped-out old destroyers. Later, it was a fighter station against an attack across the North Pole by the Russians. When the Americans left, their base was turned into the basis for a small city of 11,000 people, which seemed to be growing very fast, with new building everywhere. The biggest employer was a local paper mill, a giant production plant I could see across the bay, into one end of which trees are brought on trucks, and out of the other end and straight on to ships for Europe, high-quality newsprint was produced.

But more importantly, oil had been discovered up the coast.

There were more newspaper, television and radio queries. I arranged a schedule. It was apparent that reporters were following up each other's stories, without having gone to the web site. One charming Irishman spent some time questioning me before it became apparent he did not know what a microlight looked like, he didn't know who Alcock and Brown were, and he may have known where Shannon was because he lived only 20 miles from it. There was a priceless remark from a Canadian radio producer who asked how long the St John's to Shannon flight would take, and when told, with luck, 24 hours, asked, "is that all?".

Dinner was a T-bone steak, entertainment was "Chitty-chitty-bang-bang" on the television, and the rest of the evening was spent watching my fears emerge, isolating each one of them, and calming them down. It was a familiar occupation. When you are not naturally brave and have to work at each individual situation, there was a whole process that I had evolved to cope with all those forces that try and stop things happening.

In the George Mallory biography I had got through the war years, and the first expedition to Everest in 1921, and I was in the middle of reading about the second expedition a year later. In the account of the first, you could see by the behaviour of many of the participants how, having created an Empire, we had also evolved attitudes that made the losing of it inevitable. The deep divisions between the aims of the Royal Geographical Society (of which I was a Fellow), and the Alpine Club, jointly organising the first expedition, made any sensible attempt at climbing Everest impossible. There was a similar quality to the second expedition, but because the characters liked each other and had a sense of humour, it did much better and was more focused on the climb.

I do not think anything like enough research has been done into the pressures within groups involved in adventures, and those forces that tend to destroy them. In any group brought together to do something, there is also, often unconsciously, a will to frustrate it being done. The previous year I had written a book about what went wrong on my flight around the world three years ago. I tried to discover why I ended up all on my own in Nome, Alaska, without a partner and soon, without a sponsor, to ascertain whether it was possible to see that process happening much earlier in the adventure and head it off. I also wanted to know why the whole process was so destructive. I called the book *"The Down Time Days"*, because it was in the days when we were not flying that the destructive forces were most potent. I could see in the men brought together on those early Everest expeditions how the very choices doomed the success of the event.

This was the last night of peace of mind on the whole flight.

On Friday, June 8th, I found an e-mail from Liam, who had been negotiating for days with Transport Canada after the debacle in Halifax. He was reporting on the case, apparently prepared by Gleave after June 2, defending the changes I had made to the Flyer to enable her to fly the Atlantic. Four days earlier, Liam had said: "Just for the record, if I had handled this Canadian thing myself from the beginning, it would have been done by now." That day's e-mail was much more foreboding:

> *I have just had a long chat with Chris (Finnigan of the BMAA) and Jim (Cunliffe, of Mainair). Jim said he will phone you so I am sure he will relate to you what he said to me about the likelihood of the CAA granting an exemption. Chris was of the same opinion, almost a definite "no go" from the CAA. Now just a personal plea. I know that you are sometimes willing to risk all for the adventure. However, you are not alone in this and if laws and rules are broken then a lot of well-intentioned people and organisations will*

be implicated and affected by your actions. Sometimes adventures work and sometimes they don't Therefore I ask you, personally, not to do anything illegal that goes against the Canadian aviation regulations.

Outside, it had dawned foggy. I talked to the weather forecaster, who opened the possibility that I could get into St Johns that day. There was a low pressure area moving north, bringing a north-west air-flow to Stephenville that afternoon. I was flying south east, so it would be a tail-wind. At St Johns, the wind was forecast south-westerly, still OK. He warned me that in such conditions there was always, in any direction of landing, light to moderate turbulence on the approach to the runway, but who cared? I was on the verge of finally reaching the start line, to settle and prepare for the big one that had haunted my dreams for months.

It would be so civilised, having to leave after noon. That meant I would have time for the national radio interview that had been set up. I told myself not to burst into song.

Later that morning, I checked out of the hotel, all my gear packed for flight, and went to get another weather check. While it was a moderate north-west wind, cloudbase was 800 feet and I had peaks of more than a thousand feet to cross. I thought it prudent to wait until the afternoon to get into the air. St Johns, on such a wind, was only 4 hours away.

At 2pm I was asked to call Kim Threathaway at Transport Canada, the Canadian equivalent of the CAA. I found a phone with difficulty, sweating in my flying gear. He set up a conference call with three other officials, Marty Plumpstead, Claude Daigle and David Alton. I had talked to the first two, and Liam had been negotiating with them, but Alton was new. Claude started off. He told me he had issued me a Canadian validation of my Permit to Fly last Saturday, June 2, while I was in Halifax, which enabled me to fly a microlight in Canada.

On Monday, two days later, Claude was involved with other officials and with Liam in sorting out permissions, belatedly, because of David Gleave's behaviour, or to exemptions within the operating requirements for the Atlantic Crossing.

Claude now said he was suspending that validation.

"Does this mean I must stop, pack up and go home?" I asked.

A voice replied, "That is certainly one of your options."

10

More Down-Time Days

"What's the other option?" I asked.

"You need valid authority from the British CAA, an exemption, or a temporary exemption for some other reason, from your Permit to Fly," said Claude Daigle.

It had to be a written exemption, of course (and on a Friday night, 6pm in London, it would be impossible to even query that for at least two whole days).

This was the Flight Authority part of the official objections

There was a second series of objections to my flight because of the Atlantic crossing rules, regulations governing single-engined aircraft. They said they were not able to exempt people from these rules.

They objected to my flight for safety reasons, saying bluntly that they thought I was not safe. These were their specific objections:

1. *I was not IFR rated, I did not have an Instrument Rating.*
2. *I had no HF radio set, just two VHF radios.*
3. *I had no artificial horizon, an "attitude indicator", normally driven by a gyro.*
4. *I had no gyro compass*
5. *I was restricted to flying below 5,500 feet; above that I needed to be IFR rated.*

Liam had already replied to these queries. Briefly, the answers were:

1. *I had no IFR rating, but I had flown in IFR conditions for dozens of hours on the world flight. I had more experience of this type of flying on flex-wings than anyone else in the world except possibly Colin Bodill. Also, you cannot get an IFR rating on a microlight, because it does not have enough instruments for the regulations.*

2. *HF radio doesn't work on flex-wing aircraft. It is an aerial problem. I had spent thousands of pounds trying to modify my aircraft to accept a HF radio for the world flight, and it had been a failure. I intended to communicate by VHF with the hundreds of airliners that passed overhead on the Atlantic route.*

3. On a flex-wing, an artificial horizon continually "topples" because of the nose-up attitude of the aircraft. Because of its pendular capacity, a flex-wing is naturally stable. It does not spin and stalls only with difficulty; it must be forced into one. I had flown for hours in cloud, with safety, on a turn-and-bank indicator, which indicated the position of my wings. My experience led me to say that an artificial horizon was worse than useless on a flexwing; it was added weight and took up valuable room on the dashboard.

4. I had no gyro compass, a leftover from World War 2, because I used the magnetic compass as a poor third to the directions indicated by the three GPS's I was carrying. I believed this rule was introduced before GPS became common.

5. I accept these restrictions on the height I could fly.

They also wanted answers to queries they had put to David Gleave back in April, which Gleave had never put to me or Liam, and for which the Canadians had no answers:

Did I have an oil pressure gauge? (yes).

Was the coolant temperature indicated? (yes)

Did I have internal lights? (yes, a dashboard light and 3 torches tied to me, how else would you light so open a cockpit?).

Did I have a positioning light? (No, but they were easy to install, and when I needed to use them, 800 miles from anywhere, who cared that I was lit up at night?).

Did I have pitot heating? (Only by putting my warm hand on the pitot tube, the inlet for the air speed indicator, which was next to me in the cockpit. And with three GPS's, who cared on a flex-wing about air speed, because the GPS gave the true speed?)

Did I have alternate static? (No, I had so second electrical system. But then, I was far less reliant on engine instruments than GA pilots, aside from the GPS. I did have dual ignition on the engine).

Was Transport Canada throwing the book at me, and insisting on every single one of their regulations?

Four microlight pilots had traversed Canada on flights that ended with an Atlantic crossing, all without the slightest objection from Transport Canada. This time, for some reason, it was different.

Liam invited me to consider whether what I was writing on the Internet about the personal fears I had about the flight, had provoked Transport Canada into taking a hard line. I thought it was a loss of patience worn thin by the behaviour of David Gleave in ignoring problems they raised months ago. But Liam had to sort it out. That was his job.

Claude told me that when I went back to the British CAA, I would be asking for approval for an operating weight 30% higher than previously approved.

He also told me his validation document allowing me to fly a microlight in Canada would not be re-instated unless I had specific CAA approval for my aircraft.

One of the other officials then formally said that unless I obeyed the rules they had laid down, they had the authority to detain me and the aircraft.

I presumed that meant jail.

I had been held up on my flight around the world a number of times. I knew that Jennifer Murray and Colin Bodill, on their world flight the previous year, had all sorts of problems with Russia. This was despite Jennifer knowing people like former US Secretary of State Henry Kissinger, and Charles Powell, the former foreign policy adviser to Mrs Thatcher. These bureaucratic delays were a regular feature of modern flights across the world, and for a long time in Newfoundland I saw what was happening to me in the same light. But it was not like that.

I thought I had a simple case. Of the four microlight pilots who had traversed Canada successfully on flights that ended with an Atlantic crossing, all the crossings ended successfully. The flights were done openly, with the knowledge of the authorities. I was the first to make such a flight, entering Canada at Beaver Creek in the Yukon Territory on June 15, 1998, and exiting at Bellingham, BC, on June 19. I re-entered Canada at St Hubert, Montreal on July 3, and exited from Broughton Island off Baffin Island on July 10. The following year Mike Blythe and Olivier Aubert came from South America on flex-wing microlights and exited from Pangmirtung for Greenland. In 2000, in company with helicopter pilot Jennifer Murray, Colin Bodill flew a microlight Blade 912 along roughly the route I took. None of these flights were banned by the Canadian authorities.

It was on those precedents that I was able to raise the money to make my own Atlantic flight, and involve the charity The Artificial Heart Fund. I had had no indication that these sort of problems would arise with Canada. It was not fair for Canadian officials to say, as they were saying about the previous flights, "that was then and this is now."

There was no substantial difference between our aircraft then and my aircraft now. The only difference was the level of public interest. I did not believe, then, that the authorities had allowed the previous flights because no one noticed, and would not allow me this time because some journalists had decided our type of flying was a story.

The whole affair was an offence to natural justice.

I spent the afternoon in a state of shock. It was similar to the feelings I had in Yuzhno-Sakhalinsk in Russia, when the authorities grounded me there, too. At the end of that incarceration I had lost my co-pilot Keith, but my organiser, Charles, was still in there fighting. Where was I going to start the fight here?

I placated the various journalists who phoned by telling the truth, that I had paperwork problems, but I did not outline in detail how serious they were. I spent the evening alone, writing notes to myself about how this situation evolved, and had a solitary pizza and root beer at the bar. Not a brilliant Friday night.

On Saturday morning, I resolved to fight.

I discovered as the days and weeks developed that I was in one of the weakest areas of Newfoundland to put up a decent public battle. There were no television link points in Stephenville, and every time I went on television I had to be driven for an hour to the city of Corner Brook. The same applied to radio, though the phone was useful here. Was it by design that I had been grounded there, instead of in St Johns?

I spent the weekend reading the original accounts on my tiny lap-top computer of the down-time days I had spent in Russia, and trying to achieve the same patient frame of mind I had then. Then, I had used the Russian media shamelessly because it had no effect on my sponsor. I was not sure I could do that now. I went through the same emotions of frustration and despair in Stephenville as I had gone through in Russia, but shot through with hope and determination. The irony was that my difficulties were multiplied greatly by officials claiming to be acting in what they said was my own best interests (which they claimed were served by stopping me making the flight). I feared even then being so exhausted by the bureaucratic fight that it would materially affect me when the flight actually occurred. I never allowed myself to admit that the flight would not happen.

Liam thought there was no point in fighting on Sunday, but gathered what contacts he could. Sean Sheppard invited me to his home to meet his wife

Roxanne, and his two children, James and Jade, the names, oddly, of my own children. An unbearable irony was that, after all those days when the weather was too bad for me to fly to St John's, the whole weekend was sunny with light westerlies.

On Monday, June 10th, I started the political wheel rolling, with Liam pulling all the strings he could in England. Sean told me how politics worked in Canada, who the local MP was, a man called Bill Matthews, and I started to prepare a case for him to fight for me (in all the time I was there, I never once had a reply from Matthews about my pleas).

That was the first day I heard from Phil Hoskins, a school teacher at the little town called Baie D'Espoir, 131 miles away overland on a direct line between Stephenville and St Johns, but as the road went, at least 10 hours drive away. I called Baie D'Espoir the Bay of Despair (it may have been Bay of Hope). Phil and his ninth-grade children had been using my flight from New York to Paris as a history and geography project, following it on my web-site, excited at each day the tiny dot moved across the map of eastern Canada at a speed no more than a car. They were, said Phil, very upset at the delay, and threw themselves into writing to members of parliament and ministers, arguing that I should be allowed to continue. I resolved that, whatever happened on my flight, I would fly in one day to see those children, whose views were touching:

> "They let others go so why not Mr.Milton?"(Chelsea)(Jordan)
> "Is Canada really a free country?"(Cassandra)
> "Why has Canada allowed him to travel so far into Canada already if his plane is illegal?(Ashley)
> "His plane is in perfect condition"(Mollie)
> "He has already flown around the world."(Shelby)
> "We want to see his plane over our school!"(Dillon)
> "If he cannot fly across Newfoundland, what was the point in letting him start?"(Dylan)

It became a feature of this flight, in a way it had been in no other of my adventures, that the web site excited comment. I found the messages of encouragement helpful, in that they bolstered my morale, but there were also nastier comments coming in, criticising me for lack of preparation for the flight, and violently inviting me to go home. I had not been accustomed to this on previous adventures, living essentially in my own little world. I found e-mail useful for staying in touch with friends, but when some twerp on the web-site started to argue that I should not be allowed to fly into Shannon Airport in Ireland, because it was too big and important to take a tiny aircraft like mine, I decided not to bother looking at the chat page any longer. Phil Hoskins was one of the more useful contacts to come from the web-site.

On Tuesday, June 11th, Liam told me he had the situation in hand and I should wait for him to get clearances. He had prepared a "safety application" document to submit to the CAA:

> *I ran it past Richard Taylor (of the British Special Rules Group) and the Canadians on the phone and both agree with the content. Richard stated this is only the start of the process, i.e. merely to get the committee to discuss the principle of granting a special certificate, regardless of the technical issues involved. If they agree to take the matter further, then there will need to be in-depth discussions between the CAA and Mainair in order to document exactly what modifications have been made.*

There were stirrings among Canadian national newspapers, including Richard Foot of the Toronto-based *National Post*. I learned that Transport Canada were not actually putting up a spokesman to defend their decision, just issuing details of various paragraphs of regulations they said I was contravening. Two television crews turned up, and I went across to the Flyer each time to be interviewed. I had not seen her for a few days and was struck by how beautiful she was, despite the small garden shed of a fuel tank in the back seat. If I restored her to her original condition to allow her to fly in Canada, something we started to consider then as a temporary measure, she would be legal but it would be impossible to cross the Atlantic in her. As she was now, an Atlantic flight was feasible, but banned. If you have never heard of Catch 22, this was as good an example as any.

I was finding it odd that everyone assumed I would just pack up and go home. Where did people get such an idea? But there was one phone interview with a television station in which the presenter, a woman called Louisa, was discussing my predicament afterwards, and made the electrifying statement that I should try St Pierre, a small French island off the coast of Newfoundland which would not have the same regulations as Canada. This search for a French alternative weaves through the following three weeks, as I tried to escape the deadening clutch of Canadian bureaucracy. Liam took a dim view of the idea:

> *Sorry to be the voice of reason here, but the Canadian regulations 602.39 and 605.18 govern all flights leaving "Canadian domestic airspace over the high seas". Even if you take off from St Pierre, you will then have to fly through Canadian Domestic Airspace before getting to the Atlantic. Therefore, once again your Permit to Fly will be invalid and you will not be in compliance with the above mentioned regulations. Please ignore me if you think I am being silly.*

I knew that decisions were being made by the CAA in England, either to clarify the situation, or to see if an exemption was possible. Liam phoned on Wednesday afternoon, sounding resigned, and said it was not a good decision. No formal statement had been issued, but officials at home would not endorse the changes I had made to the Flyer. Liam had quite suddenly become despondent, as if it was all over.

I would not believe we were giving in.

Wednesday was also the first time I met an English doctor, Terry Dennis, who became so important to me later in the flight. He invited me to dinner the following evening.

I spent the evening alone, finishing my first reading of Homer's *Odyssey*; the scene in which he deals with Penelope's suitors is powerful and chilling. There were many points of morality I did not understand, and while I was diverted from the flight, resolved to sort out with Stephen Lewis. It was a bit like long range chess, to take my mind off my painful situation.

On June 13th, Liam resigned.

> *This is a very difficult letter for me to write and I know that the timing may not be perfect, but it is best to give you as much notice as possible. In addition, please read through this letter at least twice before hitting the roof and firing off angry e-mails. Due to some very personal reasons, I am afraid that after June 22nd I will not be able to continue working for you in the same capacity as I have been up to this point. I will not be able to co-ordinate all the various activities that are currently in process … one would hope that the current crisis will have passed by then … I will continue to update the website until the challenge is completely over … I do not expect any payment for this … I will, of course, follow your progress with immense interest and hope that the small part that I have played will have contributed to your success … PS: I will inform Nikki King and Paul Loach of this decision.*

Liam did not tell Paul what had happened until much later. His departure left me isolated, cut off, and fighting alone. I cannot say I was impressed.

As the debate washed to and fro, and I answered e-mails and paced the floor, talking my morale up, I could feel the same forces acting on me as had worked in Russia. One difference was that Liam was now very concerned about his reputation with Transport Canada officials, with whom he felt he had established a rapport. Though I was still paying him as my own organiser to fight for me, he was terrifically affected by the legal arguments he heard, and not at all impressed by the political ones. Inside this sea of red tape, close to drowning, I felt isolated.

Liam did send what he called was good news, that the British CAA had unofficially taken the view that they would not proactively make a move to stop this flight going ahead on the basis that it was a one-off record attempt. The problem was that, being unofficial, this would not be enough to persuade the Canadians to relax their regulations.

We got bogged down over the next few days over approval for the changes I had made to my aircraft. It is not worth going into all the hopes raised and dashed by the various moves made, but in the time scale of the flying season for the Atlantic, which had to end by the middle of August, it proved impossible. In the end, no legally water-tight way forward was found.

I think Liam would argue on his side that he saw that was going to happen to me long before I did, and whatever his protestations about "very personal reasons" this may have affected his resignation. Much later, after the flight was over, he began to try and make the case that none of the permissions process was his primary responsibility; it was really press and public relations.

Meanwhile, on June 15th, two days after his resignation was offered, he sent the following e-mail:

> *Two weeks ago I saw a man die. I watched as his aircraft dived towards the ground and then explode right in front of me at the Biggin Hill Airshow. It was not a pleasant thing to witness and highlighted the knife-edge that all aviators tread every time they take to the skies. You have achieved so much in your aviation career and you have so many well wishers, followers and admirers. Everything seems to be telling you not to go on this flight. Maybe it is time to quit while you are ahead, return to the drawing board and plan it all for a later date. The exhaustion of the fight cannot be doing you any good in your preparations for this most gruelling of challenges.*

More Down-Time Days   161

I cannot say I was pleased to get this e-mail from someone prepared to leave me on my own in the middle of one of the worst holes I had ever fallen into. I replied:

> *It is at moments like these that you don't give up. I have been here so many other times before. It is obvious that you haven't. I think the chances of dying here are much less than they were on the world flight. I did the fighting then after 60 wearying days on the road, and when the fighting in Russia was over, went on for another 41 days flying. I am not interested in giving up. I don't know what will happen to my appeal. I do know that in reaching the Minister of Transport today for it, I did so through the Regional Director of Transport Canada. His last words to me were, "good luck". The thing is, he meant it.*
>
> *I have lost nearly a dozen friends in aviation, Liam, and it never changed my own commitment. Once I lost my best friend on a hang gliding hill, with him flying a hang glider he had offered to me five minutes before he died on it. Alvin Russell, Keith Cockroft, Pepe Lopez, Chris Bulger, Paul Renouf, Didier Favre, Willi Muller, Stu Smith, these would just be names to you, they were faces and friends to me. One day I am going to die. Believe me, it will happen to you, too. But while I'm alive, there are values I want to fight for, and this is one of them. It got much worse in Russia before it got better. We were alone then. Keith Reynolds felt as you did, and began plotting a different end to the flight. Is that the way you want to go? What sort of a life do you think I would have if I walk away from this one like this? It is now a straight-forward political fight. Once in Ireland, Jim Cunliffe can come out with a truck and a spanner and change me back. I am going head to head here – Keith used the terms Walter Mitty at a similar attitude, would you like to as well? – to see where this thing breaks. Canada was not built by bureaucrats. It was built by men, and in circumstances like this, men fight. I am fighting. I know you're walking away, but don't invite me to walk away with you. I am not paying you to maintain your reputation with Transport Canada. When we are set to lose the game, tell me, who cares about your reputation with Transport Canada? Why is it of any importance at all? Please don't send me any more letters with "I've seen men die" lines. I've seen friends die, but I wouldn't dream of using that fact to kill off a man's dream …*

Impatient, battered, frustrated, I decided on June 15th to try and cut the Gordian Knot and, as I told Liam, appeal directly over the head of the officials to the Minister of Transport in Canada, David Collenette. The officials had said they had no leeway in the regulations to make an exemption, but a politician was not governed by the same rules. I did so in a long letter, outlining the arguments I have already cited, and quoting the previous precedents. I ended:

> ..."I have secured from Lloyds of London a US$400,000 "search and rescue" insurance policy, so there would be no "search"; in the unlikely event I would ditch, I would be within a few miles of the last GPS tracker signal, and easily found by Locat beacon. I also have US$1,000,000 third party insurance. It is no intention of mine to be any drain on the Canadian tax-payer ... In exercising your judgement, I would ask you to take into consideration the history of big international microlight flights through Canada (and I quoted the precedent of four previous flights across Canada and across the Atlantic, my own, Mike Blythe's, Olivier Aubert's and Colin Bodill's) ... Both Colin and I were awarded the Britannia Trophy by the Royal Aero Club, the highest award in the Club's gift, for our flights, from the Club's president, Prince Andrew. We were awarded Diamond Colibris by the FAI, again the highest such award, and I was given that year's Segrave Trophy, the rarest of all adventure trophies, and seldom awarded these days. We would not have been so honoured had the authorities thought we had broken the law ... I wish to appeal those flights as precedent. If we four were allowed through over the past three years, why am I being turned down now? I have risked US$100,000 of my own and my sponsor's money on that precedent, and think the official response to this query, "that was then and this is now", is an inadequate one. How can one plan anything in Canada on such an arbitrary interpretation of the laws? ... The history of the great flights in Mainstream Aviation is littered with corpses. It is not so with us. Since the beginning in 1971 of the New Aviation, of which, in microlights, I am a part, we have been attempting to emulate the great flights of the pioneers, but we are taking flight in a different direction. We will never grow up to be Jumbos. One day a man will attempt to fly around the world, powered by the sun; it will be to the flights of Bodill, Blythe, Aubert and I hope, me, that they will look for experience (indeed, I hope that man will be me). In all our endeavours on the great flights, we have a 100% safety record. No one has been killed, and while there have been accidents, they have been repaired and the pilots flown on to success ... I have more experience of this type of flying than any man in the world with the exception of Colin Bodill. I am pleading with you to recognise that experience, and the judgement which has taken me through extremely difficult flying conditions to

safety and success, and allow me to make the two flights that are in your power to allow to happen ... "

Meanwhile, I set out in a long range search for a replacement for Liam, before finally deciding that I could conduct the fight myself. It was not going to be resolved by any help from England and the CAA there. I had to sort it out myself.

As well as the letter to Mr Collenette, I also conducted a public relations campaign, patiently outlining to radio, television and newspaper reporters the measures I was taking to ensure my safety, and that I was not a drain on the Canadian tax-payer. One result of this campaign was that Canada's equivalent of *The Times* – the *Toronto Globe & Mail* – carried a half-page article on the dilemma I was in. But much more importantly, it also carried an Editorial:

LET THE ADVENTURER SOAR

What does it take to raise money for charity by flying solo across the Atlantic in a tiny, open-cockpit microlight aircraft? More than just skill and a wealth of experience. It also requires permission from the aviation authorities. Hence the plight of British pilot Brian Milton, who finds himself stranded in the small Newfoundland town of Stephenville.

A 58-year old adventurer whose hefty resume includes a 120-day round-the-world odyssey in a microlight plane in 1998, Mr Milton is anxious to duplicate the 1919 transatlantic journey of his countrymen Alcock and Brown. Such a feat would not just add to the roster of historic flights he and like-minded pilots have been emulating over the years, but would also, Mr Milton hopes, raise money for Britain's Artificial Heart Fund.

For the moment the mission is grounded, and the problem lies in Mr Milton's three-metre long Mainair Blade plane. It doesn't include the instruments required by the regulations for flying "blind" through clouds, and it has violated safety standards by being modified to carry a particularly large gas tank with sufficient fuel for the 3,200 kilometre trip from St John's to Ireland's Shannon airport.

Transport Canada has therefore denied Mr Milton approval to take off. Discussions are under way between the department, Britain's Civil Aviation Authority and the plane's manufacturer to see whether a one-time exception can be made to the usual rules.

164   Chasing Ghosts

> *Let's hope so. Mr Milton is no reckless neophyte in such risky ventures. His preparations include a US$400,000 insurance policy covering the cost of any search and rescue operation, should his unusual craft glide down into the Atlantic. With a tracking device aboard, he would not be hard to find. He is also willing to sign a waiver freeing authorities from any liability.*
>
> *Agreed, aviation safety regulations are essential. But an exception could and should be made in such a clearly special case, rescuing Mr Milton from the sea of red tape and propelling him up into the blue.*

I was pretty certain that the word "adventurer" was not one that Transport Canada could listen to without a shudder, but I had to accept the label. I thought if I attracted enough public sympathy, it might also work on officials. If it did not work there, then it was possible with a democratically elected politician like Mr Collenette.

That Friday evening, June 15th, facing the emptiness of a weekend when I could not continue the fight, I started to read the account of Amundsen and Scott's journey to the South Pole. I was horrified at the destruction of my mythical hero in Roland Huntford's "The Last place on Earth". This had caused a terrific fuss when it was published because it was so scathing about Scott's incompetence and motives. There was an inevitability about the hatchet job Huntford did on Scott, one of my schoolboy heroes. Back then, in the 1950s we were taught naturally about people like Scott, Gordon of Khartoum, George Mallory, Mafeking, the Relief of Ladysmith, the Sepoy Mutiny, and the residual knowledge remained with me. In modern history classes, instead of seeing Nelson's place in the history of Pax Britannica and the nineteenth century, children are asked what the victory would mean to a black, dyslexic, one-legged, lesbian, unmarried mother of six? The answers are thought worth grading.

Yet the accounts of Mallory's climb up Everest, and of Scott's attempt at the Pole, rang appallingly true. The same type of characters, Establishment figures I was running across, somehow wormed themselves to the centre of adventures and buggered them up back then. The attitudes that destroyed these great adventures were the same attitudes I was running into, when saving face and the letter of the law take precedence over common sense and an imaginative approach. Scott, of course, was deeply flawed, and Mallory was a much more attractive character. But at bottom, both had in abundance the one quality that crosses all cultural barriers, courage. It was not really enough, but without it nothing actually worked. As Churchill put it, "Courage is rightly esteemed the first of human qualities because it is the quality which guarantees all others." The fault with Huntford's book was that Amundsen was almost a perfect idealised hero, while Scott was portrayed as an out-and-out rotter. Life was not like that.

Eppo Harbrink Numan phoned that weekend. Eppo, a Dutchman, had been thundering into my chat pages, being rude to critics, as full of passion as ever. I had seen an account but never a book, about his flight across the Atlantic in a microlight, the first man ever to do so. He was helped at the time by the Canadian authorities, of all people, when he was having similar hassles to me; his were with the Danes. Contacts with the then Canadian Premier, Brian Mulroney, produced a letter from Transport Canada which enabled Eppo to get to Greenland and then into Northern Canada. He had intended to fly on around the world, the flight I made in 1998, but the Russian and Chinese authorities defeated him then as they so nearly did me. Eppo stopped in New York, my current start-point.

Eppo urged me to keep the faith, to stay strong. He said he had been two and a half months in one hotel in Iceland (how did he pass the time without going mad?) waiting until he had found the right button to punch to get his flight up and running once more. This did not cheer me up. The authorities there, as the authorities in Canada, kept maintaining the threadbare fiction they were concerned for his safety.

Sunday, June 17th, was the second of the lost days, and I tried to ration my time so I did not go insane with frustration. I got out of bed an hour later than normal, had a leisurely breakfast, and sat through the morning reading, with growing horror, the contrast between Amundsen's journey to the South Pole, and that of Robert Falcon Scott. The Norwegian did everything right, the Englishman did everything wrong. I reached the middle of the account of Amundsen's run from his base camp on the Bay of Wales, where, having reached the plateau prior to their final run on the Pole, thanks to the magnificent efforts of their Greenland dogs, they then shot half the dogs and fed the bodies to themselves and the remaining dogs, during two days of resting and feeding. They had always intended to have the dogs with them for food. Part of me feared what my own sentimental countrymen would do with the pathetic horses they had brought with them, and the two vehicles (you cannot eat a car), when I was to get to the account of Scott's endeavours.

It was not difficult to compare the thinking that doomed Scott's journey with the thinking that was holding me up. Amundsen looked at the Antarctic, saw it clearly, and planned his journey with the minimum of sentiment and historical baggage. He was nimble, preferred small instead of large, and changed quickly if circumstances dictated. Scott was stuck in out-moded forms of thought, preferred big rather than small, and failed to learn any lessons from experience.

Later, I had a call from a Canadian ultralight pilot, David Edward, upset that I had been blocked for nine days. David, a former airline pilot who had turned to ultralights, knew nothing about what was happening. He promised help by mobilising other aviators around Toronto, and threw himself into getting me free.

That day "Terry McQuade" phoned. I had never met him, but John Hunt had told me he was being spectacularly rude about everything to do with my flight on the web site. He had been criticising me daily, and was obviously miffed I did not reply. McQuade found my hotel phone number and started the argument live with a genuine listener that he could not have on the Internet. He claimed to be an experienced pilot with dozens of Atlantic crossings to his name, and an instrument rating, and he said he feared the effect of Atlantic winds on my trike. His experience of trike flying was zero. He was speaking as a GA pilot, and seemed to hold the common view that trikes were delicate little flowers and cannot take rough weather. It was a conversation in which I listened a great deal, and he repeated a number of times that he was not looking for a confrontation. I thanked him afterwards for his comments, which I also think he found not very satisfactory.

The fact remained that I had no IFR, and my aircraft had been changed to make it capable of flying the Atlantic, but those changes would not be approved. They were the only way that aircraft that evolved out of hang gliding were going to make such journeys. I suppose McQuade did not notice all the other trikes going through the USA and Canada on the way to an Atlantic crossing, or they too would have been the object of his concern. None of those pilots were IFR, and all had aircraft outside the strict envelope of a Permit to Fly. All made it successfully.

But I had to confront, philosophically, why I was alienated by McQuade's comments. If one compared aviation to mountaineering, the difference between General Aviation and microlighting was like the difference between Sir John

Hunt's team-assault on Everest in 1953, and Reinhold Messner's solo effort, without oxygen and other support, in the late 1970s. I had come across the Atlantic three weeks earlier in an airliner, and sat in the cockpit with the pilots. They were surrounded by instruments, 35,000 feet above the Atlantic, the control column moving on its own with an automatic pilot, disembodied voices telling them where they were and what to do. It was like being in a sealed office, with a lovely view, but you could hardly call the experience *flying*. They were going through the atmosphere, certainly, but they were cut off from it, sealed up, breathing second-hand air.

Was this really the apotheosis of the dreams of Daedelus, the designs of Leonardo da Vinci, the sacrifices of Otto Lilienthal?

McQuade was American, where GA flying is cheap, but in England and France microlights made up one third of all registered aircraft. We evolved from the purest form of flying there is, foot-launched hang gliders, and we learned different lessons from general aviation. It was not just that our flying was cheaper, it was culturally different. Our approach was described by Dr Paul Macready, one of the fourteen pioneers who began hang gliding 30 years earlier, as "quick and dirty". Macready had made the breakthrough in man-powered flight because he approached it from hang gliding. Within a year of starting work he had cracked the Kremer Prize for a mile-long figure-of-eight flight that had eluded mainstream flyers for decades. Macready took that approach (to which I was obviously sympathetic) into sun-powered flight, and those of us who wanted to fly big sun-powered journeys will have to go to him when we want one built. But could you imagine the reaction of Transport Canada to the prospect of someone turning up there planning to fly the Atlantic? (it will happen one day).

My method of flying in cloud, on a stable flex-wing machine that did not stall or spin, actually worked. I could negotiate IFR weather as easily as any other small-plane pilot. I was attracted to this type of flying because it took flight back to its roots, wind in the face, big-effort flight, a test of physicality, aesthetically far different from the clinical and mechanical methods that have evolved in GA flying. If I was planning to make my journey over the water, as Atlantic oarsmen (Chay Blythe) and canoeists (Peter Bray) and even swimmers (Guy Delage) had done, there was nothing the authorities could or would do to stop me. But because I was using the air, once thought free but in reality regulated nigh unto death, powers were assumed to stop me and imprison me if I tried. It also opened me to the unasked-for criticism of the

McQuades of this world whose expressed concern for my welfare I doubted (I was a stranger to him). It was an affront to natural justice, and I hoped Canadians would come to think so.

All the following week I waited for news from David Collenette. I heard he had gone to the Paris Air Show, ironically at Le Bourget where Lindbergh landed in 1927, and where I also planned to land. Eppo Numan tracked him down, and my friend Dave Simpson, who was also there, bearded Mr Collenette and pleaded on my behalf. Canada's Transport Minister indicated the matter was in hand, but must have thought there was no way of escaping me.

The *Globe & Mail's* direct rival, the *National Post*, published a mean-spirited article about my flight, inferring I was stupid to even attempt it. The reporter, Richard Foot, though he claimed to me later that he supported my flight and wished it to go ahead, wrote a long piece casting doubts on the quality of my air/sea rescue insurance. He also paraded concern for the alleged threats to safety of the rescue services who would have to pull me out of the water, this after recording the views of the rescue chief who said how much he loved his job. The article linked my flight with the efforts of Peter Bray, who had already tried to cross the Atlantic by kayak the previous year and been rescued, and was lined up for a second go. We were, said Mr Foot, going to be a drain on Canadian tax-payers, whatever efforts I made to avoid that.

(In passing, the day we stop the Peter Brays of this world is the day we should acknowledge we have moved to a Taliban style of government).

Meanwhile, I was struggling through the awful account of Scott and Amundsen's journeys to the South Pole. It was not because it was unreadable but because the flaws in Scott which killed his companions as well as him seemed so inevitable and horrifyingly incompetent. The forces that countered this and made a hero of him were also inevitable, given doubts in England at that time about our role in the world, and the challenge of Germany. Because Amundsen was a genius in his field and coped so well with all the privations, so much so that they did not seem like suffering at all, he did not emerge as the sort of hero England really took to. We liked people to suffer, and to do so in style, maintaining a stiff upper lip but also coyly revealing the extent of their torture. Scott was superb at doing this. His brilliant account of a deeply flawed expedition is far more readable than Amundsen's rather dull account of a brilliant expedition.

I particularly took to the character of Oates, the man famous for (allegedly) saying, "I'm going out, I may be gone for some time", and then leaving the tent to walk off and die. These were lines which had thrilled me as a child. His body was never found, it is still out there, and his mother always saw Scott as a murderer. I think Scott involved all his men in his own collective death wish at the end, it was the only way to salve his reputation, but the book's explanation for Scott's hold on the imagination of his colleagues (supposedly Naval discipline) was not convincing. He must have been charismatic as well as flawed.

Oddly, Huntford's account had no trace of the most famous lines to come out of Scott's expeditions, those Scott wrote when he knew he was going to die: *"Had we lived I should have had a tale to tell of the hardihood, endurance, and courage of my companions which would have stirred the heart of every Englishman. These rough notes and our dead bodies must tell the tale."* I had to search libraries later to actually find those lines. It weakened Huntford's premise that he dropped these lines.

Sean Sheppard that evening introduced me to two flying friends, Al and Debbie Skinner, who showed me their Cessna 172 and went to have a look at my own Flyer. Al, a big man with a beard who worked for Air Canada, had tried hang gliding when he was a younger man but settled on 3-axis flying. As ever, he was personally sympathetic to my plight. We discussed solutions, without coming to one.

In those circumstances, I was forced to reconsider an alternative flight to the Atlantic. One reluctant option was the Coney Run, suggested by Jim Cunliffe and Liam, and rejected earlier by me. I could remove all the changes I made to enable my Flyer to cross the Atlantic, and put back on the original fittings the Mainair Blade 912 had when it was built. This would re-conform to conditions in the written Permit to Fly. Transport Canada could nominate an official to examine it. Then, with the month of July still ahead of me, I could head south out of Canada, and no longer concern the Canadian authorities. The Coney Run would be a possible solution.

All the research for this adventure was done, I had media contact numbers, airfields, regional lists of ultralight clubs that could help, the historical research videoed. It would not take long to make this happen, so long as I got away from Newfoundland in a flying machine I could use. It could be completed by the middle of July. I would rather have done the Atlantic, but if I didn't I saw the Coney Run is an alternative. It was a sad second-best, but better than crawling home with nothing achieved. But Paul Loach and his partners were not interested in the Coney alternative. In the event, the Coney Run became a smoke screen, effective because I knew so much about it that I could string it out across my web-site. That was weeks ahead yet.

On Tuesday, June 19th, I e-mailed the National Post reporter, Richard Foot, objecting to the article he had written. He said I would be surprised at some of the criticism my flight had aroused, and which he had not used directly. Pressed on this, he claimed one major critic was my own organiser, Liam Abramson! Foot claimed Liam had told him I had not prepared adequately to make the flight. I put this comment to Liam, and, wearily, he denied it. I was not able to make any judgements on this.

After lunch, Al Skinner turned up and offered me a ride to St Pierre in his beloved Cessna 172. I had been corresponding with the French Airport chief there, Regis Lourme, so I leapt at the chance to meet him. Unfortunately, I was not able to get through to him to let him know I was coming.

I spent the afternoon looking down at a beautiful and wild Newfoundland from 4,000 feet, above most of the thermals, in the sort of weather novices pray for. The land seemed to roll on forever, with the occasional logging road cut into it. At St Pierre, I found Mr Lourme was in town on other business, so I talked over my dilemma with an English-speaker in the control tower, Yann Delamaire. The flight back from Wintertown, halfway to St Johns, took more than two hours, which was a long time for Al, who sat back and smoked cigarettes from time to time, but it was just a settling-in period with me. It brought home to me how much long-distance microlight flying is an affair of the mind.

All through this period my frustrations were compounded whenever the weather was good, and felt better when it was not. Every day I looked at the sky and made calculations about how long it would take me to get to St Johns. If it was less than five hours, as it often was, I imagined myself doing it, and sighed when I couldn't. If fog descended, or cloudbase was too low to get over the mountains to the east, I rationalised away the feeling that I had already served thirteen days imprisonment. Back in England, my friend Adrian Whitmarsh was monitoring the Atlantic weather. In his view, it had not been right for an Atlantic attempt, another source of comfort.

Another comfort was that I was making friends in Stephenville. Sean Sheppard, though much younger than me, looked after me like an elder brother. The real find was meeting Dr Terry Dennis and his family. Terry, a small charming man in his sixties, with a soft Yorkshire accent, had turned up at my hotel and invited me to a dinner at a local restaurant. He had been in Newfoundland twelve years, and seemed to have got into doctoring as a young man because it allowed him time to play rugby and tennis. He once had a trial for the great rugby league team, Wakefield Trinity, and he had been at the same school, two years ahead of the television journalist, Michael Parkinson (with whom I had worked at TV-am).

Terry fell in love with my flight. There is no other way to describe it. When he learned I was stuck, he gave me the keys to a hire car and told me to use it as long as I wished. Trying to return the compliment, I offered to cook for him and his family a beef stroganoff, and one evening I had the use of a kitchen. I met Terry's wife, Yvonne, terrifically English still after twelve years in Canada, and we toasted their 39th wedding anniversary, first in claret, and later in champagne, a Veuve Cliquot. Their attractive daughter Katrina pottered around the kitchen with me, helping with the food, and I tried to establish some sort of relationship with Katrina's daughters, 8-year old Angelisa and 6-year old Anna-Maria. Our conversation ranged around any number of subjects, not just my flight. It was telling how many local people who heard that I knew Terry Dennis who told me enthusiastically that he was their doctor, and how good a doctor he was. I thought he and Yvonne should write their own version of "A Year in Newfoundland" because of the stories they had of life there, with all the echoes of Peter Mayle's "A Year in Provence".

On Thursday, June 21, I was occupied with David Edward in Ontario, furiously lobbying his own MP, a Canadian Cabinet Minister. I also spent time looking at the legal implications of a formal waiver of responsibility, so that Canadian officials could not use this as a weapon (a waiver had been suggested by the editorial in the *Globe and Mail*). There was a QC in Stephenville, Fred Stagg, to whom I talked, and who was confident that, if I needed one, he had the precedents to draw on. We were of an age, he and I, though he thought initially I was rather younger. I think this impression was created by my hair, still having it, and it had not yet gone grey except at the edges.

Jim Cunliffe called to say that the package containing the makings to bring the Flyer back to its legal state had been sent, and was expected the following Tuesday, with three whole days in between. It included a 22 litre fuel tank to reduce my capacity to a tenth of what it was then. I resolved to wait to hear Mr

Collenette's verdict first. If he allowed my flight from Canada to Ireland, I would send the legal makings back. Meanwhile, if I needed to go back to a legal condition, it would only take a few hours to remove the two offending tanks, replace the seat frame with a standard version, drop in the seats to reconvert it to a two-seater again, adjust the fuel system and re-tie the skirt. The section cut out of the nose cone, not an integral part of the Permit to Fly definition, could be re-attached with gaffer tape. She would not be quite as pretty as she was when new, but she would be able to get into the air again and get out of the country.

For journalists, the story had gone quiet while we waited for Mr Collenette's opinion. They all urged me to stay in touch, but voiced criticism of my description of my stay there as "incarceration", as if I could be separated from my aircraft. I could not be. Where she was, I was too.

I felt there were much deeper issues of personal freedom involved in this case, aside from the pettifogging queries raised, and which I had to tackle, which were stopping my flight. I needed to articulate these issues, but I could not find the right words. I found it striking that, while in media discussion journalists struck poses or picked fastidiously through the issues, not one politician had expressed a view on my plight. It could be argued that I was a foreigner and too small an issue for politicians to dwell on, and perhaps that was the reason. Half way between waking and sleeping, in the early morning, I conducted such a debate, and the words flowed freely. In the cold light of day they came with more difficulty.

I went looking for books in Stephenville, as a punctuation before going back to read a second time the books I had brought with me. Sean Sheppard laughed when I asked if there was a book shop in a town of 11,000 people. Some books were on sale, westerns and romances, not my cup of tea at the local Wal-Mart. There was a sale of cast-off books at the local library. I bought Forster's *"A Passage to India",* and Steinbeck's *"The Grapes of Wrath"* along with a Maigret novel.

On Friday, June 24, David Edward told me about his conversations with Marty Plumpstead of Transport Canada; it was Plumpstead's committee which grounded me. David said that unless I was endorsed by the British CAA, Transport Canada would not move. I explained why that would not happen, how the CAA could not change its own regulations, and had coped with flyers like me and Colin Bodill in the past by the judicious use of a

Nelsonian blind eye. So long as no one forced the matter up their noses, or an accident happened, they stood back and watched. The only way out of a situation that Transport Canada had ignored four times in the past, but chosen to pick up with my flight, was to get a politician to make an exemption. I told David that was what politicians were supposed to be for, to make judgements, and why they were elected. Otherwise, officials could just run things. They knew the rules much better than any politicians. It was this discretion that the *Globe and Mail* editorial had appealed to the previous week.

That afternoon, I heard that Collenette had made his decision, but no one knew what it was. Because of the media row, there was a lot of crossing T's and dotting i's. Meanwhile, Transport Canada wanted a blue-print of the original status of my Flyer, which I sent off for from England. If I put the aircraft back into "Permit to Fly" condition, they wanted to know how I had done it, and what to measure it against.

Terry Dennis came around in the evening (I was well into "Maigret Rents a Room" by then), and we had a couple of beers and gossiped. Later I went to the local Holiday Inn for a steak, full of noisy night-life – teachers, I was told – and Terry turned up there too. We had a huge amount to talk about.

Saturday was a warm summer day, light winds from the west, and I wrestled with myself all morning, wondering what to do. Did I wait out to the bitter end, Collenette's reply, before modifying my aircraft? Unless there was a clear go-ahead I had to change the Flyer, and remove the two tanks that were causing such angst. At 2pm I decided I was going to prepare the Flyer to go back to its legal state. Implicitly, I had started to believe Collenette would say no. I got access through the local fire station chief, Denis Burke. Denis was of a mind, like a whole bunch of people on the web-site, for me to just *go for it* across the Atlantic. I told him, sadly, I had other flights to make, and it would not do to defy Transport Canada like that. I told him that morally, as well as legally, they had right on their side. It had, after all, been my decision to trust Liam, and through him, David Gleave.

In the Flyer, I had nearly 100 litres of fuel in the big tanks, and finding somewhere to put it was a problem. Denis lent me two fuel cans, which I took to the former ice rink which housed my aircraft. When I raised the door to see her, she looked potent and hopeful, ready to go, capable of the journey. I felt bad that I was removing that capacity, and returning her to be just an ordinary little aircraft again. I undid one of the fuel hoses, and watched the fuel drain out of her. It took more than two hours. Some went into the tank of the hire car, but most went into the tanks of Al Skinner's Cessna 172. I left 22 litres for the small tank I was going to install from England. I was able, solo, to remove the big tanks and the slipper tank, without any damage to the threads of the fuel joints. When they were lying on the ground, the Flyer looked as if she had been kippered. I left it like that, all the nuts and bolts in neat little piles, and the power points for various instruments, GPS, tracker, video camera, dangling from wires.

On Sunday, June 25th, I spent most of the day cooped up in the hotel, nowhere to go, poor weather, hour after hour reading first one book and then another. I could feel the edges of my mind go awry. There seemed to be mental states, more often than ten years ago, into which I drifted, in which I was fearful of everything. It had to do with perceptions of reality. It might, for example, be claustrophobic, a sudden feeling that I was hemmed in by the bounds of my own room. Outside, everything was normal. Inside, I could feel my breath shortening, and the thin edges of panic.

As soon as something sensible happened, like writing out a list of things to do, or going for a meal, or talking to someone, the feelings went away. I came to believe they were to do with helplessness, which is what I felt. Once the Flyer was able to take to the air again and I could head out of Canada, then these feelings may stop.

I oscillated between *"A Passage to India"*, and *"The Grapes of Wrath"*, neither the best of choices for a man in my position. Both were masterpieces, drawing you into the story and the human condition, but each outlined human weaknesses where I would rather have concentrated on my strengths. There was not much space in my little room to pace up and down, and there was too much equipment anyway. I sat at the computer and played various games, my mind in "parked", and otherwise chose different reading styles, sitting with my feet on the bed, on the table, or kneeling over the bed to read like a small boy at prayer. Occasionally I turned the television on, but the programmes were appalling. I consciously looked for old episodes of The Simpsons, as a visual comfort blanket.

Dr Terry Dennis phoned that evening and took me off to a former paper company hunting lodge, rustic and sprawling, built of wood with a nine-hole golf course next to it, by the side of Sir Harry's River. We ate poached salmon and talked nineteen to the dozen. In a remarkably short time, Terry had become a friend, with whom I was able to share confidences. This was absolutely necessary for me because, aside from the e-mails and occasional phone calls from friends thousands of miles away, I had no one else to bounce ideas off. Whatever confidences I might have shared with my organiser, Liam Abramson, disappeared when he resigned. Terry was a few years older than me, with a passion for flying, and also a curiosity and empathy with adventures. A good man to be in a trench with, Terry.

Monday June 25th was a national holiday in Canada, dedicated, ironically I thought, to its adventurous past. That meant another day's delay to my parcel from England. I swam a half-mile in the local swimming pool and felt good that despite no genuine exercise for days, I still was fit. At breakfast, Terry Dennis appeared, and together we visited the Flyer and removed both the offending tanks from the hangar, and took them away to Katrina's house to be sent overseas.

The weather was poor, with fog coming down and then half-lifting all day. Katrina introduced me to a pleasant walk through a park with all the trees and shrubs native to Newfoundland planted within it. Later she took me to the Canadian Legion Hall. It was filled with the faded photographs of young men of the district who went off to war for Britain, called across the seas to fight and die for causes never a direct concern of Canada's. I looked at the faces and wondered at the paths that had led them to their deaths.

There was a poster in one corner with the faces and details of the sixteen Canadians in the Second World War who had won Victoria Crosses, the highest of all decorations for courage. Nearly half the VC's were awarded posthumously. As I looked through the details I was struck by the fact that the poster had been issued on the orders of Canada's then-Minister of Defence, a man called David Collenette. Surely such a man, marking extraordinary acts of courage, would be sympathetic to my own modest aspiration towards the same qualities?

Why had he not replied?

On Tuesday, June 26, I got the official word. It was NO.

David Collenette decided *not* to use his power to exempt me from conditions imposed by Transport Canada. He did it in a rather clever way. His officials said that if the British CAA were flexible, then so would they be. That, of course, was impossible. It took months of work and tests to find an exemption to national aviation rules, by contrast to the simple political power Mr Collenette had to grant an exemption. A fax gave me the news, from Blake Johnston, Special Assistant, Atlantic Region, Office of the Minister of Transport, in response to a fax I had sent direct to Collenette:

> *"The Minister has asked me to respond on his behalf. I appreciate the urgency of your request for Canadian authorisation for your historic flight. However, I note that you are a British citizen with a British micro-light aircraft pilot licence, operating a British-registered aircraft that, at the present time, has an invalid British Permit to Fly as a result of unapproved modifications that you made to your aircraft. Since the invalid document is British, you must resolve this issue with the British Civil Aviation Authority. As long as your British Permit to Fly is invalid, Transport Canada is not in a position to authorise you to fly in Canada. If the British Civil Aviation Authority approves the modification and revalidates the Permit to Fly, or issues another form of flight authorisation, Transport Canada will be able to evaluate your application for a Canadian Validation of Foreign Flight Authority that would allow flight within Canada. Once this has been accomplished, departmental officials are prepared to work with you to help meet the requirements to facilitate a legal and safe transatlantic flight."*

I spent much of the day absorbing this depressing news. Liam pressed for his resignation – "for personal reasons" – to be accepted. I cleared away his expenses. The only other necessary job left for me in Canada was to see the children at the school in the Bay of Despair who had made this flight a geography and history project.

On Wednesday, June 27, I calculated I had been in Stephenville for 21 days, of which 19 were because of the grounding by Transport Canada. That beat the 18-day record I spent in Russia on the world flight. The parcel from Mainair arrived at 1145, and at 1146 I was phoning Claude Daigle of Transport Canada to arrange for an inspector to come and look at the aircraft on Thursday evening, two working days away. I drove to the Flyer, taking my small metric tool kit, spanners, a screwdriver and my Leatherman pliers, and dismantled the oversize frame within which the giant Atlantic tank had been sited. Because I was a journalist and not an engineer, everything had to be marked with sticky tape to ensure the ignition wires, for example, went into the right sockets in the engine.

Just to be actually working again was sweet. I forgot about food, drink, any comfort at all in the cold fresh wind, and constantly talked to myself as a reminder to take my time and not give way to the huge impatience I felt.

When the big frame was out, I set about installing the smaller, legal frame, which held two seats, and was slimmer than the Atlantic frame. There were significant differences between the old and the new rigging – the fuel flow switch between the reserve and the new tiny tank had to be re-positioned, for example – and again, I had to count my nuts and bolts and ensure they were all used, or have reasons why they were not.

Hours went by, with particular attention paid to installing the original fuel switch. It was the simple modification to this that allowed me to fit the huge Atlantic tank, and on which I expected the attention of the Transport Canada official to focus. I had to determine where the fuel pipes ran, between the engine and away from the exhaust system, and ensure each pipe was covered with protective metal coils.

A large fibre-glass but roughly-cut floor to the trike was included in the parcel. The original pod, not an essential part of the trike but certainly a comfort, had a floor that stretched back under my seat and was attached to a skirt to cover the small Permitted fuel tank. One Atlantic modification was the introduction of a slipper tank, and that had meant cutting away a big part of the floor to install it. Removing the slipper tank left a huge hole, covered by the rough-cut piece sent out from Mainair. Looking at the fuel tank of 22 litres, I was struck by how small it was. With the reserve, I had only 44 litres of fuel in total, enough for 3 ½ hours of careful flying, so I would have to make accurate calculations about wind speed and navigation flying in "Big" country like Newfoundland.

I kept reminding myself of the fact, not immediately obvious, that these changes were all being done in the cause of my own safety.

Sean Sheppard and another local man, Tony Pike turned up to help, and firemen appeared from time to time to watch the Flyer return to a shape they had never seen. This was the first flex-wing microlight ever in Stephenville. Sean helped by videoing the process, while Tony talked of his days helping to build hot-rod cars. I offered Sean a flight to thank him for all the help he had given me but he said he would only fly if Tony and I strapped him in before he knocked us both out. He did not fancy flying.

Wednesday, June 27, was a perfect flying morning, a light wind from the west so I could make it to the Bay of Despair quite easily, even with small tanks. I longed to fly again. There was a series of phone calls from Transport Canada in St Johns, a man called Charles Warren. He told me he would be in Stephenville at 7 o'clock that evening to inspect the work I had put into getting the Flyer back to legal status. That gave an urgency to the day, which I spent attaching the skirt to the pod and cleaning the aircraft up so she looked pretty again, rather than displaying that SAS-air of toughness which characterised the way she was set up for the Atlantic.

There was a strong gale all afternoon, rocking the tied-down Flyer even inside the abandoned ice rink. It would have been impossible to test fly her, even if I had been allowed to. Gusts of wind reached 50 mph.

I met Charlie Warren, a slightly wary-looking man with a beard, at the airport that evening, where he was hiring a car. We drove to the Flyer, with me full of apprehension. When I raised the door to show her, he audibly admired her beauty, and the simple brilliance of her design. I gave him her handbook, and took him through the changes I had made, removing the Atlantic modifications. It was apparent after a few minutes that, seeing the Flyer had fuel only for 3 ½ hours was quite enough for Charlie. There was no chance in her present state of her going out into the Atlantic.

The ceremony, returning my right to fly, was a simple one. Charlie had drafted a letter in St Johns, which he signed and handed to me. It said:

> *"In consideration of the return of your aircraft to its original configuration, we hereby withdraw our notice of suspension dated June 8, 2001. The letter of validation issued by us on June 2, 2001 is therefore in force."*

Though my wings had been severely clipped, I still felt a sense of relief. Afterwards, we talked about flying. He mentioned casually that hundreds of aircraft leave St John's every year, in my condition, that is, with a big unapproved one-off tank, and no one stopped them. How were they able to do it? I asked. They just do, he replied. I wondered if they showed up on radar, but he said the question never came up. It was because I had been so high-profile that I had been picked on. Full of relief at getting my permission to fly back, I took little notice then of these comments. But they were the beginning of a long slow burst of anger that seemed to grow in me over the next two days.

On Thursday, June 28th, I spent the morning writing to Paul Loach, a letter copied to Nikki King, about the dilemma I was in. It was a difficult job:

…"there are three options; pack up and go home, find another way to do the Atlantic flight, save something from the ruin by doing the Coney Run. I wish to discuss them.

Take the worst option, going home. I will have spent much of my budget, and face more expenses getting material home. I would also face ruin. You would, quite rightly, want to know what had gone wrong, why I didn't safeguard against every contingency, why I didn't even get to the start line on the flight, and want – contract notwithstanding – to be reimbursed for the trouble. I would not have produced a film, nor have produced a book – what can I write about what I haven't attempted? – and I would save little or nothing from the wreckage. Even worse, my reputation for bringing home projects safely, however difficult they were, would be gone. I would never get a chance again at such an adventure.

The safest option, pulling chestnuts out of the fire with little risk, is the Coney Run. There's a terrific amount of interest here in me and my type of flying, and if I'm "driven" from Canada by bureaucrats, a residue of interest in the USA to start with. I can fly down to Brunswick, Georgia, and commence the slow flight across the USA to San Diego, California, and prepare for the fast, 57h 27m flight back. All the research on the flight was done before you backed the Atlantic flight. I know the newspapers and TV involved, the slow part of the flight is quite easy, day to day, and if the fast flight is hard, it's only 2½ days, and I will sleep at night. The publicity and PR spin-offs can work pretty well, even if your main investors in Washington DC, Philadelphia, New York and Boston, are not on the route. It's the option favoured by Mainair if I can't make the Atlantic. It would take me about a week to get to Brunswick in Georgia, the Coney start line, so it would be over by August.

I still favour the third option, but must calm your fears over the word "Illegal". When the Transport Canada man came to see the Flyer on Thursday night, he went out of his way to tell me that hundreds of aircraft leave St Johns every year, all with oversize tanks, just like mine, none of which would comply with Transport Canada regulations. I suspect he was told to tell me that. My problem has been that I am so high profile, they have had to act against me. Now they have, honour is satisfied. If I then fly away and get safely to Ireland, they won't whinge, even if I have flown through some Canadian air-space. They would be roared down in horror. I will offer to go back to Canada to "face the music", but the reaction here to a successful flight will so overwhelm them that they'd rather forget it, as they forget about the hundreds of transit aircraft that illegally leave St Johns on the ferry route to Europe.

My plan at the moment is to persuade the French to let me use St Pierre. This allows the onus of the flight to be taken off Transport Canada. I intend to fly to Bay of Despair to visit a school where the children have made me a project ever since New York. Their appeals on the media to allow my flight to continue have had a strong effect, and it's my way of thanking them. I will stay at the Bay for 2 days, as guest of the local teacher. On Monday I expect to hear the French will allow me into St Pierre – all my papers are in order, I am totally legal, internationally. There I hope to persuade the French to allow me to re-build my aircraft in Atlantic mode, test it locally, and then fly away to Shannon, crossing some Canadian air space en route. Only a pedant would complain. There are numerous counter-arguments; that TC, in its concern for my safety, have forced me to fly an extra 171 miles, jeopardised my insurance cover, harassed me to distraction. They allow kayaks, tiny unsuitable boats, and illegal aircraft to leave their shores, but ban me.

Regis Lourme, the boss of St Pierre Airport, will let me know on Monday about my status visiting his island, about 60 miles south of the Bay of Despair. He is personally very keen, but it depends on Paris.

That leaves getting on to the flight and then not making it successfully. I have had a legal waiver drafted by a Stephenville QC, Fred Stagg, in line with the recommendation by the Globe and Mail Newspaper, that not only absolves the Canadian authorities of blame or any responsibility for rescuing me if anything goes wrong, but absolves you from blame or responsibility as well. It specifically says you warned me not to do anything "illegal". Fred, a former MP for Stephenville in the Province's parliament in St Johns, was so pleased with the result that he waived all fees and took me to lunch instead. He said the Canadian authorities may believe they can over-ride such a waiver, but that it was as much as I could do, legally, to counter Transport Canada's objections.

Without harassment, I have a very good chance of making the Atlantic flight without trouble. The bad period will be hours 20–23, the sleep cycle. There was, and is, always a chance that something could go wrong, in which case, I have the survival gear and, if necessary, the last spot the GPS tracker was seen working. It won't be technical problems that put me in the water, but my own failings as a man. You took a bet against that happening, and it remains a good bet despite my having to fly for an extra 2 ½ hours out of St Pierre. The imperatives for staying awake are even greater.

I would like a clear run from St Pierre, and a righteous and enthusiastic defence of the values of the flight, compared with the piddling objections to it. There are strong and deep values that attracted you to the flight in the first place, that attract every Canadian I know to it, even the TC chaps, and you should use any opportunity you can to speak to those values … What has happened to me is patently unfair, it's legally mean and must be challenged. Wherever I turn, I am offered help, of any kind, to get me on the flight.

Please transcend the "parking ticket" view of my legality, and see it as it is seen at every level here outside Transport Canada, as a great human adventure overcoming what the Globe and Mail called "a sea of red tape". I wrote about the world flight that these adventures are a test, not just of my own aspirations to courage, grit, stoicism, determination, but by extension, of a sponsor's too. You were never aware of the detail of the hassles I had to wade through to make the world flight work. They were just like I'm facing now, and it is part of this adventure to overcome them."

My great friend Valerie Thompson went in to intercede on my behalf, to gauge Paul's mood. This is what she wrote afterwards:

… It's a thoroughly concise summary, Brian. I suspect Paul will groan and feel bloated under the weight of what's happened, in that he has to explain it to his partners. I doubt he will comment, since what can he say?

Option number 1 leaves him feeling/looking like a fool with his partners, option no 2 is out because he's unlikely to want to be seen endorsing anything illegal, option 3 could be something they could leverage.

I think he is likely to say 'salvage what you can but keep us out and we'll assess the upside and downside of events, after it's over'. That's my read based on that one conversation I had with Paul a few weeks ago, and what little I know of him generally.

Liam has blown both you and Paul up here, but Paul will still consider this your fault because you chose Liam and Liam had an opt-out when the going got tough. Hindsight is a f★★★★r isn't it?

Doubt you can win anything from Paul just right now, but later yes, especially if you succeed in doing the flight from St Pierre, which I pray works out since I think it is the best solution by far. Your point that they are hardly likely to shoot you down for your safety, is excellent.

However, Paul I reckon will still be agonising over your touching, albeit briefly, Canadian air space, since Liam has shoved the illegality of matters down his throat and Paul's nature is I think to be sensitive to such things. Thus, Paul will need a way to be able to promote Lion's involvement with the flight without it implicating the firm in or endorsing anything illegal. That's what will be worrying him when he reflects on your letter I think.

I do believe in God, and that no-one can take what rightfully belongs to us and I believe that this flight belongs to you and the credit for it being possible financially belongs to Paul.

I also believe that things can happen out of the blue, that solutions/events can appear from sources unexpected.

You are doing absolutely everything possible within your power to work matters out whilst managing to keep at bay the extreme anxiety over what's happened. Working like a dog with no shred of sympathy is very hard, so you are a hero because you are bearing events virtually entirely on your own. In the City there are many guys earning multiple millions who are in charge of making money, yet they don't lose sleep, money or their social life, when things go wrong and big losses occur. They just act stressed and blame bad markets and expect sympathy, even though their losses are often a cover for incompetence and could have been avoided. The buck doesn't stop with them, except for the literal buck, which they readily accept and demand more of.

In general, City types today lack a deep sense of obligation and responsibility to the shareholders whose money they play with so freely. Your sense of obligation and responsibility to Paul and Lion however, is deep and genuine, and I do believe that Paul is aware that you could not be hurting more than you do over what's happened, although I can understand his position as well.

I believe you will make this flight successfully and that things will work out well for Paul and Lion Capital as well.

I am thinking about you.
Love,
Valerie

At that time I pinned everything on the reply from St Pierre, and planned a visit the following day to the school in the Bay of Despair. Halfway between Stephenville and St Johns, about a 3-hour flight, this was just within the envelope of the Flyer's new short range. Phil Hoskins had conducted a straw poll among the 18 children of his class, now on holiday, and they all wanted me to come.

That evening I took some of my Stephenville friends for a flight in the Flyer. Terry Dennis bought a motor-cycle helmet for the job, and thrilled at the low flight along the coast. I took Katrina out to an island and flew across it low level a number of times, to ensure Sean Sheppard had a photograph of my flying in my legal form (Sean lent the camera to Karen Skinner, Al's wife, to take the photo from Al's Cessna; it was not just microlights Sean hated to fly in). I also took Sean's wife, Roxanne, for a spin. It was striking how big that airfield was, and how few people noticed I was flying.

Before crashing off to sleep, I looked at my e-mails. There was a disjointed debate going on around the flight, focusing on values, with a lot less abuse in direct e-mails than on the web-site, where feelings were more raw. Stephen Lewis, with whom I always leave my last wills and testament when I go on adventures, had been sending me a daily diary of great insight into the political and social scene, not only in England, but where his imagination roamed. Stephen – once known as "The Fifth Horseman of the Apocalypse" because of his views as the City of London's top economist – was a George Smiley figure, and I counted dinner with him among the high points of my life. His letter that day touching on the problems of the disk jockey, Chris Evans, was particularly good:

> *"What sad reading your web site makes! High optimism descends, day by day, into despair and frustration. I think you are right in supposing that the authorities no longer want adventures to happen. It is all of a piece with the 3ft-high slides in playgrounds that children nowadays can only enjoy by jumping off the top. Partly, I think, it is a reflection of the spread of litigation and of the dominance of insurance companies' concerns. This process has gone further since your world flight, and these are very different times from the swashbuckling 1980s when you flew to Australia. Interestingly, it was in the 1980s that a marked shift occurred away from heroic values towards celebrity values. This is where Chris Evans's bad behaviour is so relevant. He can generate more discussion at every level of society by going on a binge than anyone else might through a worthwhile exploit. He was, incidentally,*

sacked from his radio job yesterday; he claims he is being made a scapegoat. Chris Evans is, in one sense, the Robert Falcon Scott ("Scott of the Antarctic") of our times. He displays, in exaggerated form and to the point of weakness, the characteristic values of his generation. This is probably why such men exercise a strong hold on the popular imagination.

"The problem you face is that your values are ones remembered only by that dwindling band who read history at school. Philosophically, you have little option, if you wish to carry on along your present course, but to maintain that some values are absolute and that, having abandoned them, the world is a worse place than it used to be. This is essentially the conservative and pessimistic conclusion that I have reached."

This was the day the scales fell from my eyes. Stephen's letter helped.

11

The Fateful Decision

That Friday morning, June 29th, I had awoken early, looking forward to flying again, even if only to the Bay of Despair. I wrote my daily journal, had breakfast, time seemed to speed by much quicker than I wanted. Terry Dennis turned up to pick up items he had lent me, a petrol credit card, his mobile phone, and I looked out at the weather with growing apprehension. I was due to leave about 11am to fly to where Phil Hoskins and the local children were waiting for me. But cloud was extending down to hills to the east of me, and as I watched it got worse. Terry went off to make house calls, visiting people at home was one reason he was such a popular doctor, and Sean Sheppard arrived to come with me to check the weather. I paid the hotel bill, C$750, packed, and in some disarray but with everything together, went through the rain to see what the prospects were. The weather forecast was poor, rain all day and low cloud. It was as if, now I was able to fly legally, Stephenville was clutching at me to stop me going.

I phoned Phil Hoskins and told him I was going to postpone for a day. Sean and I went into the Stephenville Hotel for a cup of tea. Terry Dennis joined us.

Then I was hit with blinding force by an extraordinary thought.

Why couldn't I make the Atlantic attempt from Stephenville?

I had allies, I had resources, and really for the first time, I also had the moral high ground. It was that comment by Charlie Warren that opened this floodgate, that "hundreds of small aircraft leave St Johns every year to fly the Atlantic, most of them with oversize tanks" like my own. Had Charlie Warren been briefed, however unofficially, to tell me this? Stephen Lewis had already written that morning, wondering if his conspiracy theories were running away with him? He, too, thought I might have been given a coded message to get on with the flight and stop trying to batter permission out of someone.

The comments transferred the moral advantage from them to me.

A second factor about Charlie Warren's visit also occurred to me, which could be compared with Sherlock Holmes's dog that didn't bark in the night. *Neither Charlie, nor anyone else, had once asked me where the Atlantic makings were.*

They knew I had the means to convert the Flyer back, they had the power (as they originally reminded me) to impound any of my equipment. But they didn't. Add the two together, and it made a strong case, conveniently deniable, that some sportsmen inside the flying establishment knew the only way out was the way I was (finally) contemplating. Whatever happened to me, they were covered. Were they, like all pilots (except the McQuades, of course), curious to see if the flight was possible anyway?

I recalled a similar situation on my flight to Australia in 1988, having already landed on a track in a Malaysian paddyfield, and two days later I was forced down on a plantation road by monsoons. Both were "notifiable incidents", and required officials to inspect the aircraft. In the first instance this happened, and I was cleared to fly on. In the second incident, an official, an Englishman on secondment to the Malaysia CAA, phoned long-distance and asked if there had been any damage to my aircraft in the previous day's out-landings? I assured him there had not been, and gave him my word. He cleared me to fly on without a formal inspection. Then he added: "Get there, Brian, OK? Just get there".

After further adventures, I did. I hoped that happy ending was going to be repeated, but as it was then, I would not know until it was over.

A great peace descended upon me when I came to these conclusions. If Charlie's comment was a message, well and good, I had got it. If it was not, did it matter? Whether or not Charlie would later confirm what he had said to me, it was undeniable that what he had said was true. David Collenette must have known this when he refused my appeal, so he had been hypocritical. In some instances I supported hypocrisy, but it should favour the adventurous individual, not work against him. Were Collenette's hands so tied by the rules that it was impossible for him to use his political powers to exempt me from Transport Canada's Atlantic rules? Did I have to come to these conclusions myself, and stop demanding the unattainable? I came to think so. Permission could not be formally granted, but I could be shown the way, however obscurely.

This reasoning was accompanied by a leap of understanding, that I had been contemplating risks that were too big for me to comprehend. I had wanted the French authorities to agree to take me into St Pierre, and to allow me to re-build the Atlantic mods. Al Skinner had already agreed to fly these modifications in his Cessna, including both big fuel tanks, to St Pierre (I would cover his extra expenses). If the French said yes, I would have to build a support network similar to the one I had in Stephenville. But what if the French, too, said no, as seemed likely? What would I be left with?

If I left on the Atlantic flight from Stephenville I had a raft full of allies keen to help. It had been suggested a number of times already, but it added an extra 275 miles to my journey if I flew via St Johns, even if I could get away from Stephenville Airport. The difference was the moral high ground.

(Later, David Edward's girlfriend Lynn said, "that's what you should have done in the first place", but I disagreed; moral right *had* to be on my side if legal right was not.)

When taking Terry Dennis and his daughter Katrina for a joy flight the previous evening, it had struck me how huge the airfield was at Stephenville. Every time the American Space Shuttle took off from Florida, Stephenville was one of the opt-out airfields if the mission was abandoned. There were enormous expanses of concrete and old hangars and other buildings, stretching into the distance. Katrina had told me two Americans had crashed there once, and it had taken a whole day to discover they had even died.

Al Skinner joined the three of us in the dining-room of the Hotel Stephenville, myself, Terry and Sean, as we began, without inhibition, to examine the idea. We had a bold and creative half hour. First, what were the distances involved? If I flew to St Pierre, it was 165 miles from Stephenville. From there, assuming a direct flight across Newfoundland via St Johns, it was 2,114 miles to Shannon in Ireland. If I went direct from Stephenville to Shannon, it was 2,153 miles, only 39 miles more than from St Pierre! Why was I scrabbling around trying to persuade the French it was a sporting proposition, for such a piddling advantage?

Could I cross Newfoundland and find an airfield closer to Ireland, to lessen the risks? Terry, the non-pilot, plotted a route on the map and wondered whether I could try Springdale as a final jumping-off point? It gave me a leg of 126 miles in which to test the Atlantic Flyer, and fix anything that might be wrong. Al Skinner knew Springdale, which had 3,000 feet of tarmac, fuel and a hangar, and he knew the chaps who ran the place. It became his job to arrange for me to pick up the bulk of my fuel there, avgas for safety instead of the motor-car gas I had been contemplating. The total distance from Springdale to Shannon in Ireland was 2,028 miles, just 85 miles further than from St Johns, an hour's flying with a following wind, so much less risky than from St Pierre. I was calculating real risk, of course, rather than the unapproved risk the aviation authorities had been playing with.

If I flew from Stephenville, I could not stay in the old ice rink, virtually under the eye of airport officials, while I re-built the Atlantic Flyer, so where could I stay? There were old hangars at the far end of the runway, the threshold to runway 27, isolated from the rest of the base.

Who owned them?

A self-made man called Edward Lavalle.

Did anyone know him?

Terry said he was one of his patients.

How would he feel? I asked.

Terry thought Mr Lavalle would be open to the idea.

How would I get there?

Answer, fly away to Bay of Despair, talk to the children, then secretly fly back to one of the Lavalle hangars.

Was there enough space in the hangar?

We resolved to go out and see, drove there, and found it absolutely ideal.

We took a group photograph, and I used the video camera to introduce these three characters. There was a similarity between Sean Sheppard and Al Skinner; in America they might have been called Good Old Boys, as in "good old boys drinking whisky and rye", from the song, *American Pie*. They both had a cheerful disrespect for the law, not outlaws, but a Newfoundland disrespect, what used to be called once upon a time, a "sturdy independence of mind". Dr Terry Dennis was different, more cultured and thoughtful, without the natural instinct to strike a rebellious pose. I think he had always been his own man since working his way out of a poor working-class district of England, achieving a mastery of tennis and rugby on the way through. In reaching Newfoundland, and being there 12 years, he missed a career as a senior consultant in England, but had the sort of relationship with his patients that the fictional vet, James Herriot had. He was swept away, as I was, by the romance of the Atlantic flight, but he confessed to a flutter in his chest at the thought of what we were doing. It was quite a common condition with me, I told him.

I drove to Katrina's and moved my luggage in. Terry phoned and said he had talked to Edward Lavalle, and we were to meet him at the hangars. Edward was in his 70's, a nice, kind man who did not look like a multimillionaire, but he had to be because he owned so many apartment blocks in Stephenville, as well as a number of storage hangars. He found the keys to an empty hangar and showed me how the small doors opened, and the massive hangar doors moved. They once housed F-102 fighter aircraft called Delta Daggers. The doors weighed 18,000 pounds each, and one of the hangars was now to be my hideaway.

Right then, the French option was still open, but I instinctively preferred the emerging Stephenville one. I was surrounded by people who had pledged their help, and backed it up with immediate action. It was astonishing and touching to me, to see such behaviour, and I reflected on it sadly.

I had not set out to break the law. I was also not above it, and had to be prepared to suffer the consequences. The issues involved were much greater than whether I had an oversize tank, or cockpit lighting (let alone a cockpit), or a gyro compass, or an artificial horizon, or an instrument rating. The only real justification for breaking a law could be a moral one, and I felt I had that. It was obvious that the precedent of four other microlights being allowed through to fly the Atlantic had not sufficient moral force. But I felt the legal arguments against me looked mean and threadbare against the fact that hundreds of aircraft worse-equipped than my own, and with large fuel tanks, make the crossing every year without interference.

I felt I had done everything possible, within my own form of aviation – microlighting – to meet the requirements for a safe flight across the Atlantic, including all my insurance policies, which would now be invalid because of the way I had been forced to make the flight. I was cutting myself off, in a legal way through a waiver, from any offer of help or rescue, once the flight started, because the price of that offer to help was that someone else judged my flight so impossible that they banned it. I would rather not take help offered in those circumstances. It was like stopping a man at the foot of Everest, and telling him he could not climb it because, in the judgement of someone else, his boots were not suitable, .

I knew that between making that decision and leaving on the flight I would be assailed by doubts, fearful, nervous, irritable, not always a good example of grace under pressure. But I also know that I had crossed a Rubicon. If I could get to the start line, I was going into the Atlantic with every expectation of flying across it. The full moon was the following Thursday, so I needed to go within the next 15 days.

Al Skinner phoned in the evening. He had set out to *drive* to St Johns, twelve hours on the road, rather than take a one-hour flight, so he could drop by Springdale and arrange my fuel. Al had not told them who I was, but felt they would be OK for me to deal with.

My biggest enemy between now and then was the media. It could turn out to be my biggest friend after I started. But there were no guarantees, given that they had values which had made heroes in England out of Chris Evans and Victoria Beckham. I thought Stephen Lewis, as ever, was right; there were absolute values that rose above all ages, but they were ignored. I had to find my own small way of reasserting them, and do it at the risk of my life. It was a rotten life without them.

If in the event, I did not make it, it was my decision.

I dined in the evening with the Dennis family, this time a lasagne which I cooked, too sloppy to be called good, but the taste was what I wanted. Even Anna-Maria, Katrina's youngest, ate it; she and I never saw eye to eye. We drank red wine and later watched a manic version of Goldilocks and the Three Bears, along with Little Red Riding Hood, put on with hand puppets from behind a sofa by both Katrina's daughters. It was full of script changes and little fights between them as they tried to upstage each other. It was late before I went to bed, and read some of Wilfred Russell's collection of Anglo-Indian poetry, half aloud to myself.

The following day, July 1, a Sunday, dawned with low cloud drifting across the bay, and only a dim prospect of better weather than Saturday. But as the morning progressed the cloud lifted marginally. I called Phil Hoskins at the Bay of Despair, and despite remaining doubts about the weather, I pushed the Flyer out of the ice-rink in which she had rested since June 6th. There was no wind, and smoke from the paper plant across the bay rose thickly into the air and then drifted. The weatherman sent me a message, worrying about cloud in the high terrain over which I planned to fly, hills close to 2,000 feet, no roads, bad landing-out country. But I felt confident my little aircraft could cope and packed her for the flight, trying to remember which bits went where now the big tanks had been removed.

I got away late at 11.20, for a flight of 131 miles and a rendezvous time of 13.00. This was especially apparent when I found that, turning east, I faced a head wind of 10mph. I climbed over the bay and past the paper mill, over a headland dividing Stephenville the air base and modern town from the original Stephenville Crossing – a railway junction, when there was a railway, along which Alcock and Brown had passed in 1919 on their way to St Johns – and settled into the routine of flight. Cloud base was 2,500 feet, but continued to rise as I flew east, passing through lumpy air from time to time, scraping along between cloud and mountain. It was never dangerous. There were always valleys into which I could descend if the clouds came down, but there were no roads or logging trails, and I did not fancy my chances in a forced landing.

I was never sure when my inner self, less determined in many layers than my outer self, would start to get nervous about the sensation of flight. Wisps of concern made their appearance from time to time, and then fluttered away. I felt I had not the time, in this dreadful situation I was in, to bother with wimpishness like that. Bigger things mattered. The countryside appeared vaster than the country over which I normally flew in England. The light went right to the horizon, and the hills, valleys and sometimes mountains looked unexplored and uncompromising. It was easy to imagine it under snow and ice, with 50 mph winds blowing. Lakes were everywhere; this was float-plane country, and said to be great for fishing and shooting.

I picked up Phil Hoskins on the radio at one o'clock. He could hear me much better than I could hear him. The sky changed, cloud base lifted, the sun appeared and I was soon bumped around by thermals. I looked south much of the time, down towards the French islands of St Pierre and Miquelon, seeing only a misty headland across a few miles of sea. Ahead of me I could see more lakes, the steep sides of what looked like a fjord which ended in the fishing and forestry town of Bay of Despair. I worried about flying with such small reserves of fuel, 22 litres in my main tank, and a reserve of 22 litres, and with an hour to go, went through the contortionist process of finding the switch and changing from one tank to the other. For the next five minutes I looked for places to land in case the change-over didn't work. I was also upset at seeing the *Flydat* was still on the blink, as the fuse blew once more with little or no load on it. It *had* to be the regulator, a device that modified the charge from the alternator, that was going wrong. But I could fly safely without such instruments, and after that I settled back again and prepared to find the airfield, about ten miles in front of the town.

Phil Hoskins radioed that the children picked up my microlight visually, to great excitement, in the last two miles of my flight. I roared low over the top of them and landed on the bumpy, neglected surface to taxi to a crowd of 80 people, about half of them children.

Phil, a thick-set kind-looking man, introduced himself from the general melee, and after stamping around to stretch my legs, I began to take some of his pupils flying. Only four of them, all 9-year olds, volunteered to begin with, but later another got parental permission, a 15-year girl won a draw among the pupils outside Phil's class, and of course, I took up Phil himself at the end. It was the first time anyone there had seen a weight-shift microlight, and there were all the usual comments about "never get me up in one of those" from the adults. But the children were lifted in, one after the other, a helmet fastened to them, a strap tightened, a little conversation before the roar of the engine stopped all that – I had no intercom with me, expecting to be solo on this adventure – and then we roared off to a short routine. I usually climbed to 400 feet, did a steep 540 degree turn, and then made a number of low passes, waving, before a final fighter turn and landing. As it grew bumpier during the hour's flying, especially on landing, I grew more circumspect. How many good days had been ruined by a moment's carelessness?

There was little comment from the children except a few "wows". They may have been saving their comments for their friends, in the immediate clusters that grew around them as the next child was strapped in, and then it was engine on, wave, taxi away, and back into the air. They had their lives ahead of them, and I felt it was possible they might remember that day and the experience for some time, and one day tell their own children about it. Creating such memories was a marker down to future generations, passing on an attitude of mind, countering the state of mind that had grounded me in the first place.

The children presented me with home-made cards, welcoming me to the Bay of Despair and wishing me luck on my flight, scarcely aware that, in its present state, the Flyer was incapable of getting across the Atlantic. They had done their bit by adding their voices to the petitions to let me continue. I was aware that the original start-point, St Johns, was only 145 miles away to the east, another 2 ½ hours flying away.

It was here that the deception began.

"Where are you going now," asked one of the parents.

"I want to look at St Pierre," I replied, "and I thought I'd fly south to Winterland, an airfield near the French island."

This appeared to satisfy them. The local strip out of which I was operating was surrounded by higher ground. It was not easy, two minutes after I took off, for them to see exactly where I was heading. Phil Hoskins was in on my secret, and at one time I had considered having my private base at his airfield. But an examination of the local hangar, small, open to the elements, too low by 18 inches, confirmed that my final plans were the right ones. I had a cup of tea, another pee, took Phil flying, and then, in a fatalistic frame of mind, waved goodbye and flew away.

Heading west again, my speed was above 70 mph, with an unusual east wind blowing. I turned over in my mind the actions I was taking, and could see no alternative. I saw myself going through this process for days ahead, a wearying thought. Fictional wannabe heroes never seemed to have these doubts. Despite the appearance of great and unwavering determination, I was always swept by doubts and had to thrash them into submission.

I let my mind drift through various situations as I climbed in thermals up to 3,500 feet, listening on the 122.10 Stephenville frequency for local traffic, and calculating how I would sneak back into town. Sean Sheppard was waiting for me with a radio on the frequency 122.80, and I was able to talk to him 20 miles out. He said later he grew alarmed because he had no keys to the hangar in which I was going to hide the Flyer (I had them, but he thought Terry Dennis had them). Though uncertain, he decided to stay by the car that was going to give me mobility on the ground.

The good part of an east wind was a fast flight. The bad part was it forced me into a down-wind landing; only pilots can appreciate how dangerous these can be. As I hugged the hills to the north-east of Stephenville, waiting for the long runway to come into view and descending to merge with the countryside, I looked with horror at my GPS and saw I was doing 77–80 mph, with an air-speed of just 65mph. That meant hitting the ground 30 mph faster than a normal landing. Was it worth it? I could not slip on to the tarmac in front of Edward Lavalle's hangar because there was a strong danger I would overshoot. As I picked my way, 50 feet above the trees and little hillocks to the airfield, I decided to risk a landing on the main runway itself.

I remembered it was so far away from where the main buildings were situated that it was difficult to see an airliner land; how much more difficult it would be to see me, unless one was deliberately looking? Sean, waiting for me, did not see me until I crossed the threshold at a terrific speed, whistling through my teeth and fighting for control against the turbulence, but I got her down safely and scuttled back to the deserted tarmac in front of my secret hangar. I opened the small door, half-lifted the great hangar doors (for light), let Sean in the back, then lifted the hangar doors more fully and taxied the Flyer in. Aside from a lorry driver who stopped and watched the whole proceedings, then drove away, I did not think we had been seen. We spent the next 20 minutes waiting for an investigating car, but none appeared. On our drive back into Stephenville we met Dr Terry Dennis, and drove to Katrina's home for a beer and a post-mortem.

I had flown 5 ½ hours, some of it – the last landing, for example – rather difficult, and I was tired. We heated up the previous day's lasagne which fed us all and tasted good, and then I went to bed while the Dennis family went off to fireworks for Canada Day.

On Monday, July 2, a thunderstorm brewed at 8.00 in the morning, and rain lashed down. I thought through the process of transporting the Atlantic makings to the secret hangar to start re-building the Flyer. I was unsure how I might cope with any media chasing me, and resolved to just lie low and not say anything. I had to draft my departure statement, and record it on sound and video. Along with my waiver, these were the main weapons available in my own defence when out there in the Atlantic. I wanted to make sure it got to all my friends, so they could also conduct that defence.

Three names were emerging among friends in England – Adrian Whitmarsh, Dave Simpson and John Hunt – to consult about the weather. There was a full moon due in four days, and I started to work on the presumption I would leave within twelve days. I began to monitor a high pressure area moving north east that could stabilise in mid-Atlantic, and give me west winds by the end of the week.

It was all dreamlike.

That was the day I made the significant step towards making the flight, and implicitly defy the authorities. My only sin, until then, had been to land unannounced in Stephenville. But when I started to re-convert the Flyer back into Atlantic mode, Transport Canada would be within its right to fall on me like a ton of bricks. I lived with little flutters of apprehension, worrying about whether I had made the right decision.

12

The Secret Diaries

After June 30 I composed two diaries, a real one and a second one calculated to deceive those following the flight on my web-site. It was difficult, because lying does not come naturally. I wrote the true diary first, and then struggled with the other one, not certain whether or not I should let it fade away. I did not want to alarm the media. and I knew, from queries at the edges, that there was still interest out there. I just wanted to fade from consciousness.

There were difficulties in picking a good weather site in the Internet to make my decisions about weather in the Atlantic. I was never satisfied with any suggestion. I did not have to have perfect weather, especially in my situation, just weather where it was possible. But first I had to be equipped to make the flight again, so later in the morning of Monday, July 2, carrying all the Atlantic makings except the big tank, I motored to Edward Lavalle's airfield site, four huge hangars near the threshold of runway 27, and opened the one where my Flyer was stored. Edward himself came to join me. He was a 73-year old engineer who had managed to amass 48 apartments and a number of other properties, but who had to go slow after triple heart by-pass operations. He helped me make the changes, and talked about his eleven children (Newfies had big families) and how he was going to cash in soon and consider a winter home in Malaga in Spain.

I had allocated two days for the job, but it all happened very quickly. Before I knew where I was I had the skirt off, the seat frame removed, all the hoses for the fuel changed, a new seat-frame installed, the slipper tank put in, and I was looking at installing the giant tank in the early afternoon. It was as if she was always reluctant to go back to being straight and square, but was impatient to get back to Atlantic mode.

Outside, where I looked occasionally, nervous about airport security checks, the weather started poor, overcast and drizzle, but as the day went on this stopped, and in a very short time skies cleared and the sun poured down. Edward and I went off at lunch time for a cup of tea, brought back the big tank in his pick-up truck, and in less than an hour I was fiddling with small changes, tightening bolts and deciding how I was going to portray the changes on video. I replaced the fuse on the *Flydat* again, after much fiddling around, and I was nervous that it would blow mid-Atlantic, but could not see what to do about it. It seemed to be a fault in the regulator, but where will I get one in time? UPS took five days to get a package from England. Meanwhile, I found the electrical links to the battery were loose, one possible cause of the fuse blowing, and I tightened them up.

At the end of the day the Flyer was ready to go, except for the addition of 10 gallons – 50 litres – of fuel to get me to Springdale. I intended then to start from Stephenville at dawn on the chosen day, get to Springdale, and there take on board for the third and last time a full load, 438 litres, 115.62 US gallons, including reserves, which should be enough for 34 hours flying. I expected to make the flight in 25 hours but an east wind at any time could kill me.

I ended my working day by composing – ad libbing – various voice pieces to the little video camera to try and sum up my mood. Each time I felt dissatisfied, and made another attempt until the words popped out, "I could see no honourable way out of this situation other than the one I am taking", and that felt right.

It was the positions of Jim Cunliffe, Nikki King and Paul Loach and his partners that I worried about the most, and whose reputations I wanted to ensure were not hurt.

Back at Katrina's, I heard from Regis Lourme, airport director in the tiny French island of St Pierre. He told me in a message through Phil Hoskins that, regretfully, I was allowed to enter or leave the colony *only* with a valid Permit to Fly, and I would not be allowed to install the big Atlantic tanks. That was the last lawful option closed. I had already resigned myself to this course, so I took it without the soul-destroying emotions previous refusals had induced. I persuaded the Dennis family to have roast beef and sauté potatoes, pepper and onions for dinner, went out to buy a particularly nice piece of meat, stuck it with garlic, covered it in English mustard and roasted it for 55 minutes. It turned out well. We drank red wine and Katrina's mother, Yvonne, introduced me to the poetry of Robert Service, which was terrific. I had only read the *Ballad of Dangerous Dan McGrew*, and its off-shoot, the *Ballad of Eskimo Nell*, but none of his other poems, of which he wrote hundreds. My son James would really like him.

That evening I thought, so long as I can avoid harassment, I was at peace with my own soul. This is where I wanted to be a month ago. Three years ago exactly, to the day, I had left New York to head north into Canada on my previous flight across the Atlantic. Although my original six-week window had now shrunk to two weeks, Adrian Whitmarsh kept telling me I had missed no significant weather. The only time I could have gone, in his opinion, was on the day I flew by airliner to New Jersey in the middle of May. It was all still to play for, so long as I could get to play.

I thought a lot about Transport Canada's dilemma, and I had some sympathy with it. Once someone started asking questions formally there was no official way out, or avoiding the fact that I had a big and unapproved tank. The CAA in England could do no more, or less, than it had done. The only way to cut the Gordian Knot, legally, was for a political decision to be made by David Collenette to grant me an exemption. This he declined to do; what was in it for him? It was all down-side.

Tuesday was spent looking at the Atlantic charts. I formed an initial view that, if the weather developed as forecast, the best time to go would be Sunday, five days away. It looked like it was going to match the blueprint given to me months earlier by the British Met Office in Bracknell. There was a big high pressure over the Atlantic, and a low pressure south and west of Greenland. The lines in between indicated a moderate to fresh westerly wind all the way from Newfoundland to Ireland, in a straight line, like tramways. This was set to occur three days after a full moon, giving a lot of light at night as well as a decent westerly straight into Ireland. Without all the hassle I had been through, if I was just considering this as a flyer, as Alcock and Brown did, Sunday looked the best day.

The first prospect of an Atlantic attempt on Thursday, just two days away, was raised by John Hunt. This suggestion looked fine until 300 miles from Ireland, and then north-east winds were forecast, which was daunting. These could cut my ground-speed from 80 mph to 40 mph, and bring me into the danger zone, tired and at the edge.

The question I kept asking myself was, am I putting off the day from Thursday to Sunday because I am frightened, or am I making a rational decision? Actually, I thought I had got over the worst of the fear, which had occurred during much of Monday as I was re-building the Flyer. I could always whittle away fear if I kept worrying at it.

I worried away for hours about the weather. None of the three men I was consulting in England were professionals. In my clandestine condition, I felt cut off from official weather forecasters, especially in Newfoundland. How would I be able to explain why I needed the information?

The prospect of leaving within two days came as a shock to me, because I had become so embroiled in the fight to save the flight that I had forgotten there was a terrific physical task ahead of me. It sobered me, on a Tuesday morning, to scroll through weather charts and contemplate that two days later I could be out in the middle of the Atlantic with 2,000 miles ahead of me. I searched back through accounts I had written of other frightening flights, and was reassured to know I had had the same fears then. They magically seemed to disappear as I started the actual preparations.

I resolved that Tuesday morning to act as if Thursday was going to be the departure day, one day before a full moon.

In Katrina's house I was comfortable, warm, with tea and toast and Marmite constantly available, and Katrina and her two daughters, Anna-Maria and Angelisa, intent on their own lives but moving over to allow me to play my end-game. I gathered together my equipment and laid it out in the deserted garage, deciding which to take and which to send back with the Dennis family when they next went on holiday to England. It was cut down to just an overnight bag, along with the camera bag, both to be tied to the rear suspension for the big flight, and leaving me enough clothes and equipment to complete the flight home via Paris.

Meanwhile, John Hunt had been worrying since Halifax about the way my *Flydat* fuse kept blowing, taking out all the engine instruments. I had never had this problem before. Though I had become accustomed to flying without engine information, John accused me of being too blasé:

> *"As far as the aircraft is concerned the main problem remains the fuse blowing in the Flydat. Nigel Beale, the Rotax agent, who I saw last week, is still saying that it is probably a high voltage causing it and I would say that this has to be the best bet. Did you see high voltages on the analogue voltmeter, greater than 14 volts, at any time? (No)*

"This problem MUST be resolved before taking on this flight because any voltage over about 14.4 volts is likely to take out the battery. This will stop other instrumentation, GPS's, turn-and-slip, radio, tracker etc. Please change the regulator, Flydat and I would suggest a replacement battery in case that one is already partially damaged. You might consider a spare fully-charged battery that you can use to run your instruments in case of emergency but you need to be able to disconnect the existing links in flight and just run the equipment off the battery without connecting it to the regulator.

"Please be careful and don't let the desire to achieve this flight over-shadow common sense. Everything needs to be perfect for this flight and at the moment it is not."

This same issue also came up in mail from Adrian Whitmarsh, who felt moved to go to capitals to express his concern:

"BRIAN, JOHN and I BOTH FEEL STRONGLY THAT IT IS IMPERATIVE, REPEAT IMPERATIVE YOU SORT THESE FAILURES OUT AND THOROUGHLY TEST FLY UNTIL NO FURTHER PROBLEMS OCCUR BEFORE YOU EVEN CONSIDER HEADING OUT ACROSS THE ATLANTIC. Remember what I said about gut feelings – well I've got one and it says don't start rushing at this now without the proper technical function checks and re-checks giving 100% on all systems. THIS IS NOT A SECTOR YOU CAN 'HOPE FOR THE BEST'. There is no point in heading off because you feel you have found a way through the bureaucratic hurdles if you don't make it because of inadequate functioning of your necessary systems. That will only lead the authorities to say 'we told you so' and possibly make it harder for you – or others – in the future."

My own view was that, stuck in Stephenville, five days away from access to the best packages from England, I had to shuttle between perfection and what I could achieve. I spent hours motoring around agents looking for an alternative voltage regulator, and finally found one – mail order – to satisfy those caustic comments from England. I did take seriously what was said by friends, but sometimes they needed to say it twice, especially when I got close to the action and was priming myself to get on with it.

That afternoon I bought drinks and simple foods for the flight, to comply with Dr Carl Hallam's suggestions about always eating in the air, to replace lost energy. Katrina took her children off to do the garden at her mother's house. I ate roast beef sandwiches and read more of the poetry of Robert Service, the while drifting back to animate the weather maps, and psyche myself into leaving in two days.

Meanwhile Nikki King at the Artificial Heart Fund e-mailed me to say how unhappy she was at the way things were developing. She took me to task over my views on Liam's resignation:

> *"I realise that you seem to be in a no-win situation but to try and bluff your way through it and go against the Authorities is madness. Please think of the knock-on affect it has to Paul and his backers who are sponsoring you and to the Charity. He was extremely hurt with your para: 'Please transcend the 'parking ticket' view of my legality and see it as seen at every level here outside Transport Canada as a great human adventure overcoming a sea of red tape'.*
>
> *"You simply cannot 'cut corners' with other peoples' money. If you are being sponsored and trying to support a charity, everything has to be done 'above board and according to the book'. It is simply not good enough ignore all the advice around you like an ostrich and just bulldoze your way through ignoring all the legalities. Lion Capital Partners could well be involved in litigation if anything goes wrong and you are flying through Canadian Airspace illegally. You will have far greater ruin to face or worse still leave one behind, that you have created, even if it is all over for yourself. Stop being selfish, please take warning Brian - you are not Captain Biggles in a cartoon doing heroic adventures.*
>
> *"I also noted your comments previously about Liam and you do not consider he has done a very good job PR-wise but you are wrong. I have had a lot of phone calls wanting update of your movements from the newspapers and it won't do you any favours if you fly in the face of so much adversity. If you wish to do the Coney Run then see if you can find some American sponsors and make a good show of that. Lion won't fund you for that I know, but equally they will not fund you for the Atlantic Challenge if it is illegal, either. Please be Careful. Best wishes, Nikki "*

I wrote back to Nikki to ask her exactly what she thought I should do (she did not reply). It did not seem as if the explanations I had made about how I had got into this situation, or the way I saw out of it, cut any ice with Nikki, who obviously had the interests of the charity at heart. I had no criticisms of Liam for his PR work; it was the organising through Canada I had doubts about. I had left it to him and he left it to David Gleave, who turned out to be a 'flake'. Leaving a legal waiver was one small way of meeting her criticisms.

On Wednesday I woke with a feeling that on the morrow, July 5, I would already be over the Atlantic in the middle of the big flight. It was, I thought, to be my last day there. But down at the computer, I checked the weather and saw there was forecast to be 300 miles of weather junk in front of Ireland, with an occluded front, very difficult to fly through at the end of 22 hours flying. This was confirmed later in the day when Jim Cunliffe phoned to say he was going to stop me trying. The forecast for Sunday, five days away, remained absolutely perfect, but of course, it was five days away, and a lot could change.

Gradually the tension seeped out of me as I realised that, in flying terms, I should be choosing Sunday rather than Thursday. Although I examined my own decision to see how much I was postponing through fear, I still felt I was right. One problem was that Adrian Whitmarsh started to question the quality of the weather information I was getting. He studied weather charts far more than me, and disagreed with the forecast I had. He told me to judge forecasts on how much they complied with reality later. In his experience, there was no neat relationship. The only way to resolve these differences was to debate, constantly, up to the time of departure. For myself, so long as the wind was to the west, I hardly cared about anything else. If it was rough, or cloudy, or rainy, so be it. This was never going to be a picnic anyway. A west wind meant I had a decent chance of making it in a reasonable time. Any other wind, especially with an easterly component, had the capacity to kill, and even vindicate the forces of darkness I felt I was fighting.

Adrian also raised more fundamental issues. He was under the impression, which may be more widespread than him, that if I did not do the Atlantic flight that summer, then there was always another year to have a try. He felt that the weather had not been right since I left England, and was not shaping up to be right in the coming weekend. He felt it was a braver decision to walk away, if everything was not perfect, than to make the attempt anyway. I did not feel that way.

I did not know Adrian as well as I knew, say, Stephen Lewis or John Hunt or Dave Simpson. John and Dave were flyers, Stephen and Adrian were not, though

Adrian was in the aviation business (arranging aircraft for celebrities all over the world). Given that, and also that Adrian was a supporter and had been a terrific help, I had to meet his criticisms.

I thought through a few "absolutes". The first was that there was no other year for me to make this flight. I felt I would never be able to pull together the resources again to get it to work. I could have chosen another year when the weather was better, but I did not do that. In the way my life unfolded, and the way that Paul Loach came in to support me, this year was the only year I had. That meant I was going that summer. If the weather was not perfect and success virtually certain, I would go when it was imperfect and success was only possible, and depend on skill and determination and luck to get me through.

From that, it followed that I had to complete this flight inside a certain time period. I had originally set aside six weeks, budgeted for that period, and found that the hassles with Transport Canada had frittered away four of them. Adrian said that from his view of the weather, I had not missed a flyable period, which was a relief. But I could not stay for another month, until another full moon in August. There was, I felt, only a short period left before someone in media, a newspaper or radio station, started to ask persistent questions about where I was and what I was doing. I did not feel able to sustain a direct lie, however much I dissembled on my web site, where I was just being economical with the truth. If I got away into the North Atlantic before being discovered, then all would depend on how I conducted the flight. I imagined how nasty the reaction would be if I failed, as nasty as it would have been had I failed on the world flight. This was a dilemma modern wannabe adventurers constantly faced.

To win was everything.

To lose was to get crucified for even trying.

It sounded sensible for Adrian to caution me against being so hyped-up that I made a wrong decision about the weather. But sooner or later, and it was sooner, I *had* to make a decision to go. I could not see any other choice. I did not actually mind this. Numerous times on the world flight I had faced a similar situation, and each time I had made the right decision, turning back three times in the Atlantic, for example. I hoped I had the experience and nerve to make the right decision this time. But there was no way that a decision could be postponed to another year.

I talked to Jim Cunliffe. He said that I just had to ensure he was informed when I left, and he would be on the boat to Ireland, spanner in hand, ready to convert the Flyer back into its Permit to Fly state as soon as I landed. I was deeply touched by his support. I never had anything like this from Pegasus, who had built GT Global Flyer.

Judy Leden, at one time the greatest woman hang glider pilot in the world, phoned and said Dave Simpson thought I should be using motor fuel – mogas – instead of aviation fuel – avgas – in my 912. Apparently the engine was designed for mogas, and ran better on it. I had to admit that with the mogas I put in the engine started immediately; one feature of avgas was how difficult it was to start microlight engines. I had arranged for 115 US gallons of avgas to be supplied in Springdale, and told Judy I would think again, but I wanted to see Dave's arguments first-hand. It was an odd time to be beginning such a debate.

Helen Dudley phoned, thinking it was the last time she could get through before I left. I told her I had postponed until Sunday, and we talked about life in London, so far away from where I was. In my state of mind distances were measured in old-fashioned terms, in the blood and sweat one needed to expend to cover them rather than the modern perception that everywhere is just hours away by airliner. For me it was not, and the sense of remoteness from other parts of the world was real.

I felt, philosophically, I was ready to go. The surges of apprehension were natural for a man in my position. Francis Chichester, the great pilot and yachtsman, wrote that they were natural for anyone doing something so out of the ordinary. Fears of failure came with the territory. I was glad I kept detailed records of my feelings before every adventure, because it was comforting to know I was always half-sick with worry before them all. Something seemed to happen in the actual flight that drove it all away. I was sure wartime pilots went through the same process.

On Thursday, July 4, Adrian began to have doubts about weather at the weekend, and wondered whether I should have gone that very day!

"Let me say this in words of one syllable," he began, "you will not fly the Atlantic this Sunday".

He had little time for the European weather maps I was looking at, because the far better British product showed that a low pressure area would produce hundreds of miles of cloud, and a strong northerly which would push me towards the Azores, dramatically slowing me down. I was shaken by this news, and wondered why the Europeans had got it so wrong. Adrian was adamant that

British forecasting on the Atlantic was better, that it had been proved over the years, so I stopped whatever arrangements I had been making to leave on Sunday.

If I could not go Sunday, when could I go?

"Can you leave now?" asked Adrian, which caused a lot of cursing at my end of the phone. Outside, the wind was a moderate to fresh westerly, but a front was coming in, and three hours later it arrived. Could I really have got away? It was a thought that haunted me much of the day. It may haunt me forever.

I spent more hours with weather maps, worrying that the low pressure area that made Adrian Whitmarsh in England nervous was also making me nervous. Outside Katrina's house it was foggy and drizzly, with visibility down to 300 yards. Part of me was reassured that the nervousness I had was what I had expected to feel a month earlier before getting caught in the bureaucratic thresher.

The debate continued about avgas or mogas. Dave Simpson was a senior man with British Aerospace and not someone to ignore. He felt strongly that I should use motor gasoline on the flight, even with a bigger chance it will contain some water ("drain it before you go"). This view was backed by Nigel Beale, agent for Rotax engines. Against them were John Hunt, a computer whiz who builds his own microlights, and like Dave Simpson and me, a survivor of the early hang gliding scene in the 1970s. John thought avgas was fine and he was backed by the aircraft maker, Jim Cunliffe. I was swayed first one way and then the other. I had flown around the world using avgas and had no problems, so I felt I would stay with what was convenient. It was only a 30-hour flight, after all, hardly a blip in the engine's life.

John, who felt we should have had the avgas/mogas debate months ago, started a new hare, worrying about me flying with a full load and encountering turbulence. He said he was going to start worrying about the aircraft's structural integrity "for the first 15 hours of the flight", until the fuel load was down to the levels I had on the world flight.

Charming.

Jim also felt that way. I was the pilot who had conducted the tests with a full load, and Jim had seen there was no distortion in the wing. I promised to fly slowly and not hack my way through turbulence. Once away from the coast, I felt I should not encounter it anyway. It was a prescient hare, though.

There was one bizarre danger I never expected to run into. Those reading the secret diaries were a select group, whose e-mail addresses were programmed on to one part of the computer. Everyone else read the official diary until I emerged honestly into the sunlight, blinking, to reveal the flight was on. My two oldest friends, Jay Jones and Mike Winecoff, both Americans, were both writers who had known me when I wanted to be Jack London or Ernest Hemingway. Jay wrote to me about the literary effect this situation was having on my writing – the diaries – and I sent him back the secret diaries to assure him I was still in the game. Unfortunately, my cursor drifted over to the "blind copy" button, and the first name on my address list – Liam Abramson – also got a copy of the secret diaries.

(I thought he had done this deliberately when he had adapted my computer to take a Palm Pilot, but he convinced me later that he hadn't, and I publicly apologised to him for the accusation. At the time, though, he had already resigned, expressing his grave concern about his reputation with Transport Canada. This reputation had never existed before my flight, and I worried that Liam now considered it so valuable he would release the diaries to show how upright he was. In the event, this did not happen.)

On the Internet, I kept coming across weather sites which included wind and wave charts for the North Atlantic, which showed a weather pattern similar to the European model I had been using, with no sign of the British-forecast northerly winds that were alarming Adrian. One chart showed clean westerlies all the way across, the other a cold front on the right of my route, meeting with a warm front in the middle developing into gale force winds, but from the west. I did not mind a gale if I could ride one home; someone could always catch my wings on landing. I phoned Adrian again, he re-checked his material, and came back rather less certain that there was no chance of me leaving on Sunday. Who could really predict the weather more than two days ahead? It left open the possibility of a Sunday departure again. We agreed to talk once more in the morning.

I dined on warmed-up chops and potatoes, reading Hemingway's "Death in the Afternoon", a book found amid the Stephen King novels and westerns at Sean Sheppard's house. Sean thought the Hemingway book might be a good trade on the Internet, he did not rate books as something to be read. Terry Dennis came over for a few beers and we talked about some of his doctor's problems. Though he was no more than seven years older than me, he seemed of a different, more gentle generation, more sure of his English values.

As expected, I was waking up nightly with nightmares, wrestling my way through cloud which stretched a hundred miles high, eyes glued to the turn-and-slip indicator, trembling fingers holding the cockpit lighting at the right angle as I burrowed into the darkness. I certainly believed in the stiff upper lip. To let it all hang out was just a short distance away from frightening everyone else with your own fear. It encouraged cowardice.

Friday came, a full moon day, in which I reached the lowest depths of despair. I spent much of it watching the weather develop into a good flying day, torn between driving 15 minutes to the hangar to tighten, yet again, all electrical connections on the Flyer, and hanging around the phone waiting for calls from England. My frustrations reached a new peak. I fell into the jerky motions of a man torn by conflicting desires, pulled one way and the other as they battled inside me. I dropped Katrina in town – she didn't drive – and I went to the Flyer to record my "apology" to Canada for what I was about to do, and then found I had forgotten the script. The wind blew serenely from the west, the sky clear of clouds, it was fine summer weather, and I was in despair.

Adrian Whitmarsh was emerging as my real partner in this flight, doing the job unpaid that Liam Abramson had been paid to do. I had only grown to know him after the world flight in 1998. It was his phone calls that now had most effect on me. He was very forceful that day about the weather:

> *"Again, DON'T LEAVE SUNDAY! Assuming these charts are correct – and according to the forecast on the BBC at 0930z (z = Zulu = Greenwich Mean Time), the essential message is agreed. That is, a low pressure area is plotted to the north of your present position Sat pm/Sun am will swing out due west of you then spin tightly into a real corker of a storm to centre over Ireland by 1200z Tuesday. From Sun pm/Mon am it will start to pull in northerly winds across your intended track. By Tuesday am they will be about 2/3rds across, and probably about 40kts northerly. You don't want to end up in that.*
>
> *Sorry to give you depressing news but that's the score. Brian, I can only reiterate that I believe these charts against all else you've looked at. Obviously, again, these are forecasts 2–4 days ahead and obviously there may be subtle differences but I can't see the basics being significantly different.*
>
> *Again, you HAVE to realise that it's SENSELESS to just go heading off into oblivion. No matter what you may feel the pressures are, they are only*

in your head, believe me. No one will think anything other than you are wise if you can't go because of the weather. However, if you go against wrong weather predictions you could only be remembered for taking a bad decision. I don't want that to sound brutal, Brian, but I want you to know what I gauge the feeling to be. It is certainly my feeling. This, I think, is a lot different to your world flight in that if you go, you WON'T turn back. The circumstances and performance criteria I see as being very different. I understand that being 'in it', your feelings must seem quite similar."

This was a very powerful message. I could see the days stretching endlessly ahead of me as the full moon waned and we drifted through July, all without going anywhere. In the afternoon, I wrote to my closest and most trusted friend, Stephen Lewis:

"I am at my wit's end, and cannot work out what to do. On the one hand, I am poised to make the Atlantic flight in the worst summer for some time. The weather hasn't been good enough to make the flight, except a halfway chance yesterday, and then I understand that the last 300 miles into Ireland would have been well-nigh impossible. I am not stuck to do the trip on a full moon, but doing it on a moon-less period would be difficult. There is only so long I am going to remain undetected in my current Atlantic state. The next full moon is in early August. I am being urged by some good people not to lurch into the Atlantic, with all my choices closed down, to make a gesture and keep faith with my original promises to Paul Loach and his partners, and perhaps die in the attempt. The weather there right now looks poor, with a genuine storm developing on Tuesday over Ireland. If I'm there, already on the ground, who cares? But there are some very complex things going on in the Atlantic, with occluded fronts, dangerous and full of clag from sea level upwards, and strong winds inside them. I would go through two of them within 500 miles, and they would stay with me across much of the Atlantic, including the period of darkness. Even with all the commitment in the world, I cannot see myself staying the course in such conditions.

What options have I got?

1. I can convert back to legality, leave the Atlantic makings here, and pootle around for a month, giving rides, watching the weather, and generally keeping my horns in until I become a fixture. On an appropriate day, it would take me a day to make the conversion back again to go. But once past

July, the weather options get poorer, and only early August is left, and after that, Autumn comes in.

2. I can ship the Flyer home cheaply, leaving the Atlantic makings here, and come back another day. But, who would fund this? And how, legally, would I get back? And what about my contract with Paul?

3. I can go on Sunday anyway, and fight my way through successfully. Or not.

4. I can carry on waiting for the right weather. A full moon isn't absolutely necessary. I can disguise my intentions by converting the Flyer back, yet again, to legal mode, and be seen doing so and seen flying around the island. I should close down the web-site as a security risk, even if only temporarily, after yesterday's gaff (sending the secret diaries to Liam).

What other suggestions can you make?"

It was, essentially, a primitive cry, a shout of frustration. The weekend stretched ahead of me, empty of action. I settled in to read *"Death in the Afternoon",* about bull-fighting in what was a classical period of that Spanish sport in the early 20th century. I had not known, or I had forgotten, just how much knowledge Hemingway had about the art of bull-fighting. He had written moving passages about the faces of matadors on the day of their fights, the stillness behind their eyes, their apartness and awareness of death. These lines were particularly striking to me in my current situation. The book was almost a song to death, a celebration of it, too close to give me any succour. I was both repelled and fascinated by it.

Then the phone rang.

It was Adrian Whitmarsh.

Maybe it was possible, he thought, to make the flight the following day, Saturday rather than Sunday?

13

Going for it

I was electrified by this view. Adrian had been immersed in weather charts and was not certain, but it was possible that the way things were developing in the Atlantic, there would be a short window of opportunity. He asked me if I could get to Springdale that evening, cutting 126 miles from the total journey? After rapid thought, I felt I could. Adrian went off to monitor the weather again, while I began breathlessly running around the house, trying to stop thoughts jumbling over each other, pulling together my equipment. This I divided into two, the bigger bag containing everything not essential to the actual flight. The smaller bag contained what I needed. All the books except Homer's *"Odyssey"*, which I intend to pick up in spare moments to read again, went in the non-essential bag, including the Hemingway, which had been so disturbing.

Adrian's phone call was at 5 o'clock, Newfoundland time, three and a half hours later than British Summer Time. Terry turned up an hour later, and together with Sean Sheppard, we motored to the hangar in the car Terry had hired for me to use. I shut down many of my thought processes, only thinking of what to do, rather than why. In the secret hangar, under pressure to leave, I finally did my piece to camera, to explain to any TV company that was interested why I was making the flight. I did two takes, one at a much closer framing than the other, so as to allow it to be edited (a TV journalist to the end).

It was surreal, standing there, trying to make my "apology" convincing, knowing I had to leave an explanation, whatever happened to me. I rehearsed all the arguments I had developed over the previous four weeks, and put them as movingly as I could. The key argument was the revelation that hundreds of aircraft make the flight I wanted to make, every year, all with large one-off unapproved tanks…

" ... Why was I picked on, when the others were not?
I think, because I had a higher public profile.
Is that fair?
I think not.

I had made promises to people when I came here, and fought to keep them. Coming from a society where Big Brother contestants and Chris Evans are now people of consequence, it is difficult for me to talk about honour. But had I crept home, utterly defeated, I would have been, for the rest of my life, a man without honour.

When you first read this, I will be somewhere in the North Atlantic. I converted my Flyer back into Atlantic mode after it passed inspection, with a lot of Newfoundland help, and I intend to fly to Shannon. Once, I had an air/sea rescue insurance policy worth US$400,000; that's gone by the board. Once, I had third party insurance of a million dollars; I can hardly claim on that if things go wrong. I have signed a waiver, as the Toronto Globe and Mail suggested, taking total responsibility for my decision to fly, specifically exonerating Canada and my sponsors and the charity I supported. Please don't blame them. They opposed this decision, I acknowledge their opposition. Paul Loach, Nikki King, Jim Cunliffe, you who originally backed me, this is the only decent way left; please have patience while I try it.

I am not above the law. When punishment is handed out, I will take it. But I will have kept my word. I worked for two years for this adventure, I must attempt it, even though it has been nearly destroyed by the aviation authorities, allegedly concerned for my safety. There are, for me, deeper issues here, principally of the freedom of an individual to take decisions about his own life and salvation.

Newfoundland people have given terrific support to re-set up the Atlantic flight. They include Dr Terry Dennis, his wife Yvonne, their daughter Katrina, Fred Stagg QC, Sean and Roxanne Sheppard, Ed Lavalle, Phil Hoskins, Al Skinner.

I am not being reckless. I have put care and attention into staying alive.

There are people at home I long to see again, my children James and Jade, my closest friends, Stephen Lewis, Moira Thomson, Julian Parr, Valerie Thompson, my flying friends, Dave Simpson, John Hunt, Judy Leden, Chris Finnigan, the Plaistow Squadron.

There's also a beautiful girl in London from whom I am separated by the deepest of all gulfs, not caste, not creed, not cash, but age, she's young enough to be my daughter. I gave her an uncut Siberian opal after my world flight, and she gave it back to me for this flight, expecting it to be returned again by microlight; I don't want to disappoint her.

It's going to be very difficult, the next 24 to 30 hours. I expect to go beyond fear again and again, and I hope I come back to write about it later. Whatever happens to me, please understand that in all ages, some men must try these challenges. I just happen to be one of them. Allow me to try. Don't condemn me if I fail."

Terry Dennis was visibly moved by this speech, which I was glad to see. Who knows with special pleading whether it sounds genuine or not? He and Sean helped me into my gear, and to pack the Flyer. But it was 7.15 when I had warmed up the engine, and the huge 18,000 pound weight of the door climbed up to reveal the grass-strewn taxiway I was going to use for take-off. I had arranged to be at Springdale by 8.30pm, but even with a following wind, it was going to be tight. It was a beautiful clear evening.

I got away safely, fast and low, probably unseen by people at the other end of the huge airfield. My little aircraft climbed to the north-east in smooth evening air, and I settled down to accustom myself to the cramped quarters of the Flyer in Atlantic mode. The Flydat was working perfectly, though I confess to having installed a 5-amp instead of a 3-amp fuse; I had tightened the connections with the battery, and the spare regulator, as I had secretly expected, had not been delivered that day.

It was a beautiful flight to begin with, over mountains and lakes, up past Glover Island and Grand Lake to the east of the city of Corner Brook, and soon seeing Deer Lake airfield on my GPS, over to the left. There were occasional roads, but I saw no homes or buildings. I thought over the Atlantic flight, the first real chance I had had at it since leaving New York back on May 31. Could I keep the whole operation together for that little while longer? Would I overcome my secret terror and actually line up to fly? What excuses would I use to be brave?

At 8.45, still inside my mind and out over open country with quaint names like Gaff Topsail – a little village in the middle of nowhere – I saw for five seconds a huge jet weaving over the ground, *at my height,* and heading towards me! He must have seen me and been afraid for the same brief period I saw him. We passed, going in opposite directions, 200 feet apart and at about 350 mph, and I was sure he was in the same state of shock I was for a while. What was he doing there? So low?

The sun was going down to my left and I noticed, fearfully, that fog and low cloud were creeping inland. In the distance ahead of me it still looked clear, but to the left the fog looked dangerous, and fears began to grow inside me. What would I do if Springdale was fogged in? I looked at the tracks below and thought I could land on them, but that would mean spending a

Newfoundland night alone, and would delay everything the following day. I kept flying towards Springdale, growing ever more certain and horrified that I was going to be blocked out, with night approaching. Just ten miles away I descended and tried to find a way through below the cloud, but it was not possible. I climbed and continued on, shortening the range of my GPS each time, and hoped to find a hole in the cloud through which to descend. I thought I might make an approach to the airfield, despite the cloud, flying solely on the GPS. Over Springdale I descended, but at 1,000 feet (!) I was enveloped in cloud.

I could not stand a thousand feet of this!

I opened the throttle and climbed again and circled and thought, "it's all over, I have to reveal who I am and what I'm doing". I started to head for the international airport at Gander, about 85 miles away. The sky grew darker and I switched on my cockpit light, a car map-reading light shoved into a cigar-lighter socket to the right of the dash; it did an adequate job, and made my immediate surroundings cosy, even if I was now in dire straits.

I raced east into the darkness at 70 mph indicated on my back-lit GPS, with my engine instruments on the *Flydat*, also back-lit, working well, and the other instruments lit up by the reading light. I tried radioing Gander at intervals, working on an explanation. I could say that I had been diverted from Springdale by fog, and had no alternative but to fly to Gander, but would they ask me about the big tank? Technically, I was still legal, my Permit to Fly still validated (though an examination, which is a conscious act, would invalidate it). Would this happen over a weekend? That was the prospect ahead of me.

It was now seriously dark, and I became greatly detached. I knew my body was rushing through the night air, and I could see the rim of light to the right and behind me as the sun sank below the horizon. But my mind was cushioned, fatalistic and calm. In action, when there are few choices to make, and some of them are fatal but all of them are difficult, I seemed to reach into a state of mind where I am alive for just the next few moments, and do not think of anything beyond that.

It was in this detached way that I noticed another airfield symbol come up on my GPS, isolated and surrounded by nothing, no major river or road marked. I pressed "Near Fields" on the GPS and decided it must be a small airfield called Exploits. Would that be landable? I could pick out darker patches in the gloom ahead of me, no more than that, but decided to divert

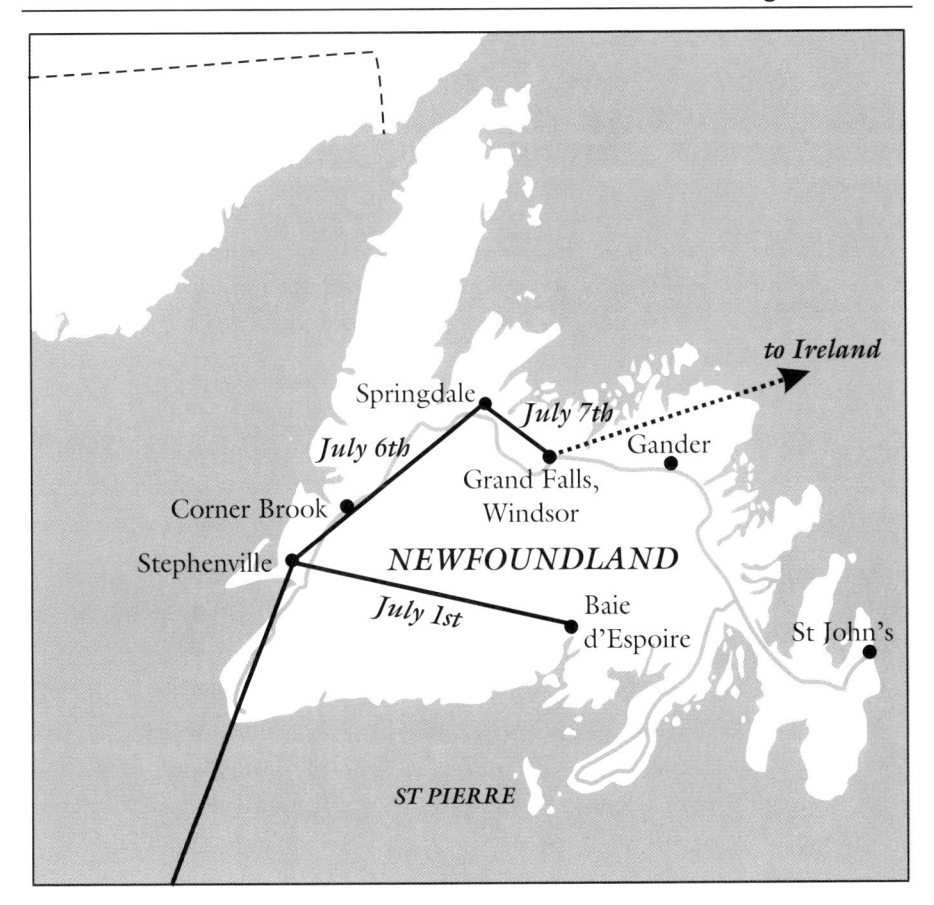

Newfoundland

there, about 30 degrees to my right on the course to Gander. The fog still crept in, it seemed to be racing me but losing, and yet there were dark patches – fog-free – in the distance. On the horizon I glimpsed the lights of what looked like a town. So long as I could see these patches I had hope. There were lakes marked on the GPS, and beyond that as I zoomed in, the town of Grand Falls, Windsor. Would I find the runway in the dark? Could I pin-point it exactly? Closer to it and slowly descending I could see the occasional car lights passing across me between the bright lights of Grand Falls, and a town I later learned was called Botwood.

Inside myself I was able to sit on my natural fears. I cleared my mind and concentrated on getting the Flyer down safely. I knew I had enough fuel, about 12 litres, sufficient but only just to go on to Gander if I couldn't get down. But I reasoned that the Atlantic flight was still on if I landed at an obscure airfield like Exploits, where no one would know who I was. It was, I thought, worth the chance.

Having taken so many chances, what was one more?

The fog oozed in from the left, tendrils reaching forward to shield the road. To my left there was an orange flashing light, like a small lighthouse. Close to the road and descending into the gloom, I was naturally drawn to this light, shining in the enveloping mist. It must, I thought, have a logical purpose. I drew near to the ground and everything became misty, except for this one light, flashing. For a few dreadful moments I was suffused with fright, on the verge of banging the throttle open but still descending, and then I looked to my right and suddenly saw lines marking an airfield's threshold.

I could see the ground!

Keeping the airfield in view through a left-hand turn, I made a fighter approach, low and steeply banked and lined up. The head-light on the Flyer illuminated the ground so I could see down through the mist, enough to know when I crossed the threshold. Not caring which way the wind was blowing, I put the Flyer on to the ground. My first reaction was relief. I burst out laughing.

I turned and taxied back to the life-saving light, stopped the engine, listened to the quietness of the night, and then set off with a torch and wearing my bright GT Global flying suit. I walked half a mile to a road. No car stopped when I hitched on my thumb, but the second car I waved down contained the Cooper family, Don and Janet, and their 20-year old daughter Emily, on the way back from dropping their daughter Sherri at her boyfriend's house in Botwood. Don drove me back to my aircraft where I picked up an overnight bag, and after hearing about my plight and my intentions ("Can you find me a hotel, a taxi-driver and an open gas station?"), they offered me a bed (Sherri's) for the night. The more Don heard about what I was doing, the more committed he became to help. He said later it was the most exciting weekend he had ever had.

Back at the Cooper home I phoned Terry Dennis in Stephenville to let him know I was alive. Oddly, it had never occurred to him that I was not. Then Don rousted neighbours out of bed to collect five 5-gallon fuel cans, we drove to the only all-night garage in Grand Falls, filled up, drove back to the Flyer – it was now 12.45 at night, 45 minutes into the day I was going to attempt the

Atlantic by microlight – and using a cut-off plastic bottle as a funnel, poured the motor fuel into the big tank.

As I did so I laughed wildly at the genteel debate which had been going on over the Internet about the fuel I should use on the Atlantic flight; it had been decided for me anyway in these bizarre circumstances, with this committed stranger's help.

I suggested I needed some sleep, and Don, a hospital worker with the geriatric unit, drove me to his home again. I crashed out, my mind at peace, at 2am. I woke at 5am, looked at the alarm, and luxuriated in staying there for 30 minutes before driving myself out of bed. Don and I set out at 6am to get more fuel, out again to the remote field, more hassle pouring every drop in, back once more to a garage, another fuel-run and filling, and then back to Don's home to change out of petrol-stained shirts at 8am. Lindbergh did not go through this, nor Alcock and Brown.

Adrian Whitchurch phoned to discuss the weather, which was not panning out as expected. There was only so much he could find out from the charts and Internet. He was anguished because of the role I had allocated to him, of being my confidant in deciding whether or not to fly. It seemed, to my relief, he was as fearful as me, but also as committed to doing the flight, and we oscillated between this position for nearly half an hour. In the end he told me I had to get separate and official advice, despite my clandestine condition. Full of trepidation, I phoned St Johns weather centre to ask for low level weather crossing the Atlantic. I am sure the forecaster must have been puzzled that I also wanted to know Sunday's weather as well as Saturday's – other aircraft take less than a day to cross the pond – but to my intense relief he gave me a forecast I could both understand, and which was relevant. There would, he said, be layers of cloud between 1,500 and 24,000 feet, and he emphasised "layers", which meant I could fly between them. East of the 30W longitude, it was fully overcast in layers between 8,000 and 16,000 feet. I could fly that too, I thought. It would be difficult getting away from Gander, because of haze and mist, and there was a stationary front 50N,40W, with a low pressure at 50N,35W.

But the key was the winds.

At 5,000 feet, these were forecast as follows, along the 50th North parallel:

50N-55W – 230/27
50N-50W – 220/25
50N-45W – 270/19

50N-40W – 290/15
50N-35W – 290/14
50N-30W – 270/14
50N-25W – 270/12
50N-20W – 240/12

To those who are not pilots, the figure before the forward-slash is the direction the wind is expected from, and the figure after is the wind speed, in knots. These figures meant that if I flew the 50th North parallel, roughly the course I wanted to go, I would have west winds all the way! A west wind is 270 degrees, so 30 degrees either side of that, which most of the above winds were, there was still a substantial tail wind. More importantly, no head-winds! Given that there was a lot of cloud out there, the Atlantic was possible that day. What about Sunday? He tapped his computer again and got the following:

50N-55W – 240/41 (a strong to gale force wind)
50N-50W – 240/35
50N-45W – 230/25
50N-40W – 260/15
50N-35W – 310/08
50N-30W – 290/10
50N-25W – 280/14
50N-20W – 280/10

These were also tail-winds! The cloud was now irrelevant. It took a little while, a few minutes, for the implications to sink in. I phoned Adrian in a daze, and we talked again, but I was talking to myself as much as to him when I said it was right to go, and I had better get on with it. I could hear Adrian's sharp intake of breath at the news. I had to go.

I had to go.

I put the phone down, and the Cooper family, each member of whom had followed this breath-taking sequence of events, began to bustle around, getting me ready. I was driven back to the field in a very detached state of mind.

By now it was past 10am, and the wind had increased, until an hour later it was coming from the south-west at 15 knots, gusting 25. This was the right direction, but there was a feisty quality about that wind that made me fearful. The fog had cleared, which cheered up Don Cooper, but made me gloomy, because I could see in front of me the effect of the sun on the ground. But all options had now closed down. Whatever the situation, I was going. I prepared with as much speed as I could, the while muttering to hear myself at work, to ensure I forgot nothing. The wind blew fiercely through the trees behind which I was sheltering with two normal aircraft on the deserted strip. Don worked as a sort of squire – as Stepan had done in Evensk, Siberia, on the world flight three years earlier – fastening my suit zips. I watched the pile of gear diminish until I had accounted for everything except the flask of hot tea which Katrina had given me. No room for that, sadly.

I started the engine, with difficulty. It would not catch for two minutes, but then burst into life. I warmed her up, looking – I saw from the video shots of my face – full of tensions and pressure. Oh, to be suave and cool, instead of a bag of nerves. Don, Janet and Emily watched from the distance. Once, Don ran over to say I was leaking fuel. It was my back pressure on the tank forcing fuel out of the overflow, and where the hell was it falling on the engine? But I was too far gone. I just muttered thanks, leaned forward, the leak stopped, Don went away, and I taxied out, commenting on the gusty conditions but saying I thought I could fly. I told myself to stop whinging.

"Lindbergh must have been just as nervous, and so were Alcock and Brown, so get on with it," I told the camera.

Later, I am certain of what happened, but at the time I was living it and dwelling in my own small world where I tried to be brave. The wind was quartering on my left face, rolling over the trees that surrounded the strip. It caused a rotor which bashed around another light aircraft I saw take off there later in the day. I lined up and opened the throttle, starting the take-off roll. As expected, it took some time for me to get airborne with such a gross load, but instead of rising steadily into the air as I had done on the loaded test flights, the rotor held me and thrashed me around. The bar whipped from side to side in front of me, far worse than I had expected or previously experienced. Fighting to control more than half an imperial ton of aircraft, I managed to rise to about 50 feet before again being held and thrashed by the rotor. Halfway down the strip she still would not climb. It was the conditions as much as the load itself that were holding me down. I needed to break away into cleaner air, but it was not happening. I could see trees ahead of me, not much lower than me, and dreaded the prospect of being over them and sinking.

Would she climb?

No!

Then land while you have enough runway.

I cut the throttle, sank sideways, still fighting the bar, and put her on the runway, not as heavily as I had sometimes done in the past in a normal microlight. But there was no suspension, I had to rely on the pneumatic tyres, and the left leg strut folded inwards. This in turn bottomed the tank on to a restraining strut, which buckled. I skidded off the end of the runway into the shale beyond, where the propeller was shredded before I was able to turn the engine off. Conscious it could burst into a fireball of flame at any moment, I got out as quickly as I could, and then started stripping it.

14

Aftermath

Had I made the flight, to paraphrase Captain Scott, I would have had a tale to tell of aspirations to hardihood, endurance, and courage which would have stirred the heart of every Englishman. These rough notes must suffice to tell the tale of failure.

I could have sat on the story, told no one, and slunk off home. Don Cooper had been briefed to phone Sean Sheppard in Stephenville to say I had gone, but Don had not seen me fly overhead. He remained sitting in the car with Janet and Emily and wondered what to do. I soon stopped packing away equipment and, thinking they had gone, walked disconsolately up to the other end of the runway, where I found them still there. Though the damage to the aircraft was repairable with two or three spare parts sent out from England, I had no confidence I could remain concealed for another attempt. The secrecy had been stressful to me anyway.

We drove to a telephone and released the news of the attempt, and then spent the rest of the day breaking down the aircraft. It remained very gusty. Janet was genuinely frightened at times, holding the wing, of being blown away. Don and his neighbours took the spare fuel, more than 100 US gallons; it was like the film, *Whisky Galore*, but in this case, Petrol Galore. Emily wielded a video camera, and I tried to summarise the flight. I was obviously miserable. So much effort, all for nothing. I could understand how Raynam had felt in his Martinsyde in 1919 when the same thing had happened to him.

The Coopers looked after me while I made arrangements to ship the Flyer home. The aircraft lay in bits in the garage next door to the small frame house in King Street, Grand Falls, NF, in which I stayed on my last days in Canada. I slept in the bed of Sherri Cooper, an 18-year old would-be model, alone, I hasten to add. Sherri slept on the couch during the two days she was there with her boyfriend, Justin. Don and Janet Cooper, not the wealthiest of people but certainly among the kindest and most straight-forward, looked after me from the first time we met on that dank and foggy Friday evening, in what seemed like another era. The only down-side was that they did not touch any alcohol, no wine, no beer, and being sober for a long time was difficult; it would have to be in England that I had an evening drowning my sorrows.

Much of Sunday, the day after the accident, I was in shock, writing the account of what happened during the previous two days. On Monday, a Mountie visited, asking for me. I went out to show him the wreckage of the aircraft in the next-door garage. He was quiet for a bit, and mumbled something about being a braver man than he was *(but I had failed!)*. He said Transport Canada wanted to talk to me. I agreed, with resignation.

Jim Cunliffe had a shipping agent in Newfoundland, and arranged to get the aircraft back.

"Let's try something else," he said.

My heart warmed to him. The Japanese have a concept of personal debt called ON, and I have ON for Jim which I must repay some day.

One figure continued to urge me to carry on the flight, however illegal my condition. Eppo Numan contacted Stephen Lewis on the night of the accident, and passionately urged him to convince me to stay in there battling. Eppo was a hero out of his time, an epic figure who should have been a Viking, and conquered lands. He had ruined himself financially flying the Atlantic in 1990. He wanted me to join him in his own Valhalla, and this may have been because it was lonely there and he needed the company. He told me he wanted to fly all the way from New York to Paris, non-stop, 56 hours, in a microlight. I still have to meet him one day. I am sure I will be overwhelmed by him.

Journalists started appearing again. Because of video pictures I took of the crash, even though they were lifted off the screen of my small recorders, my story led the news in Newfoundland. It later ran nationally. One question the reporters kept asking was why I had so much help, given so unstintingly, by everyone I had asked; they went off to Stephenville to find out. The reports on my flight were sympathetic but, personally, reporters were rueful. No one had chased me down after the decision by Transport Canada, so I had never had to tell any lies to them, aside from the economy with the truth on my web site reports. More than half my instincts would have been to have shared the secret with them, but who would I have been able to trust? They wanted to know if I had been threatened, and I mentioned the Mountie.

I welcomed the return to honesty. I had hated the false diaries. It was an added strain writing them. Rumours swirled that I was to be deported, charges laid, arrested. Part of me was spoiling for a fight, part of me was cautious. I intended to act deliberately, as coolly as possible, openly making my arrangements to leave and watching to see if the mood changed. I intended to monitor that mood through media interviews.

I was obviously a big story in the local paper; nothing much else happened in the area. The subject occupied half the front page and quarter of the second page, with most of my "apology" published, and a sympathetic three-column lead editorial which ended:

> "Whether you agree Mr Milton should have broken the law to realise his dream is irrelevant. The real story is the fact that Mr Milton has followed through on his dream, rather than just live it in his mind, as many arm-chair philosophers tend to do. Though his mission was unsuccessful this time, one can see that he will someday make it – maybe not this year, but soon. And that is most admirable. Let's hope the law is on his side."

The aircraft bits were shipped by container to Halifax, arranged by an agent in Liverpool in England who also flew a Mainair Blade. Jim Cunliffe's Mainair pilots constituted a brotherhood in a much different way from Pegasus pilots, who formed no such community. The bits returned by ship to Liverpool and Lancashire. I returned by airliner arranged through Air Canada by Al Skinner, a few days later.

Before that, a senior Transport Canada official, Kim Treathaway, a Regional Manager in the Aviation Enforcement department came around to talk. It was Mr Threathaway who had convened that conference call a month earlier when I was in Stephenville, grounding me. He was the epitome of good manners, but had at least sixty questions. I did not, he said, have to answer any of them, but I elected to answer them all honestly. As I had said in the "apology", I had not gone to Canada to commit any crimes, but to try and fly the Atlantic by microlight.

Mr Treathaway said at one point in the interview that Transport Canada did have the discretion to let me make the Atlantic flight, even with my aircraft carrying an unapproved tank. They had decided not to exercise that discretion. This comment ran directly counter to what I had been told earlier by other Transport Canada officials, who had maintained throughout that the rules were the rules, and they had no discretion to change them. That was why I had opted to make my appeal to David Collenette. I was not able to evaluate Mr Treathaway's comments.

I had dreamed of learning of the limits of courage, of going to that place beyond fear that I had found on previous flights, of measuring myself against the standards of Scott of the Antarctic and George Leigh Mallory and Edmund Blunden. I had also wanted to discover again, in the midst of the tensions of a huge adventure, an idea of England which I wanted to be inspired by. I was concerned with values, about aspirations to courage, stoicism, loyalty, commitment, steadfastness, and about the Englishness of such qualities. I had hoped that whatever I experienced, on the way to St Johns and on the long flight across the trackless ocean chasing the ghosts of great men, I would glimpse something of what made them great, and experience what they had, and what I feel we, today, have lost. I do not want to be alarmist, but I feel that, as a people, we are going to need to rediscover such qualities again soon. I am not sure where the gates are, but I know the barbarians are just outside them, baying to get in *(this was written before the attacks on New York and Washington DC)*.

Holding the likes of Chris Evans and Big Brother contestants as people of consequence is not a healthy state of mind in which to cope with these barbarians.

But I was not able to advance such researches. Instead, I was hammered into banality by debates about the size of my fuel tank, about whether or not an airport as big as Shannon should possibly accept an aircraft as small as mine, and wondering where to turn when the very man I relied upon to get me through the paperwork urged me to pack up and go home before I had even got to the starting line.

There were five possible outcomes to the flight. These were, making it across successfully, at one extreme, or slinking home without trying, on the other. In between, I could have flown off, ditched, and been rescued (despite my waiver). I could have flown off, ditched, and died. The fifth was crashing on take-off, and living through the experience to fly again. As John Hunt said in discussing the outcome, it was the second-best of them. I am glad I did not ditch, but I never had any intention of not trying, easily the worst of the outcomes.

This venture has been the most dramatic of the clashes between the two aviation cultures, Mainstream Aviation with its roots in the Wright Brothers, and the New Aviation that evolved out of hang gliding in 1971. We were able to ignore such clashes in previous flights, such as my Australian journey and later world flight. Eppo Numan had similar hassles on his Atlantic flight in 1990, Guy Delage did in 1992 crossing the South Atlantic, and Colin Bodill did – with difficulty – in 2000. Some of the puerile criticism on my web site just had to be accepted, but there are serious and sympathetic lovers of flight in both aviation traditions. Between us, if we want to explore further limits of flight, we need to work out exemptions to rules that work for one tradition but are being questioned by the other.

My worst critic is me. I always doubt my own motives, disbelieve my own excuses, ignore an up-side in favour of the down. I have examined my own motives on this flight and feel, simply, that I acted honourably. I did not succeed in the flight, but I did everything I could to make it happen. Of the five ways the flight could have ended, only one was clearly and unequivocally shameful. I would rather have had any of the other four, including falling in the sea and never having been heard from again, rather than suffer that dishonour.

What an odd word that is – *dishonour* – in this day and age. Yet it still has power.

Could I have done it successfully that day? Yes, it was possible. If I had started with the advantages of the modern world, that I had counted on as plus factors when putting the adventure together. It would have been helpful to have started from a big airfield, for example, with a long flat runway, and the permission to use it. I would have had a better chance if I had been able to have daily discussions with weather experts, to get a day's notice of good conditions, instead of the hole-in-the-corner way I did learn about the weather. My chances would also have improved if I had been able to re-fuel the previous evening in quarter of an hour, instead of the four hours of struggle Don Cooper and I had driving and lifting and pouring in the fuel through a cut-off 7-Up bottle. It would have been safer to have started at dawn, as I had always known, when wind conditions were generally calm, so that by the time the wind rose I was out over the sea and away from the turbulence that thermals and trees caused.

But surely the outcome, the crash on take-off, justified Transport Canada's concerns; surely I was not capable of making it? The reply to that question, which was put by a number of journalists, was that if you tie a ten pound weight to each of Linford Christie's ankles and then ask him to run 100 metres in under ten seconds, and he cannot, it is hardly fair to say he was not capable of it in the first place.

The time I decided to fly was, I believe, the only day in all the month of June and earlier July when it was possible to have made the flight, and succeeded. During that period, until July 7, Adrian Whitmarsh was adamant that flying conditions were too dangerous.

The saddest outcome of the whole adventure was the results of an experiment conducted by Al Skinner, which he revealed to me as I waited through a foggy night in St Johns to take an airliner home.

"We took those weather forecast figures you published on your web-site," he said, "and checked to see the weather broadly did behave as forecast. Then we ran a simulated flight, using a Cessna computer model, but limiting its speed to 65 miles an hour. Do you know, if you had got away, we calculate you would have landed in Shannon after 28 hours and 12 minutes."

And I had fuel on board for 34 hours flying.

There was one piece of good news. As I was finishing the first draft of the account of the flight, I read a small item in the *Daily Telegraph* on September 6, 2001:

> *A 44-year old lecturer last night became the first man to paddle across the Atlantic in a kayak. Peter Bray, from Pencoed, near Bridgend, had spent 75 days at sea in his 24 foot craft before arriving on the west coast of Ireland.*

Sucks to Richard Foot and the *National Post*.

Other books by Brian Milton to be published by NEP Travel

THE DALGETY FLYER
originally published in hardback by Bloomsbury

In 1987/8, Brian flew a tiny microlight aircraft, powered by a puny 447cc engine, from London to Sydney, in 59 days. It was, for 10 years, the longest, fastest microlight flight in history, despite 9 out-landings. These included being wrecked on a Greek island by cross-winds, and glueing the aircraft back together in six days. Brian landed on a road in Jordan, 1,200 feet below sea level, next to the Dead Sea, when his engine abruptly stopped as he was about to enter a mountain range, but next day he came under the patronage of King Hussein. He had three out-landings in the Saudi Desert, once because of a sand-storm, twice with rotten fuel. On Christmas Day, flying across the Persian Gulf at the height of the Iran/Iraq War, his engine stopped while 32 miles out to sea, and he ditched. Iranian gun-boats attacked two tankers just to the north, killing seven people, but didn't see Brian, who was rescued by an oil company helicopter. Six hours later he went back and rescued his microlight, dried it off in Abu Dhabi in five days, swapped engines (his mechanic, Mike Atkinson, on a First Class flight to Australia with 25 stop-overs, carried a spare engine as hand-baggage), and flew on. He had an out-landing in India, and nearly lost his reason for three days, haunted by a Djinn. But after further adventures, he finally reached Sydney, too late for the Bicentenary, but alive and with his aircraft still capable of a 4,000 mile flight around the Outback.

… Brian Milton is a fluent writer and a natural story-teller, and his account of the race to reach Australia is as gripping as any of the stories from the pioneers of aviation. His aircraft weighed less than 330 lbs. There are lawnmowers with engines more powerful than the two-cylinder Rotax which pushed it along. He took risks many pilots would find unacceptable. I'm glad he made it. But I wouldn't like to fly with him …

Peter Grose, *London Evening Standard*

… Brian Milton makes an honest and courageous attempt to look at the relationship between the attraction of danger and a pilot's fear of flying, a subject which few aviators are prepared to discuss or even touch on in any depth. The book opens with an account of an almost unbelievably lucky escape in a hang-gliding accident which was recorded on film and shown on television. It sets the scene for an undercurrent of apprehension that continues throughout the book, surfacing here and there as an almost tangible dread. That is not to say that fear dominates the book, far from it. It was a trip of epic proportions, and there is a wealth of useful advice for anyone contemplating their own 'wheeze'. I must admit it has fired my imagination. I couldn't put it down. Recommended! …

Miles McCallum, *Flyer* Magazine

… It is an intensely personal story. All the fears, the worries, the difficult decisions and the mistakes are discussed with complete frankness. Brian makes no attempt to portray himself as a fearless hero; he describes in great detail how panic set in over India and he was possessed by an almost irresistible urge to jump out of the plane. So open is the style that the reader comes away feeling that if he met the author they would not be strangers …

Norman Burr, *Microlight Flying*.

GLOBAL FLYER
originally published in hardback by Mainstream

In 1998, two men set off to fly a microlight around the world; 120 days later, one man came back in it. *Global Flyer,* by Brian Milton, is a thrilling account of the first flight around the world by microlight aircraft, no more than a large kite with a motorbike slung underneath. He and a friend of 20 years, Keith Reynolds, set out to race their little aircraft around the world in 80 days, chasing the ghost of Phileas Fogg. They were buzzed ten times by a Mig-21 jet fighter trying to get out of Syria, but the Mig didn't shoot so they were able to reach Jordan. In the Saudi Desert, the engine "blew up" seven times, discharging all their cooling fluid, despite changing their engine. They twice landed in the dark. It was only by rigging a Heath Robinson cooling system, tie-wrapping the radiator to an undercarriage leg and sending an Arab fireman out with $50 to find 8 feet of tubing and six clips, that they were able to get away. They crossed India plagued by a heat-wave, and 800 miles of jungle-covered mountains in Burma, Laos and Vietnam. China held them up, then Japan, and then – for 26 days – the Russian authorities. Keith had to fly by airliner to Alaska while a Russian navigator took his place, but he lost heart in Anchorage and went home. This left Brian to cross 3,000 miles of Siberia, sometimes covered in ice, with a Russian stranger in the back. From Nome, Alaska, Brian flew on alone, down to San Francisco, chased by tornadoes across to New York, and then the first solo west-east crossing of the Atlantic Ocean by microlight, where for three hours he was in a place "beyond fear". The flight won the Royal Aero Club's *Britannia Trophy*; there is no higher award in the gift of the Club. It also won the prestigious *Segrave Trophy*, once won by Amy Johnston.

> … In all his ventures Brian had a strong sense of history and the romance of aviation. As a journalist he approached his circumnavigation as a story that he wanted to tell well, something that Keith could never understand or empathise with. It was an amazing achievement, of dogged bloody-minded tenacity and the taking of some huge risks by a man who was fighting his fear and, at times, just about everyone around him. It was a great adventure …
>
> Sir Chris Bonington, who included Brian's microlight flight in his account, *Quest for Adventure*, of the greatest individual adventures since World War Two

… I read it at one sitting because, although I already knew the outcome and the major twists and turns along the way, the story is utterly engrossing and I felt I had to find out what happened next. The book succeeds as a 'ripping yarn' but does so on other levels too. There is the thread of a political thriller, with various approaches by Richard Branson to influence the adventure. This is a microlighting classic that should be on every microlighter's shelf. It may even rank among other travel classics …

David Bremner, Editor, *Microlight Flying*

This book is an account of one of the greatest flying adventures of all time. It is also the story of a man cast in the heroic mould yet strangely flawed, driven by a desire for the recognition he felt he was denied by his peers. It is, without a doubt, the best microlighting book yet written – go out and buy it now. The flying itself is a fantastic read, with almost non-stop drama and adrenalin. It is also very much a character study of Brian Milton, and he has shown himself to us honestly, warts and all. His achilles heel is that he is scared of heights – a relic of a bad hang gliding accident in the seventies – and his accounts of his battle with this fear, and the unusual weapons he used, are candid and revealing. Hero, adventurer – but also a hard man to live and work with on a daily basis.

Nick Bowles, *Internet Aviation* site